MW00659101

Roger Treagus was born in Sydney to a fashion journalist mother and educated in a privileged private grammar school, where he failed at everything. Assisting his mother in her oddball career inspired Roger to embark on his own career adventure, which spanned five continents in search of that next big job. He started as a printer's assistant, then a sewerage worker, postman and gardener, became a spy, a weatherman, lighthouse inspector and filmmaker, eventually making it as a scientist with a tally of 45 separate jobs so far. Roger now resides on Sydney's Northern Beaches with his medical journalist wife and teenage son.

This book is dedicated to both my wife, Jan McLean, and my son, Lachlan Treagus.

Roger Treagus

Odd Jobs

Austin Macauley Publishers™
London • Cambridge • New York • Sharjah

A CIP catalogue record for this title is available from the British Library.

ISBN 9781788488006 (Paperback)
ISBN 9781788488020 (E-Book)

www.austinmacauley.com

First Published (2019)
Austin Macauley Publishers Ltd
25 Canada Square
Canary Wharf
London
E14 5LQ

I want to acknowledge Janet McLean, my wife, who greatly assisted me with an initial thorough edit of the early drafts, resulting in the removal of irrelevant passages and copious waffle that permeated the text. Janet then developed the concept and drew the outline of the book's cover picture.

I also want to thank all those friends and work colleagues who shared many of my experiences and who, therefore, could fact-check my recounting of the past.

And finally Norma Martyn, my mother, though deceased, these many years helped with her diaries and articles that fleshed out the details from the 1960s, when I was still her Odd-Job Apprentice.

The History of Odd Jobs
(in chronological order)

The job – What it was	**The job – What I did**
The Family Business	Printer's assistant
Holes in the Ground	Street labourer
The Composing Room	Newspaper copy boy
The Mail Gets Through	Postman
Pigs in Pitt Street	Press photographer
All at Sea	Ship's photographer
Serving at Selfridges	Butcher's assistant
Gumshoe	Industrial espionage agent
The Sherwood Forest Story	Stately home gardener
Chocolate Entrepreneur	Cherry Ripe importer
The Big Blue Bus	Photo journalist
Towards Australia	Ship photographer
Inside the Weather Bureau	Weather observer
JACMAS	Flight path storm spotter
The Air Force	Honorary sergeant

Administering the WW2 Top Guns	Personnel clerk
Bean Counter for all seasons	Systems auditor
Airports of the Future	Information officer
The déjà vu Airport Study	Media and community advisor
Frogs and the International Terminal	Environment officer
The Voyage of *Argonauta*	Photographer
Amazon Botanical Gardens	Film maker
Thunder on the Ohio	Midwest TV presenter
Assisting Enlightenment	Self-development course mentor
Hostel in Paradise	Youth hostel warden
Selling the Vision in the Bush	Audio-visual producer
Alpaca in Australia	Alpaca garment importer
Reunion and Rescue	Taxi driver
Ending a motor race	Motor sport regulator
Moving Mountains	Mining noise regulator
Hyperactive neighbours	Local Government advisor
Noisy bikes and Noisy bikies	Bike noise control policy maker
The Steinway Evacuation	Volunteer firefighter
The Great River Walk Expedition	Walk leader and route finder
Changing the Industrial Landscape	Government policy maker
Windfarms and the World Bank	Scientist in Canada

The Great Caribou Migration	Resident Caribou 'expert'
Copper in the Congo	Environmental assessment author and global coordinator
Power and First Nation – the BCP Project	Coordinator
Counting Orcas	Killer whale researcher
The Wind Farm Voyage	Technical specialist
Counting Heads on the Peninsula	National Census manager
Woodstock Down Under	Pop Festival noise monitor
Bats out of Hell	Bat scarer
The Bob Miller Story	Editor and compiler
The Lake Eyre Rumble	Researcher

Starting at the End

Sydney's Royal Botanical Gardens is a very quiet place at 4:30 in the morning. There is just the faint hum from city buildings, the soft gurgling of creek water cascading towards the harbour and the rustle of leaves in the breeze. But this was no normal morning, because on this morning in May 2014 it was my job to hit the start button, a round red knob on top of a black box. As soon as I hit it, the response was immediate. The Berlin Philharmonic in its full glory bellowed out the famous passage from Tchaikovsky's *1812 Overture* through a bank of loudspeakers scattered around the Gardens. The explosive sound of Russian cannon fire bounced off the east face of Parliament House echoing back across the Gardens towards the Woolloomooloo finger wharf followed by equally loud strains of *La Marseillaise* signifying the sullen retreat of Napoleon's army in the face of a resolute foe. The clashing of rubbish bin lids being belted with hammers completed the cacophony. My team looked skywards anxious to catch a silhouette in the lightening dawn sky of the returning pathfinders, showing the rest the way back to their favourite roosting trees. Was all the noise deterring them from roosting? We wanted to know.

This was but one of many odd jobs that mapped out my 'career'. I was a bat scarer. My task was to stop the bats from returning to the Royal Botanical Gardens where they were slowly stripping their roosting trees and killing them. These were not ordinary trees. They were all heritage listed, part of an irreplaceable floral bank of the unique Australian vegetation first documented by Sir Joseph Banks on Captain Cook's discovery of the Australian East Coast in 1770. These trees had to be saved.

My career path had come to this point from inauspicious beginnings 54 years earlier. Between my first job as printer's assistant and this one as bat scarer were 43 other jobs. My 8th job was in industrial espionage complete with getaway car. By job 16 I was a systems auditor discovering Norfolk Island's secret. Then in job 20 I was a travel photographer on a ship that hit an iceberg near Cape Horn and later abandoned in the Magellan Straits. Soon after I became a warden in a beautiful youth hostel, but I shifted gears when I became a volunteer fireman evacuating a Steinway grand piano on a barge in the face of an encroaching bushfire.

Coordinating the environmental and social assessment for one of the world's biggest copper mines in the Democratic Republic of the Congo followed my work attempting to predict where the great caribou migration was going to occur in Arctic Canada. In between times, I led the first documented expedition down Australia's longest east coast river.

So my career pattern was clear. There was no pattern. My journey from the first job to the last was an illogical series of jumps. Each jump was a piece of a giant jigsaw puzzle whose final complete picture was itself a puzzle.

"What do you want to be when you grow up?" I hated grownups asking this of me, when, as a small boy I was clearly unqualified to reply. A career was always something to think about when I was older, much older. I was very interested in the stars, the planets and the weather, but I knew I had to be brilliant at school to be either an astronomer or a weather forecaster.

This account is not about a smooth path mapping a career. More like a rocky pathway of jobs, lots of them. Most were unrelated and with no natural progression; many were simply odd. These are told in chronological order, which is the only order they possess. The story is a series of hairpin bends and blind corners with the occasional straight road.

***

My mother, Norma, was very worried about my lack of prospects after leaving school, a privileged church school known for producing white-collar professionals held in high regard by The Establishment. After eight long years of the best private schooling, I had no credentials, no evidence of academic attainment. Clearly I was not clever enough to aspire to join the production line of fresh-faced apprentice accountants, stockbrokers and lawyers. My mother's huge financial investment in my education had not worked. I was a failure. I had let her down.

"I've worked so hard, Roger, to give you the education I never had," she lectured. She was understandably bitter about being forced to leave school when she was 15, simply because she was female and therefore expected to merely help with the running of the household. Her brother, on the other hand, who had neither her ability nor her drive to have a successful career, was made a director of the family business.

"I've sacrificed so much for you, you know," she would say wistfully. "You are so lucky. But you have to work hard to be successful in life, Roger. Work hard to get what you want."

Indeed, Norma had done just that. Rather than settle for a life of drudgery looking after the men in the family, she secretly wrote a letter of application to become the teacher of a country school. That meant she had to raise her age by three years and pretend to already have some qualifications for the role of an educator. It must have been a convincing letter, because she scored the job as the sole teacher at a bush school near Queanbeyan. She managed to escape from her parents' home, initially without their knowledge, and so begin her own real education and her colourful career, which subsequently spanned many occupations, from public relations consultant, to radio and TV presenter, fashion expert, TV talent school proprietor, author and diplomat.

Norma's life was drama on an international scale, from being stranded on a remote South Seas Island after the crash landing of a Pan American

Stratoclipper; to an affair with a card carrying KGB Officer; to the expose of sex and scandal in small town Australia in her first best-selling novel; and to almost marrying one of America's great war correspondents whose friends included three US presidents and two WW2 generals, Macarthur and Patton.

My mother certainly had the motivation, the drive and determination to be successful in whatever she undertook. But that hadn't filtered through to me. I had been so unmotivated at school. 'Could do better', 'Needs to try harder', 'Disappointing result' – these were typical comments in my school reports.

Then there was the truancy record. For some years while I was attending high school, my mother, anxious to pursue her own career, left me in the care of my grandmother, while she absconded to Mother England. I was never keen on school, partly because of the years of bullying and taunts about my split lip and nose deformity and my speech impediment resulting from a cleft lip and palate. Numerous operations and my mother's elocution lessons eventually corrected these defects, but the stigma and feelings of inadequacy and inferiority remained for many years. One day, a schoolboy's taunts pushed me over the edge. I grabbed the offender by the seat of his school shorts and threw him forcefully through the open classroom window. In the eyes of the school, he was the innocent victim and I was the culprit, to be punished for my violent behaviour.

Staying out of school as much as possible was the way for me. Besides, I much preferred exploring the great outdoors to attending school, as well as following my great passion at the time: ten-pin bowling. When I should have been focusing on the school blackboard, my gaze concentrated on the direction of the big black bowling ball. I was a proud member of the junior state champion bowling team, the only success in my life.

In contrast, my mother was a high flyer; she was called 'a career woman' in the 1950s. That meant she wasn't a housewife. Indeed, she wasn't remotely housewifely. And a caring housewife was what my father craved. They were totally unsuited, brought together by The War, when she became a "camp follower," moving in with him during his battalion's manoeuvres. As with many war brides, disenchantment with ordinary, somewhat boring peacetime reality soon followed the wartime romance, independence and excitement.

War time, however, continued in our home. The battle lines were drawn. Norma's world centred around her high-profile work. My father hated it. Apart from his wartime escapades as a gunner, he worked the same job all his life, in the accounting department for General Motors' Holden. On his retirement, he was rewarded with a gold-plated clock. And indeed, for him it was as if time stood still once he retired from that one job. His life seemed over already.

My father was meant to be the breadwinner, but he wasn't. Frustration, jealousy and alcohol were a toxic mix that sometimes boiled over. Dad saw his masculinity eroding away and sabotaging Norma's career seemed a solution to restore his rightful place as provider and head of the family.

In 1955, Australia's biggest ever fashion parade was planned for the Brisbane City Hall with, for the first time for Brisbane, national radio, newsreel and press coverage. Norma was the compère. The Lord Mayor and several newspaper proprietors planned to attend. As usual, my father and I were left at home in Sydney. Early one morning he announced that the two of us were going on a trip. A day later he parked the car outside the Brisbane City Hall. I was puzzled. What was going on? I didn't know where I was, let alone the fact that my mother was on stage inside. Reeking of alcohol, Dad led me inside and found his way up onto the stage, past a battery of journalists, newsreel cameras and radio mikes. He dumped me in the centre of the stage and attacked Norma, grabbing her and tearing her dress as he desperately tried to drag her off the stage. Incensed at this very public invasion, she hit him over the head with a loose microphone. It hit him hard. Blood flowed from his head. I ran over to them, vainly trying to separate them, thinking that if I could just do that, the situation would be saved. I looked around and saw a packed audience of thousands of faces staring at me, blood on the stage floor, a retreating father, a screaming mother, all illuminated in split-second grabs by flashbulbs going off, completing a surreal scene, picture-perfect for the tabloid media.

I never really got over that trauma. And nothing I could say or do saved the marriage. I blamed myself for that failure, which was bad medicine for my self-esteem for a long time.

My parents divorced when I was 12. My father was cast as the bad guy, and as he provided no ongoing financial support, Norma (I was never allowed to call her 'mother', let alone 'mum') had to work harder to support us both. When TV came to Australia, Norma had her own daytime television program on Sydney's channel nine canvassing women's interests. It seemed all so glamorous, but in those days it was still poorly paid, particularly for women. Then came the day when she had the British actor John Mills as her guest on the show. Shooting live to air, an entire set collapsed and crashed into her guest, narrowly missing Norma. The guest survived but the show did not. The Channel's proprietor, Sir Frank Packer, was watching and was horrified by what he saw. Frank's son, Kerry, who was producing along with Norma at the time, commiserated with her and offered her a compensatory job off-air as permanent producer, a plum job at the leading Sydney TV channel. But she would have none of that and stormed out. She was headstrong and outspoken but as a personality very marketable. I couldn't imagine a more dominant and powerful mother.

So eight years of Shore School had prepared me for nothing much. Having left without attaining the acceptable standard to get a 'proper job' and with Norma's expectations for me to produce a long awaited income as a professional something, I looked grimly at the job market. Skilled jobs were out. They required some sort of test. Having disgraced myself at the school Leaving Certificate examinations by not passing at the first attempt, further aptitude tests seemed a waste of time. This left the unskilled job market. I wasn't devoid of job experience. Norma had arranged a temporary job for me during school holidays. I didn't see it giving me any experience as it was for a very specific purpose.

The Family Business – Printer's Assistant

Leaving school was always going to be traumatic, regardless of how much I disliked school at the time. The unknown was frightening, especially when I was turfed out into the world with no clue about what work I could do and no qualifications or skills to do it.

I obviously wasn't cut out to join the family printing business either. A year earlier my mother had arranged work for me during my school holidays at the venerable HC Martyn and Sons, Legal Stationers and Printers, established by her great-grandfather in 1832. The only reason I agreed to the job offer was the prospect of being able to save enough money to buy a telescope from Esdales Scientific Instruments Pty Ltd, another branch of our family business. My mother hoped this exercise would not only instil me with a sense of responsibility and an appreciation of the value of work and earning and saving money, but that it would also bond me to the family. To cap it off, I could then spend my money wisely as I was a keen amateur astronomer and perhaps discover a new galaxy or two.

Being involved in the family business had been viewed as an important tradition for the men of her generation; the women of course could play no part in HC Martyn and Sons, apart from ensuring their men were well looked after at home. My mother had suggested I would have lots of fun serving eminent customers like barristers and solicitors in the prestigious one Castlereagh Street office. Norma applied her elocution teacher talents to my presentation to the point of practising my spiel in pseudo-cultured British tones: "Good morning, sir. What forms can I supply to you today? Ten A16 divorce forms perhaps?"

I had imagined the scene so vividly, but such a refined experience was not to be. I suppose management had a problem. They were under a family obligation but had trouble placing an ignorant boy in his first job. "Send him out to the factory where he might be of some use," my grandfather said.

I was stunned. What was worse, the factory wasn't in the glamorous CBD financial district; it was in the seedy, smelly inner-western industrial suburb of Chippendale, somewhere quite foreign to me, a north-shore boy. With a mix of distaste and trepidation I fronted up to the uninspiring grey HC Martyn factory block on an appropriately dull, grey Monday morning.

My cousins greeted me warmly and showed me around the noisy factory, which belted out all sorts of forms via an assortment of huge guillotine machines and a clutter of letterpresses and hot-lead printers, their spindly arms waving about like aliens from the War of the Worlds.

"These guillotines cut down the work, if that's the right word," explained Brian, the factory manager's assistant. He pushed a series of levers forwards and shoved a thick slab of paper under the blade. "Watch this."

The guard dropped down and the blade effortlessly sliced through the 4-inch slab. "Now if I stick a finger under the guard, this is what happens," he continued. I didn't want to look, nauseated by the thought of a decapitated digit.

"Keep watching, Roger, it's OK, see?" He pushed the levers again. The blade refused to move. "You see, the guard automatically stops the machine!" he exclaimed triumphantly.

He pushed more levers with finger still in position. This time the blade moved. His sudden piercing screams filled my ears. Workers rushed to his aid. "Push the emergency stop button!" yelled someone. The big red button was pressed. The blade and guard retracted. But Brian continued to scream. Half a bloodied finger lay on the white paper, staining it crimson. I stared at it, frozen in horror, then raced to the toilet to throw up.

When I finally emerged from the bathroom there was an unexpected silence. Then the whole factory exploded with laughter.

"We got yer going!" sniggered Brian, throwing me the severed red rubber finger.

"Brian does that to all the new boys," said a staffer, wheezing with laughter. "But it worked best on you."

My older cousins soon figured out that I was good at counting copy numbers from each of many stacks, but that was all. No higher skilled job seemed quite right for me. This was to fill eight hours each day of the week plus Saturday morning, the standard working week. Counting endless mountains of white forms was so tedious, I decided to simply compare stack heights, assuming stacks of equal height had equal numbers of forms. Cousin Terry clicked his tongue disapprovingly.

"I'm disappointed in you, Roger," he reprimanded. "If you miscount across the stacks, you'll lose us many, many pounds. We can't afford slack shortcuts, Roger. If a job's worth doing, it's worth doing well. If you want to join the family business, you have to have a good attitude to work."

At least by the end of the school holidays I had earned 19 pounds 10 shillings, enough to buy the prized telescope. It gave me pleasure over many years of dark nights as at various times the great nebular in Orion, the 4-star array of Castor in Gemini, the rings of Saturn, the craters of the moon and the girl in the house across the road came into view. Objects several light years away looked sharp but I had problems focussing on much closer objects, tantalisingly just out of reach.

Holes in the Ground – Street Labourer

After finishing school in 1964, I had time on my hands. "You have to get a job, Roger," commanded my mother. "I'm worried about you. You'll never get a proper job with no qualifications, but job experience will help so get off your bum, no more lazing around!"

So feeling a failure and full of trepidation, I entered the rather austere Commonwealth Employment Service office, the CES, or the cesspit as some called it. Could I cope with working as an unskilled labourer, digging ditches? It didn't take me long to find out.

At seven the next morning, fingers numb with the winter chill, I fronted up to the foreman at Ridge St, Hornsby, ready to dig a trench to house telephone cables.

"So you've never used the drill, sonny?" scoffed the brawny foreman. "Christ, what are they sending me! You better learn pretty quick." He clicked his fingers at one of the workers. "Charlie, make sure he's diggin' OK before smoko!" he bellowed.

Charlie picked up a pneumatic drill and handed it to me. I immediately dropped it on my foot. Ouch! How could Charlie lift that lump of lead so easily?

"Look kid, yer let the tip take all the weight and yer lean on it like this," Charlie demonstrated. "And yer pull on the lever here and lean into it, see?" Charlie's whole body shook wildly as the vibrations from the machine convulsed through him. I blocked my ears. "No sonny, that's not the way. See, yer need both hands on the handle to keep the drill steady, see?"

Charlie heaved the leaden monster over to me. This time at least I kept it upright, away from my wounded foot. I tried to lean into it as I fearfully depressed the handle. It immediately sprung into life, jumping up and shrieking like a wounded beast, leaping out of my hands and falling down dead in the ditch.

Charlie shook his head. "Go down and get it up and give it another go, mate."

I was out of breath after hauling the massive weight up, out of the ditch. This time Charlie was grabbing it from behind me. Our combined strength made me more confident. The drill was upright and the drill bit was hitting Charlie's mark. I wrapped my hands around the handle and again leaned on the drill. It vaulted again but I clung on for dear life. Charlie eventually let go. I was going solo. My whole body was shaking. The ear-splitting hammering was painful. No ear plugs had been offered. Would my new partial denture plate jump out of my mouth?

Thirty seconds was all I could bear for my first run. The vibrations abruptly stopped but the din from the other drills continued. I glanced at Charlie's mark.

The chalk was still intact and a hole, pathetically small, appeared well below the target. The drill had slipped. Had I leaned on it the wrong way?

Charlie inspected the hole. "A bit off the mark, eh kid, but at least yer didn't lose it down the hole. Keep at it and yer'll get it kid. Can't expect too much after thirty bloody seconds. "

I leaned on that drill all day. My hands were numb, my ears were singing. By the end of the day I was on the verge of collapse, but I felt strangely proud of my 6-inch deep hole. Charlie shook his head.

"Yer gotta hit the spot, kid," he shouted. "Look, kid, look!" he gesticulated. "That's the line of the cable, that's where it's gotta go!"

After three days of grilling and drilling, the Foreman announced: "Yer gotta go, kid, yer gotta go!" And I did, much to the relief of the Foreman. But I was given a second chance, on another site, this time digging a trench to connect the sewer to the then new suburb of Bradfield, carved out of the bush as a soldiers' settlement development. My job was to help dig a trench 10 feet deep and two feet wide all the way from the Bradfield ridgetop to the Lane Cove River, through soil, sandstone, tree roots and down a cliff line.

Joe, my new foreman, tossed me a drill. I held onto it with a flourish of confidence. "Throw it down there, mate." Joe pointed down to the muddy trench bottom. "Now, for Chrissake don't jump onto it cos you'll break it." Aiming for a different dark spot, I leaped into the murky unknown and landed in soft, squelchy mud. I thought I knew how to operate a drill by now. But I didn't. Every few minutes I shut down the drill, wiped the sweat and mud from my face and inspected my progress. There was none.

After what seemed an eternity, Joe peered down the ditch from on high and yelled "Smoko!" above bursts of drill noise. By the time I managed to climb out of the hell hole the other workers were well into their first cigs and a smoke haze hung above the huddled group. I sat silently with them, chomping on my smoked cheese sandwich.

"Like your new job?" asked one worker.

"Stupid question," chipped in a second. "Who the hell would like this shit, mate?"

"It's just for a quid, isn't it, Sam, just for a quid, eh Sam?"

The worker nudged Sam's elbow. "You alive, Sam, you old bugger? Hear me Sam?"

Sam didn't respond. "He's been down the hole too long," Joe explained. "Hearing's gone." No one was wearing any ear protection despite the dangerous drill noise. Back in the early 60s, occupational health and safety standards were in their infancy.

Sam looked disconsolate. His skin was black and wrinkled, cooked by the sun. He squinted all the time and occasionally said something in English but mainly rabbited on in Macedonian. His dark crumpled clothes matched his skin. He seemed a dead man walking.

Another worker nodded towards Sam. "Sam's been at this too long. Yer gotta know when to get out. But fer us there's not much choice. We get what we can. Shoulda stayed at school, then got a decent job but Mum needed the mulah."

"C'mon youse blokes. Get movin'!" cried Joe. "Smoko's over."

Joe followed me back to my ditch, peered down into the depths and angrily scratched his beard. "Whatcha been doin' all morning?" he roared. "Where's yer bloody cutting marks on the wall?"

He glared at me and gave me no time to reply. "If your bloody trench isn't happening by the end of today, it's over for you." He thrust his hand like a knife across his throat. Clearly my job as a labourer was over before it had really started. I was hopeless. I watched the other workers with envy. For them the drill seem to slice through the rock as easily as through cream cheese. I decided I wouldn't simply walk out immediately. It was better to be ordered off the site after giving it another go. So I wearily slid back into my hole. More drilling, more noise, more ringing in the ears – and still no progress.

I ate a lonely lunch at the edge of the ditch. Karl, one of the labourers, sensed how dejected I was. He came over to me and put a consoling hand on my shoulder.

"Joe givin' you a hard time?" he enquired gently. "Don't let it bother yer. It's like that for all the first dayers." He climbed down into the dank darkness of my hole and disappeared from sight. A minute later he emerged, laughing. "He's bullshittin' yer, mate," he smirked. "You got the claw!"

"The what?"

"He's trying you out, kid. Putting you on the claw. He's given you the bloody ironstone collar to punch through."

Joe now confronted Karl, having overheard his comments. "The kid has to learn quickly, so I put him in at the deep end," Joe said. "I don't have time to train him up. This is not a bloody school, Karl. I'm on the line if he stuffs up, not you."

I knew I had to do something that afternoon. With grim determination, I pulled the heavy drill up and put all my weight behind it, pushing the bit into the trench wall. I kept it pounding for minutes at a time, until it was too hot to touch. At the end of each period I inspected the wall but there was nothing happening. I had attracted attention with the occasional labourer leaving his own site to come over to see what I was doing. Half way into the 5th period, I felt something give and the drill fell forward. I stopped and inspected the wall. My eyes had adjusted to the gloom of the trench bottom. A large hole appeared right in the middle of the wall with soft rock and mud on the other side. I heard clapping and looked up. A small group of labourers witnessed my triumph, with a signature thumbs-up.

"What youse blokes doin? Get back to it!" yelled Joe. The foreman moved to the lip of my hole and peered down. I looked up at his dark form. Maybe I imagined it but I thought I detected a faint smile.

The next morning I reported for work right on 7am and promptly resigned before the supervisor showed up. This wasn't for me, I knew that. But I had proved something to myself. I was determined enough to punch a hole in that ironstone wall and felt more confident that I could pound my way through future obstacles, somehow.

The Composing Room – Newspaper Copy Boy

My mother was a newspaper journalist covering fashion, travel and the social scene. She was well connected as social journalists needed to be with a scattering of influential friends and acquaintances. It was because of Norma's connections that I landed jobs that were definitely a little odd. The first of these occurred just after I left school.

Norma ran an advertising column for Sydney's *Daily Telegraph* newspaper called *Counterpoints*. The column was made up of stories about products that businesses in the fashion and beauty industry wanted to push. It was paid advertising dressed up as editorial. She wrote copy for her Wednesday column ready for dispatch to the newspaper every Monday night. Not wanting to travel back to the city after a day's work in her job as press liaison for David Jones Department Store, she saw a valuable role for me as a courier. For submitting her copy to the compositor, waiting for the proofs, then delivering them back to her she would pay me 10 per cent of her earnings for the job.

It was five kilometres from our house in Kirribilli to Consolidated Press in Park Street in the Sydney CBD. I figured it was quicker to run there than to catch the infrequent night trains, so off I went over the Harbour Bridge into the city running through the Rocks, then George Street, across to Pitt Street and finally into Park. Arriving breathless at the *Telegraph* building, I raced up to the second floor where I was greeted by a cacophony of metallic clashing sounds. I had arrived at the comps.

The floor was full of linotype machines that made the hot metal plates, an integral part of the letterpress printing process. These machines seemed like gangly monsters with their swinging metallic arms, molten lead pots and their hissing of compressed air. The air was thick with steam and the smell of ink and the deafening clanging of hundreds of metal slugs clunking into position to lay down lines of type. Men were rushing everywhere on the floor, some carrying the copy to the linotype operators, others moving the metal galleys produced by these machines to "the bank," a desk where the plates were laid out. Ink vapour hung heavily in the air and droplets splashed on everything, clothes, walls, even the ceiling. Added to this was the fog of cigarette smoke blown around the floor by the blasts of compressed air emanating from each linotype. Everyone was shouting to be heard above the din.

I handed the copy to Mr Mensa, the chief compositor and King of the Comps, a man feared by his staff. He was short and gruff with a wrinkled face and lilting brogue as he talked. His trained editorial eyes scanned the document in seconds.

"Tell your mother to shorten her copy by four lines," he said sternly. Then he came up really close to me and made steely eye contact. "I know it's a tough call Rog, she being your mother and everythin', but yer just gotta get through to her. I can't be wasting my time fitting in her extra lines like she always wants. She has to bloody prune them, right. Tell her that, eh kid. She might listen to you. She's as stubborn as a mule to me."

Although I nodded in agreement, I knew it would not be easy to tell my mother to alter anything to do with her copy. Norma saw all editors as the enemy. Mr Mensa handed the piece to the copy boy, who ran to one of the linotype machine operators.

Despite the deafening noise from the shuddering machines, no one wore earplugs. They just smoked endless cigarettes. I watched the operator type in Norma's copy. After typing a line he pressed a button on the panel and suddenly the machines meccano set of arms started moving back and forth and bits of metal spat out of a slot near the top and ran down a channel to a collecting point. Line by line the copy was built up into a hot metal plate. The copy boy was shouting something indecipherable to the linotype operator who shouted something back. I was only a few feet away, but the clamour of the comps machines drowned their words.

Within 15 minutes the galley proofs were delivered back to Mr Mensa who handed them to me.

"Four lines, just four. Got that," Mr Mensa growled as if I needed reminding.

I ran Norma's copy back and forth between home and the paper for three years and loved it. Each time I hit the lift button for the second floor I had a sense of anticipation and I was never disappointed. Mr Mensa eventually even allowed me to operate a linotype machine for a short time. It was a thrill to hit the button and watch as the clattering overhead signalled the issue of hot lead. I had been operating the machine for more than my allocated time when Mr Mensa spied me.

"Christ, son, you're not doing all the galleys!" he exclaimed. "The union will be on to me!"

So ended my brief taste of being a linotype operator for an afternoon city newspaper, a career prospect that has sadly gone forever.

The Mail Gets Through – Postman

The CES (Commonwealth Employment Service) knew I liked the outdoors as I listed bushwalking as a hobby, but they also knew I didn't like hard physical work after the cable trench experience. So they thought a job as a postman should suit me perfectly. After all, it was a bit like bushwalking with no real hard yakka, and I was given a bicycle to boot. I was assigned to the Dee Why mail exchange and told to start at 6am. What? Did I hear correctly? "But you'll be finished by two," said the employment officer reassuringly.

The cold early morning air bit into my toes as I rode my two-speed Honda 50 step through to the mail exchange that first Monday morning. Dee Why was just waking up with only the bakeries showing an early morning light in the gloom.

In contrast to the outside stillness, the mail exchange was busy and boisterous. Posties were shouting as they shuffled letters from huge mail bags strewn around the floor into clusters of pigeon holes covering the walls. The supervisor spotted me at the entrance and called me in.

He directed me towards a short, rotund postie who was singing above the din. "This is Mr Moon. You go with him for the day and we'll sort you out a run. You'll need to start your own run by tomorrow so you have to learn quick. Ever done this before, Rog?" I shook my head. "Never mind, we'll sort you out. Mr Moon here knows some good sorts, not just the mail." The supervisor looked around for some laughter but only got a snigger. This was likely an old joke.

Mr Moon shook my hand with exaggerated cheerfulness. "Just watch me, son, and remember all the labels." I looked closely at the pigeon holes. Each had a street name and a set of numbers. Street names were repeated on other pigeon holes as well.

"You see, this sort gets the mail into running order. Simple, eh?" Mr Moon looked at me for a response. "Well, it ain't, 'cause you have to get it finished by 8. George over there gives you a boot up the backside if you're late."

It certainly wasn't simple. I had to know my run backwards to sort the house numbers and the streets in order, and I felt as if I was sinking in a sea of white envelopes. Delivery vans dumped mailbag upon mailbag and their contents cascaded across the floor. Not even the fastest sorter could keep up.

"There's lots of mis-sorting," Mr Moon's shouted above the din. "Some fellas dunno their run. Dunno which way is up. Isn't that right, Charlie?"

"Give it a rest, Full. I never see you back in the office on time," Charlie shouted back.

"What's full?" I asked.

"I am, according to those fuckers," replied Mr Moon, pointing to the 25 or so other posties in the room. "That's their name for me, Full Moon, get it? But don't let me hear you saying that, son." Mr Moon cleared his throat and struck up the *Toreador* aria from Carmen, until the protests got too loud.

The nickname truly suited him, as Mr Moon seemed almost as round as he was tall, with a pudding-like body and chubby-cheeked, chortling face, constantly animated with giggling and singing.

Two hours went by and the piles were finally going down. A shrill whistle brought the hive of activity to an abrupt standstill as if a switch had been turned off. "Smoko!" shouted the supervisor.

Flasks of hot tea and boxes of vegemite sandwiches were opened. A couple of posties came back from a local shop with hot meat pies. They smelled so tantalisingly good. I just looked on, wishing I had come prepared.

"You done this before, Roger?" asked one postie, chomping on his pie.

"Course he hasn't," said another. "Can't you see he's bein' trained up."

"You won't like it, Rog. It's bloody hard, specially in the rain," said a third postie.

"Even harder being trained by Full," the supervisor butted in. Everyone laughed, except Full, who stopped giggling and looked serious for once.

"Give the bloke a break, George. He knows he's with the best," said Full. I looked around the smoke-filled room and the smiles on all the sorters. Egging Mr Moon seemed to be the local sport. George slapped me on the back hard. "You'll be right, mate. I'd better show you your bike."

He led me outside to where a chunky, rusting, black bike was propped against a wall.

"This is your standard post-office-issue bike. Hard saddle, stiff chain, thin tyres and bloody heavy."

"Can I get one with gears?" I asked.

George scowled. "You'll get what yer given, mate. Just toughen up."

"Where does the mail go on the bike?" I asked Mr Moon afterwards. Mr Moon responded by singing: "Where does the mail go, ho, ho, where does the mail go?" Full handed me a canvas bag. "Take this satchel, Roger, put your name on it, and for Christ's sake, don't lose it."

I carried the satchel back to the sorting tables and pigeon holes.

"See what I do, watch closely." Mr Moon said. He skilfully tied all of his mail in bundles with rubber bands and packed them in the satchel in the order that they stood in the pigeon holes. "Keep watching. If you get them out of order, you're fucked." The satchel filled up, then a second one with Mr Moon's name plastered all over them.

I swung the satchel over my shoulders. The straps were thin and not padded. They hurt as my shoulders took the weight. I deposited the satchel in the bike basket after a few seconds of worry that I might have to carry it everywhere.

"It's your bike. You fix it when it breaks. The repair kit is in the little back bag, here. Don't let anyone take your bike and don't take anyone else's or you'll be hanged. Let's go." Mr Moon looked comical as he mounted his bike with his short stumpy legs and started pedalling.

My bike was all wrong, Saddle too low and too hard, chain very dry, tyres not pumped up and wheel not quite round. I followed Mr Moon for a couple of blocks till it became unbearable. I stopped to make adjustments to the saddle while Mr Moon disappeared over the hill. At least all my years of having my own bike with its Sturmey Archer 3-speed hub gears and leading-edge accessories (such as a speedometer) held me in good stead for this situation. I was about halfway through making the adjustments when Mr Moon came steaming back, shouting at me to move.

"C'mon. Git orf yer backside and go, go!" He glared at me until I mounted my bike and followed him up the hill.

Being a road labourer was terrible. Now this. My original thought that I could enjoy being a postman was evaporating fast. So what could I do? I had to get qualifications, just had to. But how? I had tried and failed, so what was my future? Did I really know what I wanted? I thought I did. It was either becoming a Qantas pilot or a weather forecaster. Right now both seemed fanciful prospects. One needed buckets of money spent on getting light aircraft experience and an unrestricted license, and the other required a science degree in physics. So if not these then where was I going? All these thoughts raced through my brain as I struggled up the hill on a gearless bike with wheels not quite round.

This was my current job crisis. It wasn't just a matter of cruising around the streets and leisurely inserting letters into boxes, then stopping off at the local milk bar for a long, cool, chocolate malted milkshake. No. It was getting around as fast as possible, hoping that the letters stacked in my satchel from a 6am start were in the right order, handling bulky parcels as well, negotiating tricky bush paths, avoiding snarling dogs and pedalling on a bike with an impossible saddle that chafed the skin on my crutch. And delivering all the letters and parcels correctly on a schedule that seemed physically impossible. I faced two deliveries each weekday and one on Saturday morning. It was a terrifying thought.

On that first run, Mr Moon was surprisingly helpful. Maybe he could see I was in some pain. My beat was a part of Cromer, a bush suburb on Sydney's northern beaches. In the 1960s, cows and sheep still grazed on rural paddocks, roads were without footpaths and the sewer was just being introduced. Consequently there were deep muddy ditches everywhere to house the new sewer pipes, when they eventually arrived. In the meantime they could easily swallow a postman and his bike if he wasn't watching where he was pedalling.

It was a complicated run that took two weeks to imprint indelibly into my memory. It wasn't a matter of going up and down each street. The design that Mr Moon mapped for me had me coming in and going out of the same street many times at different points. It was all about minimising run times by minimising distances.

Then there were the houses without numbers, houses without letter boxes, houses with dogs that ate postmen, houses with trick letter boxes that jammed down on fingers and houses lost in the bush connected to the outside world by a slippery and narrow bush track festooned with spiders' webs. Two streets even had a downhill so steep that my brakes faded on the way down. All that hard won altitude was wasted by having to walk down the hill.

I had the benefit of Mr Moon's tutelage for the morning and afternoon runs of that first day. Then I went solo on day 2, trying to repeat exactly what he did. I failed. Everything was wrong. I stacked the letters in my satchel in the wrong order. I couldn't remember which way the numbers ran on various streets. I dropped a bundle snapping the rubber band holding them in place. Consequently I returned to the depot late.

On day 3, my bike chain broke and it rained, so I came back very late. And each time this happened my arrival back at the depot coincided with the beginning of the afternoon letter-sorting process. There was no lunch, no leisurely chocolate milk shake, no let-up. Then there were days when I awoke to the sound of heavy rain on the tin roof of my house. And rain always sounds worse on a tin roof. Those days were the pits.

But there were moments. Coming back to the mail exchange tired and hungry after a run I was generally greeted by the strident notes of a solo trombone emanating from the locker room. It was Mr Moon. "Full does this every day, if he's not back too late. We like it, even if he's not Stravinsky," said George.

Then there was the time when I actually beat Mr Moon back to the mail exchange after the morning run. "Hey, where's Full?"

"Haven't seen him. Even later than normal." As the postie spoke, a round, brown figure, resembling a sultana-studded plum pudding with legs appeared at the entrance. "Bloody hell, it's Full, full of stinkin' shit! Get the hose onto him!"

Mr Moon was a sorry sight, gashed and bloodied, coated with sewer sludge from head to foot. He limped into the sorting room.

"This new dog was chasing me and biting at me back tyre. Bloody bitch of a mongrel. I tried to outrun 'im but the tyres slipped and I ran right into the sewer trench off Willandra Road. Just my luck it was full of shit. I couldn't stop! Me bloody bike's brake shoes popped out." Laughter erupted throughout the post office. "Fuck off, yer low life. Hit a man when he's down," he grunted on his way to the showers.

These were some of the fleeting lighter moments, though in the first weeks the discomfort and pressure of doing the rounds on time and in all weathers got to me.

But then a magical thing happened on my fourth week as Cromer's new postman. I suddenly knew the correct house order, the letter bundles didn't unravel, the letter satchel seemed lighter, the bike was comfortable, my run times dramatically decreased and the sun shone. The dogs got to know me and accepted me and some even followed me just to be social. Residents came out of their houses to chat and even to offer me a cup of tea. Soon cups of tea and cakes were being left out for me all over my run. I seemed to become an accepted part of the social furniture. I even found time for a leisurely chocolate malted. I was known universally by my first name and was consulted about the weather, the political situation, the cost of beer and cigarettes and even the illicit goings-on at number 43 Pikara Avenue.

For the first time I was enjoying working.

Even so, it was ultimately unfulfilling, it wasn't something I could work at forever. But, realistically, I had failed school, so I couldn't expect a professional occupation. Then at the back of all these thoughts lurked a simple truth and I knew it. Hard work and application to a task over an extended period was it, something that I had never really done. I had to pass exams to get anywhere and hard work was the way to do it. But where would I get that type of discipline? I just didn't think that was in me. What I didn't realise at the time was that this job was actually a stepping stone to other jobs. I was developing a modicum of 'people skills'.

"Good morning Roger. Don't give me bills."

"Hello, Mrs Ponsford, looks like I may have a cheque and a bill."

"Well, you can take that one and I'll have this one. Ha-ha, just having you on!"

"One may pay for the other, Mrs Ponsford."

"Have you heard anything about Mrs Crick's son? I heard he got run over." Mrs Ponsford thought I knew everything about everyone.

"Didn't know about that but I haven't seen Mrs Crick lately."

"That's because she's run off with that Lander bloke, you know the one, up on Willandra Road. He's crook as Rookwood."

"I think I've seen him once. He rides to the shops on his horse."

"Yes I know that, but what about his mail? What does he get?"

I learnt quickly where to draw the line and respect people's privacy. "I have to run. Got a lot left to do. See you tomorrow!"

With that I cycled down the road, leaving a clearly disappointed Mrs Ponsford behind me. Knowing how to deal with people, what was appropriate, what was not, how to be approachable, how to be discreet without appearing secretive, how to be trustworthy, how to be and appear to be empathetic in a work situation – all of those workplace skills grew from this job.

The War

It was 1965 and I had been out of school for a year. The Vietnam War was escalating and our Prime Minister, Mr Menzies decided that conscription was a good idea not apparently to bolster the war effort so much as to maintain the numbers in the services at home. But it turned out that conscripts went to war anyway.

The method of selecting the cannon fodder the government wanted was curious. Males were selected by a ballot of birthdays, like a lucky dip where marbles are drawn out of a hat in a secret ceremony. It applied to 24-year-old men, who, if balloted in, were subject to two years of full-time service in the Regular Army Supplement, followed by three years' part-time service in the Regular Army Reserve. National servicemen on full-time duty were liable for what was called 'special overseas service', which included combat duties in Vietnam.

This last aspect of the plan raised the hackles of my mother. My grandfather went to the Great War; he fought at Gallipoli. Then my father went to the sequel. So it seemed that wars were spaced a generation apart, catching my family every time but never those whose birth dates were about 10 years removed from this arithmetic sequence. This seemed basically unfair to my mother and she wasn't going to let her only son get caught up in it. She planned for us to escape the country and go to England where, theoretically I couldn't be touched. The government was wise to this ploy and prevented 20-year-olds from leaving by withdrawing passports and outlawing ticket sales.

Norma always had a formidable determination to get her own way. She was both a dedicated mother and a best friend to me. I was close to her, which seemed very natural to me as an only child of a now single mother. She was described by her peers as a 'career woman', which implied that few women at the time had one. She could be scheming and manipulative, traits that were now focused on rescuing her son from the horrors of war. But how were we to escape the country when the legal door had already been shut?

Rewind nine years to 1956. Norma was in New York studying television techniques to prepare for the introduction of TV to Australia. Candy, one of Norma's friends, had agreed to look after me on weekends. We did what was traditional in those days, the Sunday afternoon drive. On the way home from a trip to view the new Warragamba Dam, I ran across the highway to buy an ice cream. I recall a loud thud and a sensation of flying. A woman had run me over in her Morris Minor. In a moment of panic she had hit the accelerator instead of the brake and run me down again. Faces stared down at me as I lay on the grass. I was important enough to have a siren blaring in the ambulance. My main injuries were a broken leg and arm. I was still in a plaster cast when I limped out of hospital 6 weeks later. My mother convinced the orthopaedic specialist from the insurance company that my limp was noticeable 12 months later. Her lessons in limp walking, ensuring I limped pitifully on the correct leg, paid off, the insurance money going on a few terms at the elite Shore School.

But my injury was to have a much greater benefit nine years later. Norma had, through some research, selected an eminent Sydney Macquarie Street orthopaedic specialist with connections with London doctors. After discussing the merits of his art collection on display around his walls, his attention turned to me.

"Roger, I want you to walk up and down my room a few times. I'll tell you when to stop. Just walk naturally."

I put in my best effort, at pains to emulate my practice runs. The specialist studied my movements intensely.

"Well, there is something there, but it looks a little tenuous." I kept on walking. I had got into the limp rhythm. "OK, you can stop. I think you've walked a mile already. You'll be wearing out my carpet." After a long silence, he capitulated and wrote a referral for a second opinion with a Harley Street specialist. "He may spot something going on there." Norma raised her eyebrow, a silent sign of victory. On leaving the specialist's rooms, Norma held up the letter like a trophy. "This is our ticket out of here. We start packing when we get home."

We had slipped through the loophole. Exemptions from the ban on 20-year-olds leaving the country were given where dire medical need was only available overseas. My need was not particularly dire according to the letter, but at the same time my condition was confirmed, however subtle, and the Immigration Department gave me the go-ahead to leave the country. The scheme had worked, as Norma knew it would. I had my passport.

There was now only one problem. We had no ticket. This was because we had no money. But that was no obstacle to Norma. She had spied a new shipping line in Australia, eager to promote its new flagship on her maiden voyage. A little extra publicity would help, and Norma struck up a nice business relationship with a Mr Papandreou from Chandris Lines. The outcome was two free passages on the maiden voyage of *Australis* from Sydney to Southampton in exchange for a series of complimentary articles about the ship, illustrated by me, her photographer, for the Sydney newspapers.

Greek shipping lines in those days were cut-rate down-market affairs, ferrying migrants from England to Australia and returning disaffected migrants to The Old Country. Later they took these same whingers back to The Lucky Country when, in the light of their Australian experience, they realised just how bad The Old Country really was.

Australis was second-hand, like all Greek liners of the period. Its former life was as the much more glamorous *SS America,* plying the rich transatlantic trade with its sister ship *SS United States*, the fastest liner of its time. The Greeks stripped down all of the finery and increased the passenger capacity by making the ship one class, sardine class. Even so, it was still a fine ship with both an indoor and outdoor pool and a grand dining room that really was grand. It was the flagship and the biggest ship of the Chandris fleet. And this was its maiden voyage under its new colours, a great advertising opportunity for the line as it competed for passenger trade with Sitmar, Lloyd Triestino, P&O, Flotta Lauro and others.

Pigs in Pitt Street – Press Photographer

Norma's deal involved two components, her story and my pictures. A selling point was that as well as her proven track record as a journalist, I was billed as a trained press photographer adept in the skills of capturing the essence of life aboard the party ship *Australis*, the joy on the passengers' faces, the fun life with poolside cocktails, elegance at the Captain's Table and the majesty of the ship itself. This part of the deal presented a challenge on two fronts. Firstly my photographic skills amounted to shaky home stills with a box brownie and the sort of shipboard life I was to 'capture' departed when the Greeks stripped the old *SS America* down to function as public transport for migrants.

"Now I know you can do this, Roger." Norma's tone was determined and imperious rather than reassuring. "I've been recommended to a Mr Caswell who used to work for one of the papers. He agreed to take you on and train you up in 6 weeks. I think in that time you will have learnt something."

"But I don't even have a camera," I protested.

"Mr Caswell said he could give you one from his stock quite cheaply. At least we can afford it. It's one of those new cameras where you look through the lens so you know the picture you are getting. You know the ones."

"Yes, a single lens reflex," I said confidently.

"See, you know something already."

So I did my 6-week intensive with Mr Caswell and, to my surprise, I did learn the basics. I went around town photographing everything, statues, faces, traffic and the new-fangled parking meters, Sydney's latest innovation. After I had covered exposure and composition, Mr Caswell sent me out to photograph newsworthy events captured when walking around the city streets. The trouble was I never encountered one remotely newsy event. So Norma manufactured one for me. She was promoting an upcoming fashion parade and her PR machine came up with the idea of walking a group of pigs through the crowded lunchtime streets. The logic was that if you could dress up a pig to look attractive with this fashion collection, how much better would they look on a modern western woman?

I was given the inside information as to where to be to get the best shots for the downtown pig fashion parade. It was the corner of King and Pitt Streets at noon on a particular day. So there I stationed myself, camera at the ready. Noon came and went. Doubts were beginning to seep in to my thinking when at 12:45, I heard a commotion down Pitt Street with a crowd moving in my direction. I moved around to get the best angle but the crowd blocked me. I then shouted "coming through, coming through!" in an authoritative voice and magically the crowd responded and parted for me revealing the perfect set-up, with four pigs dressed in lacy skirts and pink bows on designer collars. The pigs, way out of their natural habitat, were squealing loudly. Each was cradled by a lovely model dressed in Haute Couture, followed by a clutch of policemen trying to control the crowd. In the middle of the foray was a beaming Norma, looking up at the camera as I shot one priceless shot after another, well before any of the newspaper photographers could get there. Strangely enough, they had been fed the wrong information about the location of this unique event.

I had the scoop! I raced to Consolidated Press, only two blocks away, with my treasure. The paper grabbed it, giving me front-page pictures in the *Daily Telegraph* the next morning under the sub-editor's headline of *Porky fashions stop city*. My career had been launched. Mr Caswell was very pleased with me and said he had never before heard of a novice like me getting ahead of the professionals and scoring an exclusive.

All at Sea – Ship's Photographer

Norma and I departed for England in September 1965 on *Australis's* maiden voyage sailing via Suva, Panama City, Port Everglades and Southampton. The shipping line installed us on Z deck, somewhere near the propellers. We seemed so close to the waterline that opening the porthole might sink the ship.

"There must be some mistake," Norma protested to the purser in her best posh voice. "We are here to promote the ship. We can't do that if we are living where you house the cattle." Norma flashed a few letters in front of the purser signed by Chandris executives and suddenly cabin stewards were called in to move all our luggage up to the empty staterooms on the promenade deck.

The purser personally showed us into our new palatial digs. "Will this be suitable Miss Martyn?" She nodded in approval. I had my own stateroom on the same deck but I had to share, which was welcome, as I was reaching a stage in life when I was happy to associate with anyone who was not my mother.

I tried to capture all of the high-class elements the ship was billed as having, but sadly for me they were missing. The passengers were returning disaffected English migrants devoid of any joy or exuberance. The dining room felt more like a canteen and the poolside cocktail bar was often swamped by waves from the pool because the ship had no stabilisers. I snapped at anything and everything and even caught a couple dancing who were not meant to be a couple, according to the wife of the man and the husband of the woman. Once the couple knew they had been snapped, they pursued me around the ship for days, demanding that I hand over the filmed evidence. But I was keen to evade them as my film also had important shots depicting the 'elegance' of the ship. After Panama, I never saw them again.

Norma was in her element, fraternising with all the important people on board, namely, the captain, the ship's officers and the only pseudo-celebrity on board, a chess champion from Eastern Europe. This spawned a chess tournament at Norma's suggestion, which embarrassingly, Norma won.

In Norma's later life, ship contra deals became standard operating procedure for her. On one occasion, when she was running an on-board shop, the Captain sought Norma's advice after a passenger had passed away moments earlier and the chronically drunk ship's doctor was too inebriated to either try to save the poor man's life or certify his death. The small ship had no morgue facility and the Captain wanted to act quickly to avoid upsetting passengers, so Norma promptly cleaned out some food from one of the ship's fridges and helped haul the lone ex-traveller into it for safe-keeping until they reached port.

My mother was certainly resourceful. On another occasion, she was in Hong Kong wanting to return to Australia but without the funds to do so. So when she saw a cargo ship known to take passengers to Australia about to set sail, she ran to the wharf and started waving madly at the crew. It was assumed she was a passenger about to miss the boat, so the crew came to her aid with a lifeboat and she was hauled on board through the cargo hatch. The Purser was not impressed when she said she was desperate to get to Australia and would like to buy a ticket on board. As always, she was able to sweet-talk her way out of this tricky situation. She had her seaman's ticket, she argued, and could earn her passage by helping with the accounts and writing a ship's newspaper. Norma said she enjoyed her voyage back to Sydney via Yokohama, Guam, Rabaul and Noumea – and of course dining with the Captain and fellow officers.

I had none of Norma's bravado, and frankly I felt I would be lost without her guidance. Aboard *Australis*, I was merely her assistant, a photographer meant to be taking pictures of people enjoying the luxury of life afloat. But photographic artistry seemed beyond me on *Australis*. Each night the same oily potatoes were served up, despite the menu giving them exotic names like *gratin dauphinois* and *duchess*. Each night the same music blared over the PA. The pool, on the few days when it was open, looked similar to those old council pools in Australian bush towns: a small pit filled with water and a nearby change shed. Not much to photograph there. The evening stage show was my best source of material as the lighting was left over from the vessel's luxurious past and the costumes glittered in the stage light. This was my best chance to show this touch of elegance especially since it was too dark to show the audience.

In the end I sweated over a result as the five rolls of Kodak Ektachrome were being developed when we arrived in London. Norma selected 15 good shots which pleased her to accompany her copy back to *The Daily Telegraph* in Sydney.

A month at sea served as a transition from one life to another. We crawled up the Solent to our final berth, but despite the steely-grey, cold Southampton afternoon, I was excited. A new world, and a restart to my career of sorts. I was very vague about that, as I viewed our new residency status as being on a holiday, though I knew we would both have to earn some money soon.

Having settled in to London's Australian ghetto of the 60s, Earl's Court, Norma and I travelled to Harley Street to an appointment made half a world away. Harley Street was where the specialist's specialists had their rooms. Their street represented the epitome of medical knowledge, at least in the Empire. This was where one would have to go to secure the ultimate second opinion.

Norma produced the trophy letter and handed it to the immaculately suited specialist. He scanned the letter and looked down on us in a faintly censorious manner. "Do a walk for me, Roger," he ordered. "Just walk the way you would outdoors."

I tried to emulate my Macquarie Street amble with built-in limp.

"Hmm," the specialist grunted as I paced the space. Eventually, after my 4th circuit he turned to Norma. "Well, it's good news I'd say. Roger has managed to compensate for the diaphyseal tibia shortening that came about from the poor job that hospital did on him. It wasn't significant to start with, according to your specialist's report. I don't think it's worth going further."

"No, no," said Norma, in agreement.

"Well that's that then." The doctor led us to the door and into the waiting room where the secretary typed up our exorbitant bill. As soon as the typist ripped it out of the platinum roller Norma was searching for the total and raised her eyebrows in disbelief.

"We were only in there for 10 minutes. I suppose we didn't actually have to come here. Getting to England was sufficient. And it's in guineas, not pounds," she sighed.

One month later, in Canberra the short straws were being picked behind closed doors out of the gaze of the media. This arrangement was considered best by the minders as hands dipping into hats and picking straws as the State-sponsored means for assigning young men to war wasn't a good look. Journos could only report on what they were told. I missed out on national service by two days, as the birthday two days away from mine was picked. And now Norma and I were in England because of that danger. We were both facing an uncertain future.

Serving at Selfridges – Butcher's Assistant

It was October 1965 and getting cold with the English winter closing in. Norma and I shared a pokey little room let out by the Overseas Visitors Club, the OVC, next to Earls Court Road. Our money was running out and I had to find a job to tide us over while Norma trawled for a journalist position through her BBC contacts. With Christmas approaching and the shops becoming busy, the obvious source of unskilled labour was retail. And in London, like bees to a honey pot, Australians gravitated to Selfridges, the Oxford Street department store institution.

Everything was on a grand scale at Selfridges. The employment enquiry area housed a labyrinth of interview rooms with a crowd of young colonials in a holding area waiting to be called. The queues advanced very quickly, too quickly for me to get myself mentally ready for what I thought could be an inquisition. But it didn't go like that.

"Name," commanded the flustered looking interview officer. I gave my name which she ticked off on a list.

"You're in food. Go over there." She pointed to another interview room where a group of youths like me was congregating.

I followed her directions to the new room and then waited to be called. No one came.

"Do you know what work this is?" I asked one of the youths.

"Search me, mate. Where you from?"

"Sydney."

"Melbourne, here. We're all Aussies except Dave here. He's from South Africa. They just said food so I figured we have to sell it, not eat it," the youth responded.

Just then a white-coated, grey-headed man marched in and pointed to us.

"You, you and you. Come with me. My name is Mr Broad. I'm going to show you around and train you up to be ready to start tomorrow at eight. Clear?" Mr Broad walked and talked fast and spoke with a thick North Country accent.

"What are we doing?" the youth asked.

"What, you don't know? Geez, those personnel people." Mr Broad looked at us and said, "Butchery, lads."

"What? You mean cutting up animals?" The youth grimaced. Mr Broad nodded.

"That's it. I'm not staying. Bye. You comin'?" He looked at the others and in silence, three of the group walked out with him. This left the South African and me.

Mr Broad just stood there watching them go. I took my opportunity. "Pardon me Mr Broad, but do you think there's another job going apart from butchery?"

Mr Broad glared at me. "Look, son. I don't question them and if I did, I know what they would say, if you don't like what you are given, then you can look elsewhere. Got it?"

I nodded meekly and followed the boss into the meat preparation room where he introduced me to the butchers. "This is Roger, gents. Show him around and get him familiar with his job. OK?" The four butchers in the room gave a thumbs-up sign and Mr Broad turned and left.

I was shown around the whole process and the longer the butchers explained my job the better I felt. "So all I have to do is to wrap the meat that you've cut for me and take it out to the display. I don't do any cutting, right?"

One of the lead butchers called Sam spoke up. "Hey, Roger. No one expects you to do any cutting or boning. That's a skilled job best left to the experts, hey mates?" All the butchers in the room nodded. "You just make sure the cuts are arranged nicely for the display out on the shop floor. And you must, repeat must, know the different cuts and types. We'll give you a test after afternoon tea."

"So a true butcher butchers."

"That's right, lad." Sam handed me a long, shiny cleaver. "Look, have a go and see for yourself what it's like. "Have a go at this carcass, whack it along the muscle line here to get a nice Selfridge cut," he said, pointing to the impact point I was to target.

"Stand back," I warned and with everyone in the room at a suitably safe distance I brandished the cleaver up in the air and flashed it down, delivering a forceful karate chop. The cleaver hacked straight through the carcass and into the first inch of chopping board. The meat parted, becoming shrapnel instantaneously flying through the air like carnivorous rain peppering all who stood in the way of the fallout. Just then Mr Board entered the room and collected a small meaty sample on his lapel.

"Jesus Christ, what's going on!" He glared at me, then tried vainly to brush off the globule, now sliding downwards.

My butcher mentor was doubled up with laughter.

"Sir," he panted, "we just were showing the boy the skill needed to become a butcher." The words wheezed out in spasms. Everyone in the room was hysterical. Mr Broad looked around and sized up the situation.

"I dunno what you were thinking you were doing." Mr Board paused for a reaction but none came, just laughter. "Clean all this up, now! Get that cleaver! The boy's not to have it. Right?" Mr Board turned and left, still brushing his jacket. The show was over.

It wasn't long before I built confidence under the skilled tutelage of Sam the butcher. I got to know chucks and loin, round steaks and sirloin steaks, chops and cutlets, pork ribs and spare ribs and everything in between. I passed my test with flying colours and felt ready to face the customers the next day as the new carnivore expert.

I bundied on the next morning. My first challenge was to work the Bundy clock with my new employee card. I had never seen such a machine before. Then I took the long walk to the food hall and the meat island display and counter.

"Are you Roger? Because if you are, you gotta be inducted," said a thin man in a white dustcoat behind the counter. I nodded and was directed through a maze or corridors to a cavernous auditorium where about 40 inductees were already assembled.

"Good, we'll start," said a man on the stage in front of me. He signalled to a projectionist behind me. What followed was a two-hour advertisement for Selfridges, tracing the retailer's history from Gordon Selfridge's first shop to the current empire. Portraits of the man himself adorned the walls of most of the administration offices. By the film's end, I knew a lot about the firm but still didn't have a clue on how to sell meat.

Arriving back at the meat counter after the ritual calorie-laden morning tea, the real induction began. Before long, I was advising customers on all things carnivorous. What was the best cut for them, thin, thick, chuck or shank, British or New Zealand, lamb, beef or pork? The enjoyment was in both being 'the expert' and in engaging and advising people. I was the expert because I had the jargon. The 'expert' element was missing from all previous employment and it made being a butcher's assistant my best job yet.

Being November I arrived at Selfridges in the dark and clocked off in the dark. I had never experienced such short days before. Sunlight was scarce and only viewed dimly during my all too brief lunch hour. It was a faded primrose orb hanging weak and low over Hyde Park, giving light but no heat.

Then it was back to the island counter. There was an undercurrent of infighting and petty jealousies of the staff towards one another, so talking with the customers became an escape. But that too started to weigh on me after a while. Then boredom set in like heavy sludge. I had tired of my encounters with customers as they had assumed a sameness in my mind, always asking the same questions, spending inordinate amounts of time inspecting the appearance of even a minute chop, reluctant to part with pennies as much as pounds.

There were highlights. One day I served a very special customer. He was dressed fashionably, looked suave, spoke commandingly and possessed that air of importance that the upper classes perform so well. His walking cane appeared gold-tipped and the handkerchief displayed out of his jacket breast pocket neatly complemented his bow tie.

"Good morning. I wish to purchase those two cuts and these three sausages."

"The cuts with the marbling?"

"Yes, they're the ones. It indicates quality my man, but of course, you know that."

I got the sense I was being tested and felt uncomfortable. I quickly wrapped the order and took his money. With that he abruptly turned and was off.

"You know who you served then? You know who that was?"

"No."

"It was the Sheriff of Nottingham."

"What! Do they still have them, after all these centuries since Robin Hood?"

"Of course. Didn't you know that? You served Commander Francklin of the Royal Navy who is this year's Sheriff."

"This year's?"

"Yes, there is a different one every year, as there has been since Robin Hood's time."

And that was the highlight of my Selfridges job as shop assistant in the meat department.

Gumshoe – Industrial Espionage Agent

Being a Selfridges' employee, I was qualified to join the exalted ranks of an exclusive Mayfair club, Selfridge's Employees' Club. It had rooms near Grosvenor Square sporting billiards, an indoor pool, a gymnasium and a small cafeteria. The facilities were not as important as the status of membership, a Mayfair club no less.

However this attraction could not compensate for the boredom of serving meat, day in, day out. By February the job was starting to pall but the money paid our bills, the rent for the tiny bedsit Norma and I occupied, the coins to feed the gas meter heating the space and our food, either to cook from the supermarket or the very cheap Asian restaurant in Earls Court called The Pot where you queued up for a table and then ate furiously so you could vacate the table ASAP for the next diner.

Norma was scouting for work as a journalist and her BBC friend, a substantial and cultured lady, Constance Paul, who had 'society' contacts came up with a work offer for her. The brief was to write a story about a soft drink manufacturer.

"What they are actually after is information on what rival manufacturers, their competitors, are doing," said Norma on returning from an introductory meeting. "I'm to interview all these other people. I'll have a cover story, that I'm doing a study on how soft drinks will look in 20 years' time, where the market is going – something that sounds legitimate and not like I'm after commercial secrets."

"But you are, really, after secrets."

"Well, yes. I have to convince them it's a real and independent study so I've been given fake letters of accreditation from an overseas university. I have my media pass as well, which is the only genuine thing I can show them."

"So what do you want them to tell you? What are you meant to get?"

"I hope they will tell me what they see is the future, in other words, their plans."

"Why would they tell you their plans? Their competitors might get to hear about them. They won't tell you that. How many companies are we seeing?"

"Twelve."

"Well, you might get one or two to give you an inkling."

"They don't expect much from that source. It's just a cover story anyway. So that's where you come in."

"Me?"

"What they really want is what you can give."

I suddenly became very attentive. "You see, it's because of you we've got the job, and well paid too. Puts your Selfridge pay to shame. I told them you are a trained press photographer working with a Sydney newspaper, OK? So here's the deal. They want photos of their factory setup, bottles on conveyors, brand labels, volume, production line machines, numbers of personnel, all that sort of thing."

"Hell, how do I get all that and what with? I've only got my little Pentax SLR that was given to me from Mr Caswell's training course."

"That's fine. Anyway, the smaller, the less conspicuous. My idea is that while I am interviewing the chap from the company you can look around for a good view through to their factory and then take photos from the best angle. You've got your telephoto lens. I'm sure it will come in useful."

"What if someone stops me and asks me what I am doing?"

"Say you are with me and are just getting a bit of exercise."

"Getting exercise taking photos of their conveyor belts and production lines? Sure they'll swallow that?"

"Say you are photographing a rare bird."

I started laughing, but Norma looked serious.

"Look," she said impatiently, "use your common sense, say whatever you think will work on them. By the way, you have two jobs and get paid for each. Your other job is as my driver."

"Good. I'll like that," I said. "What sort of car do we get? If I'm driving a spy around, I will need what Bond has, an Aston Martin with an inbuilt missile system and smokescreen deployment."

"We have the budget for a mini. Don't call me a spy. I'm just a journo getting a story." The voice was serious, but Norma's face was all smiles.

"Not even a Morris Cooper S," I pleaded.

"Just the mini. That's all we need. We can't be conspicuous. It will be good, better than standing behind a meat counter." I had to agree to that.

Over the next two days we worked up a plan. The 12 soft drink companies were dotted around the countryside, in the Cotswolds, Home Counties, Birmingham and even Wales, all the better for sightseeing.

I negotiated time off work at Selfridges stating urgent family reasons. I figured that would cut it better with personnel than applying for 'spy leave'. Norma and I planned a logical route and then teed up interviews that fitted with our driving route. We spaced the timing of the interviews to give me adequate snooping time. Fortuitously all but one company accepted Norma's story and granted interview time and not just with the PR person but in three cases with the head honcho.

Setting off early one cold February morning we headed up the new M1 motorway to our first factory near Coventry.

I was nervous stepping out of the car, unsure of what I was meant to do. Norma quickly disappeared into reception. I started to walk around the factory perimeter, listening for production line noise. It was a dead quiet factory. I found a gate and walked in through to a loading area. Rounding a corner, I saw ahead of me a small room with the noise of glass bottles clinking against one another coming through the windows. I looked around for a vantage point that lined up with an open window.

"Hey there!" A man approached me. I shoved my camera into my bag. "Don't see your pass, do you have one?"

"Well, no. I'm with my mother. She's inside talking to your rep. I just wanted to stretch my legs while I was waiting for her."

"You're not allowed around here, you know."

"I didn't know."

"You'll have to go back to reception."

"Can't I just walk around and get a bit of fresh air. I've been inside a car for hours so this is really good."

"Sorry, the boss would go bananas if you stayed. Just the other day we had a chap wandering around actually taking photos, would you believe? C'mon, I'll take you back." And with that I was led back to reception to wait for Norma until her interview wrapped up.

"What happened to you?" she asked as we left the factory.

"I got caught. Security didn't like me wandering around. They caught someone last week taking photos. But don't worry, they didn't see my little camera."

"This is going to be harder than I thought. I got nothing from that interview. My only hope is you. Let's see if we can get a shot from the road." We walked back to the car and drove off a short distance to park out of the view of the plant. There were a few small hills adjacent to the road that looked promising. We walked up the highest and to our delight had an unobstructed view directly to the factory. The windows were all frosted and closed except for one.

"Of course it's winter, isn't it, so they close the windows. We're lucky to have one that's opened," I said. Then with my telephoto lens on extreme magnification and with my camera looking very professional on its tripod, I took my pictures. The lens was so good, one window almost filled my frame, but all I could see were a few bottles moving by on a conveyor belt and periodic clouds of steam. After taking a sufficient number of pictures to justify our visit, despite the unchanging scene, we moved off.

The next company was just down the road. We followed the same routine. Norma disappeared into reception while I cruised the grounds. This time there was no one out to stop me, but this was a much bigger plant. The manufacturing building was hard to identify with processing noise emanating from every building. Suddenly, there it was, a line of soft drink bottles on a conveyor belt, in full view through a clear glass window. I got my camera out and was focusing in on my subject when a huge squirt of steam rose up, completely obscuring the scene. I waiting for the fog to clear but workers were starting to spill out of the building towards me, so I took quick fuzzy pictures of bottles of uncertain type and left quickly. Two unsatisfactory visits, 10 to go.

Over the next week we criss-crossed the country, going from one manufacturer to another, often returning to companies visited earlier for 'follow-up' interviews and a second crack at getting better photos. Worcester, Stratford-upon-Avon, Gloucester, Coventry, Reading and Bristol – I was getting to know the English countryside very quickly.

At our final destination, Norma was refused an interview, but our brief had emphasised the importance of this particular enterprise. I had to get good pictures here. We circled the perimeter several times to spot a weakness in their defences. There was not, not even a hill to climb to get a better view.

I was never told exactly what I was to photograph, just a general view of the production line. But by now, I was starting to understand what was important: something about production costs, and how new production line techniques brought down those costs, allowing that company to undercut its competitors. The complex wasn't even visible from the road. There was no way inside apart through the manned boom gates. Workers streamed through these gates at 6am for the day shift and 3pm for the afternoon shift. We watched one of these changeovers from a distance on our first day. It was a big plant with over 200 workers per shift. The boom gates were lifted and they all walked through in one big group from buses coming from Salisbury and other towns right on 3pm, like clockwork. We noted that there was no ID check. They just walked in.

"You're going to have to be a worker for tomorrow's morning shift, Roger," Norma announced.

"What? You're crazy. What am I meant to do when I get inside, pull out my camera and get everyone to pose?"

"Look, it will be pitch dark at 6 and everyone dresses the same. You won't be spotted. Safety in numbers. Follow them and you'll get to the production plant. Go to the toilet and wait your chance to slip into the main area and get your pictures."

"I'll be spotted by someone for sure. As soon as I peek my head around the door they will only have to look up and know I'm not a worker."

"There are hundreds there. You could be a new recruit. There's no argument. We have to get the pictures. It doesn't matter about not getting good pictures at the other places, we have to get them here. You have to do it. What's the worst thing that can happen? You get kicked out for trespassing."

"No. The worst thing that can happen is I get exposed as a spy and get interrogated, tortured by MI5, or MI6, I never know which is which. And my getaway car is just a Mini, not the Aston Martin I wanted."

"Stop arguing. You're going to do it and that's that."

The alarm went off in our little room at the local pub at 5am. I struggled up and threw cold water at my face to wake up. I donned the heavy outdoor worker's clothes that Norma had purchased, checked my camera for film and battery power and walked out to the car.

Bright floodlights illuminated the factory entrance. I quickly parked the car and joined the throng of workers massing outside the gate, keeping my head down and my jacket collar wrapped around my neck, in good Hollywood film-noir style. My camera was safely tucked away in a pocket. I was just another worker, just another grey form in the pre-dawn gloom. A siren marked 6am as the gates opened and we all streamed in. Groups starting splitting off once inside, but I stuck with the largest group which fortuitously led to the main production room.

The group slowed down approaching the main door and a loud clicking sound became evident. As I got closer I realised it was a bundy machine and each worker was bundying on using their personal card. I was going to be found out before I could get any pictures. I just knew it. I hung back to see if there was some escape route as the queue I was in advanced all too quickly. What was that door just before the bundy? People were going in and out of it. Edging closer I realised it was the toilet. I made a bee line for the door, slipped in, found a cubicle and locked the door behind me. This was just like Norma had planned. The toilet was busy at first but quickly emptied as workers had to start promptly after clocking on. At 6:15am I was all alone in a cubicle in the men's toilet about to start the most dangerous part of this exercise.

I opened the cubicle door and crept out, making my way towards the noise. At the end of a short corridor I came to the entrance of the main production room and had a close-up view of a quite different bottle processing setup from what I had seen at any of the other factories. This one had conveyors slipping into a number of parallel lines, increasing the throughput of product. The mechanism looked vastly more complicated than anything I had seen. In front of me was the Clapham Junction of conveyor belts. The room was vast and workers were tending the lines everywhere, eyes down, intent on their jobs. At any moment, any of the 50 or so workers I could see in the room might look up or turn around and see me at the door.

As well as the workers there were supervisors who cruised around the factory floor checking on the workers. I suddenly saw my opportunity to become a temporary supervisor and started to cruise closer to the work stations, keeping close to my exit route. I took my camera out of my pocket and held it under my jacket, popping it out momentarily for quick shots. I couldn't afford the risk of lining the camera up with a subject by looking through the viewer and hoped that at waist level I could judge the right direction. In that initial foray near the door I attempted pictures of the overall room view and close-ups of the multi-conveyor setup.

After just a minute or so, my instincts told me my luck was running out. I turned and headed back to my door. As I turned into my exit corridor a quick glance around gave me the warning I expected. Two supervisors were moving towards me. I disappeared up the corridor, into the toilet and back to my favourite cubicle. I waited and listened, but no one approached. That first inspection was good, very good. I was sure I had most of the pictures, but I needed another visit to the shop floor as a backup and to cover the activities I had missed first time around. One more visit, that's all I needed. Then I could leave.

I waited for about an hour, a time interval that I hoped was enough for the supervisors to have forgotten about me. I emerged, all ready to get the quick pictures. I came through the door and into the main room. Someone turned around and saw me. They stood up from their position and started moving towards me before I could move back out of sight. Then the alarm went off. Was this a call to arms that security had been breached? I backed away and turned. Then the entire floor moved as all the workers headed for another exit. Morning tea. My timing had been dreadful, but I made it safely back to the toilet. I closed my cubicle door as the toilet suddenly became busy and cubicles either side of me became occupied.

Fifteen minutes later, another alarm sounded which I took to be the end of morning tea. I waited for about another hour and hoped that this time I had judged it right, emerging into the room to the same scene as before. I looked around for the supervisors and saw them well away from me, patrolling the more distant activities. This was my best chance. No one was looking up at me. I shot a whole roll of film on the scene, long shots, close-ups and panoramas. I hoped to God my exposures were OK as my camera had no meter and I had to guess my aperture and shutter speed for the conditions. It took three minutes, the longest three minutes of my life, to reach the end of my roll of film. I had taken everything. I quickly returned the camera to its hidey-hole.

"Hello there. Can you check on gate four please?" It was a supervisor standing right next to me. I had been too engrossed in taking furtive pictures to notice I'd been noticed.

"OK, gate four then," I said and moved off.

"Where are you going?" the supervisor asked. Clearly I was not heading towards Gate 4.

"It's OK. I'll get there. I just need to check something else. Be back very shortly." I pointed off to near my door and moved that way. I could feel my heart pounding and sweat was forming on my brow despite the cold. I could sense suspicion being aroused. Then I felt something else in my pocket. It was a notebook. I took it out, opened it up and looked as if I was taking notes as I walked slowly towards the exit, looking up every few seconds to assess the activity, seemingly to check it lined up with my notes. I turned. The supervisor gave me a friendly wave and moved away. I exited the room and rushed to my cubicle sanctuary. I sat on the toilet, door locked, head down with globules of sweat dropping off my forehead and onto the floor. Eventually my pulse slowed. I was safe.

I was dozing off on the toilet seat when the alarm went off. My pulse rocketed. Had I been discovered? Gate four was never checked. What had become of me? A search had begun for the supervisor missing in action. Any moment they would inspect an obvious place, the men's toilet. Then I realised it was the alarm for lunch. Once again the toilet filled with workers. I sat on my toilet until 3pm when the end-of-shift siren sounded. I waited until I could hear the sound of a crowd leaving. My bum was numb. I got up stiffly and opened my cubicle door for the last time and looked back at my little haven I had spent most of the day in. The exit corridor was jammed with people, just the way I liked it. The crush moved me along into the grey drizzle outside. Buses were waiting beyond the raised barrier. Freedom was on the other side like beyond the Berlin wall. I attached myself to a talkative group as we passed the guardhouse and the raised boom. I was blessedly out. My last worry was whether my car had been identified as foreign and impounded, but it was still standing there, looking innocent. Maybe the Aston Martin with on-board guided missile systems and retractable wings would have stood out in a car park full of Minis, Austin A40s and Ford Anglias.

"Where the hell have you been?" asked Norma on my return to the pub.

"What do you mean? I was doing my job."

"I thought you might be gone for an hour, not the whole bloody day."

"I couldn't leave on my own. The guards might have stopped me, sneaking out before my shift had finished. I had to wait till the end of the shift and go out with everyone else."

"Did you get the pictures?"

"Did I get caught? The answer is no. Did I get the pictures? Yes, with difficulty."

"Difficulty?"

Look, there I was, looking like a supervisor cruising the shop floor taking what I could until spotted by other supervisors, then I left."

"Left. Where?"

"The toilet. I was there for most of the day."

"You were in the toilet for all those hours?" Norma burst into shrieks of laughter. "I wondered what had happened to you. I expected you would take the pics and be back here for breakfast. I was contemplating a visit to the police station when you arrived back. It's great to see you. I was worried. Did you get everything?"

"Yes everything, including all the new production setups, as close ups."

"Well congratulations are in order. It's wine for dinner. I think the travel budget can stand that."

Two weeks later Norma gave her report to the commissioning agency and the scant feedback suggested it was well received, especially the hard-won final factory pictures. Our fee for the job was paid and we could breathe financially again. But what now? Did I need to go back to the meat department at Selfridges? This seemed a retrograde step after all the excitement. But it never happened, as an entirely new career phase was about to open up.

The Sherwood Forest Story – Stately Home Gardener

Constance Paul, our BBC insider and documentary filmmaker, gave Norma and me the gumshoe job. Her greatest gift to us jobwise came next. It was Sherwood, my life-changing job. One of the BBC's many tentacles reached into the aristocracy and Constance's titled network was at the heart of this. The mid-sixties was a time when the Labour Government was increasing taxes on the upper classes, many of whom were asset-rich but cash-poor. Their assets were their castles, and they discovered that these could become a cash cow simply by opening them to the public. But they didn't know how to run an operation like this and sought outside help. One of Constance's friends was a countess who was in this position. Constance asked Norma and me to help. You bet we could. Where was her castle, her seat? Right in the middle of Sherwood Forest.

I remember those misty and dank autumn afternoons of October. In the English midlands they appeared, ponderously, day after day excising their brief brightness. Through the stillness of the country, bulky oak trees appeared limp and dormant while the giant elms and beech trees of the forest reached beyond the view of ground dwellers as the fog closed in. Disembodied tones of cuckoo and owl were heard somewhere beyond the faint forms of meandering branches and dripping bracken, calls that were weakened now, anticipating the coming cold that turned down the volume of forest life for a season.

Into this landscape I arrived, in the autumn of 1965 from a loud and energetic London, 120 miles distant. Sherwood Forest was to be my new home for as long as I could plan. Each day brought new excitement as I continually adapted to new situations in my late teens, as an apprentice traveller of the world.

Opportunities born of world travel needed clever engineering as well as knowing the right people. My mother provided both talents in abundance. It was because of her that these experiences were possible. I was in fact one of many support acts for a picture whose star and executive producer was Norma. The exciting element in this production was that she had little or no control over the plot.

The Dukeries

In this part of the country, known as the Dukeries, there were many such grand aristocratic seats: Clumber Park, once owned by the Duke of Newcastle; Rufford, former seat of the Earl of Rutland; and Welbeck, still occupied by the Duke and Duchess of Portland. In the middle of this gentrified huddle lay Thoresby Hall, my very own albeit ephemeral seat, presided over by the Countess Manvers, her Earl having departed his earthly estate some years previously.

All of these great houses, abbeys, halls and castles lay hidden from rude public view by the cloak of the forest, wrapping them in thousands of acres of Sherwood. Although mystically invisible from the public roads, these aristocratic seats exerted their influence on the public landscape in the sculptures of cast iron fences and massive entrance gates, with their grey rock gatehouses. Such structures could never be mistaken as entrances to ordinary dwellings. This was not the England of stone-hedged grey villages of slate, sheltering under the brow of the moors, although that was close. Neither was it the assembly lines of coal-dusted terraces sprouting from volcanic-like coke stockpiles, with the smoke of the Nottinghamshire pits seeping into every living crevice. That, too, was close.

The Dukeries were, and are, an aristocratic island in a proletariat sea. As the aristocrats would have it, life from this sea was trawled to sustain the island but was kept from possible submergence by the imposition of class and autocracy by the pedigreed. The maintenance of this system to the present day is testament to the honour and respect held by the English people for institutions, rules and authority that permeates their society like no other.

The closeness of Sherwood Forest, preserved by the great landowners of Eastern England, did many things. It was a haven for wildlife, a restful green space away from the 'industrial revolution' cities, and a buffer that kept the great houses aloof, safe from the traders, merchants and the crass marketplace whose dealings were fit only for servants and agents on regular forays out from the forest edge.

The trees of Sherwood sped past me as I pointed our car down Nottingham Road. It was near dusk and a moon was rising in a clear sky as we approached the first dense clumps of forest and grew stronger in the fading light of day. The Pole Star shone ahead of me, pointing the way north. We entered through the North Gate in twilight. I was nervous, as my mother and I were to be met by the Countess herself, and invited to supper. Once within the estate the forest seemed to rearrange itself into choreographed forms in scripted movement, in response to the unseen hand of a master gardener. Every leaf on every tree seemed a planned part of a manicure on a grand scale.

As we drove in towards the Great Hall below regimented lines of beech vaulting above us, I felt an unfamiliar pressure on me, the pressure to conform to a set of rules, a rigidity, a duty to keep the order. Unfamiliar to me perhaps but I sensed it was a well-known precept to the forest and its tenants.

The glow of the October dusk outlined the Victorian turrets and cupolas of Thoresby Hall. A light shone above the main door, which was so vast that the door knocker's size seemed puny and ridiculous, rather like the comedy of a large man wearing a small hat. The door swung open and the butler to Marie-Louise Roosevelt Pierpont, the Countess Manvers, introduced himself.

The Countess

"My name is Judkins," announced the dour, black-suited butler. "M'lady has been expecting you for some time. We have delayed supper, follow me."

The brusque welcome over, Judkins turned abruptly and headed up the stairs, past the suits of armour and into the Great Chamber. The butler was a tall but stooped figure, dark and Dickensian in the half light of the Hall. He seemed to lurch forward rather than simply walk. Beyond the cavernous space of the Chamber, whose dimensions I could only guess at in the gloom, then passing the gallery, the State Dining Room, the Sherwood Library and the Blue Salon, we finally arrived at the private dining room.

"Oh, thank you for coming. You must be done in after such a journey. Would you care for some sherry?"

Before we could respond, Lady Manvers pushed a discreet button under the table to summons back Judkins for sherry decanting duty. The countess was softly spoken with an air of grace and decorum learnt rather than bred as I recalled from Norma's briefing. I perceived the difference as her delivery did not sound quite natural but customised to her life situation. The Lady was plump and cheerful with a ruddy complexion. Her movements suggested a vagueness and indecision, a known aristocratic trait, meant to confirm her station in life.

"I would like you to meet Mary Worthing and Guy Marson."

Lady Manvers gestured towards her bemused dinner companions. Before I was able to demonstrate my rehearsed etiquette, the evening's first crisis of convention occurred.

"Now, where are we going to put you? Guy, could you move over to that chair? Roger, I'll put you here. Norma, you can sit here next to me." Then, after a pause, "Is that right, no, no! Mary, can we put you here?"

Poor Lady Manvers, in search of a niche where none existed. The ever elusive balance of dinner table personae had been rent by blow-ins from the colonies.

My mother, from whom I was expecting some covert semaphore on aristocratic table manners, was obliterated by a pile of oranges surrounded by a spinifex-like dahlia arrangement. If I crooked my neck to one side, I could make out the frown of her brow between the flower stalks. Alarmingly the countess was in line of sight, a perfect position from which to observe the inferior product of an antipodean education.

I improvised, as so many of my forebears must have done, faced with similar dilemmas. Applying my good common sense to the soup, I scooped the cloudy fluid away from my person in a graceful arc before bringing the spoon and most of its contents delicately to my lips. To avoid slurping I cooled the soup down by blowing on it, discreetly enough so as not to cause wind waves on the surface.

Judkins collected our soup bowls with a body language suggesting aggression. The lamb chops arrived in a pile on one serving plate. There was one chop per person. Each appeared pitifully small to a degree where identification was difficult, and hardly cooked. Judkins displayed practised skill in conveying each mini-chop to its destination with an ill-fitting pair of tongs that faintly reminded me of something I had seen in an anatomy class. On grabbing my knife and fork, I detected a motherly frown from between the daliah stalks and the Murano vase. Immediately I sensed what was amiss and made the correction. My fingers retreated up the shafts of my utensils until only a third of the lengths of each participating finger remained in physical contact with the implements, now largely uncontrollable but at least correct.

Beyond my intense personal struggle, polite table conversation had sprung up. It was in French between a countess, a princess and a first cousin to Czar Nicholas II of all the Russias. I observed it rather like one would observe the sounds of newly arrived extra-terrestrials from a noticeably more civilised planet. At intervals the conversation reverted to English, whereupon Lady Manvers would ask the unilingual Norma for an opinion and in her best stilted BBC tone Norma would reply. Lady M, Mrs Worthing and Guy would then continue their conversation in French, in its Parisian form so I believe, neatly cutting out Norma from any further contribution. It was assumed, of course, that Australians would have no knowledge of language as they were observed to have difficulty enough with the mother tongue. There was a coldness in these French sounds that seemed to have nothing to do with the language and everything to do with the company.

The crisis came for me quite suddenly, at dessert. I had survived a difficult patch and had become dangerously overconfident. My guard was down. Lady Manvers handed me a piece of fruit, not with the tongs provided but with her bare hands. This I was later told revealed her commoner background, marriage and not birth determining her current station. Flying solo, I applied my commoner sense once too often. I washed the fruit in an eminently purpose-built wide bowl, especially relevant after handling. Frantic eye signals from beyond the orange pile prompted me to observe the strange custom of my fellow diners dipping their fingers in these same bowls. Whether the faux pas went unnoticed or not I cannot say, but I remember the next occasion that we were invited to supper was the night before our departure from Thoresby, bound for India, two and a bit years later.

Perhaps it was a little unjust that my sins were not offset by the incident of Lady Manvers' teeth. As I was told later, it was her habit to remove her bottom dentures when they irritated her. At that first supper, the irritants concealed beneath a serviette were knocked to the floor by person or persons unknown. The situation may have passed had not the alert butler scooped them up with his tongs and presented them to their owner with a flourish: "I think these may be yours, madam."

And this was but day one of our life in Sherwood.

The Art of Sherwood Forest Gardening

My experience of those two years changed my attitude, my perspective and my accent. I learnt about the cycles of the seasons, the majestic succession contained in an English garden: spring yellow daffodils followed by splashes of red and yellow tulips, then white and pink chrysanthemums followed by blue wallflowers in a strict arithmetic progression. Each new bloom heralded a new page in the seasonal story, so well regulated and so different. So different to the endless sameness of Australian seasons, warmer weather, cooler weather, it made no difference there. The olive green hues of the eucalypts seemed eternal. There is no excitement where there is no change, so I thought then.

Our head gardener was Mr Mac, a lowland Scot raised in Ayrshire, home to the great Robbie Burns. He was sombre, inflexible and dedicated to his garden and to every living thing in it. Mrs Mac, a grandmother figure to everyone, cooked scones for morning tea more wonderful than I have ever known. Mr Mac was assisted by Fred Wydennorardnic, an earthy Ukrainian and war refugee, and John Stokes, recently retired coal miner and proud Derbyshireman. Fred had escaped the Ukraine after the war. He had served in the army of the Soviets. He told many tales but his experience of the war and the fate of his family were a closed subject. His deep etched features and half closed dark eyes were story enough. I knew sufficient from our unspoken communication to respect the peace that he sought in his adopted country.

John Stokes was Derbyshire. He wore its culture in the straightness of his back, the prominence of his chin and in his cherished cloth cap. John was as sure of his identity as any man I have known. He was born of generations of Derbyshire coal miners, working in the pits and drinking in the ancient stone pubs, knowing all the time that they were at the heart of the greatness that was industrial Britain. I felt it a privilege to work and talk with these men and to hear their stories, and to tend the Countess's Victorian gardens and Capability Brown landscapes.

It must have posed quite a dilemma for Mr Mac when Lady M introduced a raw Australian lad into his employ who knew nought of English flora and its regimes. Mr Mac was a wise man. He knew the job that suited my qualities of enthusiasm coupled with ignorance, a job of tedium requiring patience rather than skill, unremarkable but very necessary and now no longer falling to his experienced and overqualified hands: mowing the estate's acres of lawns.

It was a daunting task. There were so many lawns: the west lawn, with its gazebos, daffodil and tulip beds; the north lawn with its pleasant walks between beech and alder, where the cutting of grass in narrow strips partitioning flower bed from path demanded technique; and the entrance lawn, an island of green circumnavigated by the grand entrance driveway where dignitaries would be driven to be received by the Countess. Surely this lawn had to be excellently cut to create the correct first impressions, as much to a visitor from a grey Derbyshire village as an aristocrat from the Home Counties. Even the rose garden and the gazebo had their own lawns.

The west lawn though was *the* great example of Victorian order in Thoresby's landscape. It filled the feature window of the Blue Salon, the showcase French baroque room of Thoresby with the perfect Sherwood setting, a manicured formal garden framed by a cricket field, and deer in the misty distance grazing beside ponds on the River Maun.

I immediately realised the responsibility of the job. The results of my labours would provide the first close-up impression visitors would have after buying their tickets. I rose to this challenge, powered up the cylindrical grass cutters and the heavy rollers and got going. But this grass was strange. It bent, it was soft and it had a thing called grain. Where was the Aussie buffalo, sharp as a razor and metal tough, interspersed with bindii lurking to stab unwary feet?

It seemed that all of the cultural differences I was experiencing in this country were encapsulated in the horticultural chasm between an English garden and the Australian back yard. My childhood memories were of our lawnmower man who used to come every second Monday to 'do' our front yard with his Victa rotary (never our back yard as it was a hopeless jungle). The Victa was a proud machine, wonderfully suited to Australian conditions. It was tough and coarse. It could handle the rough stuff of pebbles, fallen branches, dog poo, old garden cuttings, garbage that had blown in from over the fence, shavings from wooden pegs that had dropped off the Hills Hoist, and occasionally it seemed, grass, anything in fact that reared its head above a lowest common denominator, earth. All this material was cut, mulched and ejected like bullets out of the side of the Victa. The rotary mower was designed to sever and flatten, not to cut and roll. When our mower man was about, the air was thick with missiles. The yard was a no-go zone and if you had any sense, you would clear out to collect tadpoles in the local creek, not to return before you heard the mower man's Holden Ute drive off. You knew our mower man had done his work when everything in the garden had been reduced to a short stubble, like grass, flowers, shrubs or the door mat that had just been put out to dry. It was like a very large crew cut. The slashing of the Victa seemed right for the raw, untamed wildness of the buffalo, a clashing of uncultured emotional forces in a hard and raw continent where fertility came with the weekly blood and bone mix.

At Thoresby, the grass was long, soft and pliant, tamed by centuries of care, a rich deep soil and the perennial dampness of the ground. The relationship of the English to their grass lay in the way they cut it, by a cylindrical blade that swept the grass back into the catcher, cutting in the same direction, with the same blade velocity and with a surgically accurate cutting height, all finished off with a roller that set the grain of the grass like lacquer, all beautifully controlled and choreographed.

I piloted a fine piece of English engineering that 'processed' the grass whilst gently rolling each blade into position. The grain, so created, appeared as alternate strips of light and dark providing a sense of order and civilisation. Far from the menial, tedious task it was taken for, in my handiwork I had in fact created a metaphor for the English condition.

As my confidence grew, I began to make statements in the lawns. My initial conservative rectilinear patterns were followed by bold diagonals and checkerboard designs often reserved for weekend viewing where these statements became very public and assertive, often remarked on by visitors. My art was, I believe, even mentioned in dispatches. The aristocracy know how to nurture a good thing! My disappointment came when the season was over, the grass stopped growing and the tools of my art hibernated for the winter.

I experienced two complete summers in the gardens of Thoresby Hall, being two complete cutting seasons. Mr Mac would say as Easter had passed and the night frosts became rare, "Aye, she'll soon be in need of a cut." In the peak, between Whitsun and the Bank Holiday, when the British knew it was safe to venture outdoors, the grass grew so quickly that a cut was needed every second day. It was my job and no one encroached upon my territory.

Life in the Forest Estates

On many summer afternoons, I would cycle into Worksop, the closest large town. I had my own secret route, following private estate roads, tunnels through the verdant green of a deciduous forest at its height of flower and leafiness. Crossing the northern estate boundary, I coasted down a long decline to a small stream and its perfect stone bridge. Out on the bridge I would always look right at the reflected image of an upside down church standing perfectly on a hill above the stream. Church and trees seemed both part of the earth and no manmade structure was at all foreign amongst the greenness. The land seemed contented with what man had done upon it. It was if an accord had been struck in the distant past to ensure the certainty of a continuing equilibrium in its reclusive state. And its sounds were of ducks, low murmuring breezes through leaves and the distant drone of bees.

My journey took me through the famous Lime Tree Avenue in Clumber Park, a public open space and one of the dukeries of Sherwood Forest. At the end of this avenue my spell was broken as I passed into the twentieth century and a post Industrial Revolution landscape. I was now on the main road leading into Worksop, a town serving the pit communities of the cold borderlands of Nottinghamshire and Yorkshire's West Riding. It was a world of coal trucks, brick chimneys and council houses where the fabric of society has held together by the mortar of smoke and ash.

My time in Sherwood coincided with that phase in life where the attainment of institutionalised knowledge marked by pieces of paper called qualifications was considered important by some of my peers and all of my betters. Worksop had a college of some reputation in these parts. It ran courses that led to the British A (advanced) and O (ordinary) level examinations, for university entrance.

I was to prepare myself for a future in science, although I never believed that at the time. It was too remote a prospect. I was living this life, a step away from time, time out from the expected orderly progress and the grim reality of my future, which existed at another place, in another time. Right now I did not want to be anywhere else. I was too embroiled in my own conversion to the beauty of the English landscape and the colour and wisdom of the English countryman. I treasured everything that happened to me and around me. I knew these were Arcadian days that would not occur again. My true preparation for life lay in learning from these real experiences, these real people.

There was Mr Tapper, the estate manager, who oversaw the agricultural activities at Thoresby. He doubled as the gamekeeper who kept a proprietorial eye on the local pheasant population, as well as the local peasant population, as I am sure he regarded them.

Mr Tapper saw himself as the squire, whose house on the hill overlooking the estate workers' village clearly announced his elevated station in the scheme of things. I once crossed him by shooting at a rabbit that was closing in on Lady Manvers' vegetable patch. It happened that this was both the first and last time I ever used a firearm. The rabbit escaped to eat again. I was relieved that I was such an unskilled marksman.

I had been observed however. The squire sent a curt message to me that on no account was I ever again to venture forth onto the estate proper bearing arms without his expressed permission. All of the estate's rabbits were his and were not to be interfered with by unauthorised personnel. The squire's order was directed to me through the estate's very public internal mail system so that my fall from grace could be shared by everyone. If one rabbit had caused this much commotion, I speculated what might have become of me had I taken potshots at a pheasant. I met the squire only once. I felt for his insecurity. He worked hard to attain aloofness rather than allowing it to fall to him naturally.

Then there was Mr Boland, the estate's teacher whose politics displayed a definite reddish hue. He was on a proletariat mission to democratise the serfdom of which he had become a part. Having become acquainted with Norma and myself, Mr Boland sought an entree to our home, Thoresby Hall. On the pretext of visiting us, he could bang on those great aristocratic solid oak doors with the round brass knobs. He made a great racket in the dead of night. This was a way to boldly demonstrate to the serfs that class lines could and indeed would be crossed and that no one need be subservient. The persistent thumping had the force of a battering ram, seeming to shake the foundations of the Hall. Unbeknown to Mr Boland, however, this door was never used. It was too big and inconvenient to open. Everybody used the side door, even the Lady. The only time I ever saw it used was on a vice-regal visit from Marie-Louise's next door neighbour, the Duchess of Portland, an event where there was much prostrating and touching of forelock from aristocracy of lower rank. To have such a door opened at such an hour to the local teacher, was as Mr Boland saw it, a sign of the revolution soon to come, where the workers toiling in the fields and the miners in the pits would simultaneously down tools, turn east into the rising sun and march to the strains of the Internationale, singing joyfully as one, comrades in arms much like Nelson Eddy and his band of cossacks had done decades earlier in the movie *Balalaika*.

Judkins frowned and pursed his lips as he opened the door. "I wish to see Norma and Roger," said Mr Boland.

"This must not happen again," reprimanded Judkins. "Only the side door is to be used."

Judkins reluctantly escorted Mr Boland to the bottom of the staircase in the Great Chamber. Indicating that he had been severely put out, he shouted for us from the bottom of the staircase, shattering the cold silence of the void in a tone likely to awake the Hall's residents, living and dead.

The irony was that Mr Boland was busily constructing more class lines than he was conquering and helping to preserve some hidden ones. He taught the northern dialect to the local schoolchildren as he was directed to do by the government in London. These children would be forever stamped as northerners. They would have their place.

Thoresby's social boundaries were too well entrenched for the likes of a local school teacher. The pressure to retain the system came from the villagers as much as the proprietors. The villagers saw change as a threat to their jobs and their security. It was a stable manor-serf micro-society flourishing in the heartland of 1960s Britain.

Like a child's playpen, boundaries were the security for those within its walls and conventions. The breaching of etiquette was deemed to be only acceptable for 'the Australians living in the Hall'. Perhaps the estate people regarded us as colonials pushed into the Thoresby playpen, without choice and without the necessary training so that such observances would not be expected of us. As crude colonials we may have been regarded as incapable of appreciating, much less practising, the niceties of social form, place and tradition, like the drunk who stumbles and weaves across the busy highway, oblivious to the danger and therefore without fear, lucky to have crossed unscathed but never appreciating that luck.

I visited Mr Boland's school once to present a geography lesson about Australia to 30 curious serf children. In their strong North Country accents, they asked about this south land a whole universe away. Professor Higgins could have placed them to within the shadow cast by the Perlethorpe church. Mr Boland, the class system destroyer, was its greatest protector. He seemed a happy man. I guessed the dichotomy never dawned on him.

The estate doctor, Dr Emery, seemed an efficient foot soldier for the National Health Service. All manner of maladies were presented to him by the serfs. Higher echelon personages either consulted their private physician in Nottingham or if the situation was dire, travelled up to London to see their Harley Street specialist. The convenience of Dr Emery's location right in the estate for this group of people seemed insufficient to overcome his deficiencies, either perceived or real.

The doctor handled all manner of complaints, maladies and full-blown diseases, daily. I was impressed on the few occasions that I attended his surgery by how he handled them all with a direct simplicity. His response was a system of coloured pills, with each symptom allocated its own colour. I never knew what the pills were but the doctor's patients seemed happy with the arrangement. Dr Emery proudly boasted that his patients mostly never came back sporting the same complaint.

I knew some of the good doctor's patients. They said they felt secure with an understandable medical system such as this, particularly when Dr Emery himself seemed to have such a good grasp of its complexities. However, people did say they found his explanations rather predictable. He was well-known for his 'big two' which seemed to cover almost everything. Either 'there's a lot of it around' or in the case of his older female patients 'It's The Change'.

Major Robinson was the manager of the Thoresby Hall Organisation or THO. The organisation ran the great house as a business, opening it to the public every Wednesday, Thursday and Friday afternoon between 2 and 5pm and longer on weekends to cater for the ploughman's lunches and high teas in high demand by the mostly English clientele.

For two shillings and 6 pence the public could enter selected rooms in the Hall plus the outside lawns and gardens. With an explanatory guide book, price 2/-, they had the means to better understand the riches and traditions on display. The rather ornate chest of drawers in the Blue Salon was in fact a Buell Cabinet, a priceless rococo piece from the 18th century French Court. The Sherwood fireplace relief was commissioned by the architect Salvin and fashioned out of a single piece of oak.

As Lady Manvers often recounted, "All of my friends and acquaintances know these sorts of things. It is such a pity that the public need a booklet. English education is really in a poor state when people are not taught to appreciate such works of art. I suppose we can be thankful that they can read the guidebooks at all. That awful Harold Wilson is doing all this, setting us on a course backwards. I don't know what's to become of our people. It's really all so tiresome."

Major Robinson oversaw the running of the Hall, including the catering, the outdoor exhibits, the basement exhibitions, the promotion, the advertising and the finances. It was a lot to ask of an ex-army officer whose departure from Her Majesty's armed services was cloaked in mystery. When faced with a crisis, his scarlet face would redden further and he would do a peculiar thing. Major Robinson would stick his head in closets, bread boxes or other convenient cavities, possibly meant to indicate action rather than the proverbial ostrich head in the sand approach. It was done with a very purposeful air and made obvious the impression that he was hot on the trail of the solution. Continued observations of this behaviour showed however that even when the nature of the crisis varied, the trail to the solution never did. I think the Major had spent time in Africa. Perhaps in studying the ostrich he got the idea. The major enjoyed an affinity with alcohol, especially gin, which he sought refuge with once the crisis had passed. His cheeks blushed pink, matching his bloodshot eyes. After the first such incident, the THO staff referred to the Major as Pink Gin.

The vagaries of Lady Manvers and the unseen hand of Mr Tapper constantly undermined the Major's plans. After a day in the office, he would retreat to his rented estate cottage with an air of defeat, which I felt was all too familiar to him. Here was a man whose spirit had been crippled. Thoresby was, I suspect, just another hiding place, perhaps another fresh start, like being a handicapped runner in a race with the young and the strong. Nobody notices the inequality at the start line, before the competition is under way. Beginnings may wipe out the last bad ending but are, by their nature, ephemeral, and, in the end, disillusioning. Only an ostrich would disagree.

On the African plain, the crippled animal, exposed and wandering, soon attracts predators keen to seek out an advantage. The English plain is no less fierce but its victims carry the added burden of good form, where the niceties are observed and the appearances maintained. The kill is not immediate. English predators maintain the injured animal to serve them and enhance their position, the way a cat plays with its still alive victim. They may squirm and protest but all the animals of the plain know it is broken, and it is only a matter of time. The swift and merciful kill of Africa is a long way away.

Judkins played the role of an ill-at-ease butler and occasional waiter. Like most other men of the district he had spent most of his working life 'down the pit' in the perfectly preserved imperfections of DH Lawrence's Nottinghamshire. Lady Manvers had married into class and as such did not present an appropriate situation for a professional butler, hence Judkins. He impressed me as not just being rough around the edges but positively serrated. Whenever I was in the presence of Judkins I felt his contempt. He breathed it and lived it but its dark force dispersed amid the vagueness of the Countess, who I think saw his disposition as simply a lack of finesse that one would expect from the stock drawn from these parts.

Judkins made up one side of a triangle. His tall, masculine Yorkshire wife and his short, young Spanish mistress comprised the other two sides. Mrs Judkins, a dim and austere woman, either didn't know or didn't care about the Spanish maid's other role. I had only heard the rumours until one day when opening a strange door under the private staircase, I discovered them locked together, panting heavily as their clothing strewn across the floor. Intensely embarrassed, I quickly closed the door, leaving them in the darkness to which they were accustomed. I dreaded the inevitable encounter to come but it turned out to be the most honest exchange I was to have with the butler. I was severely dressed down by Judkins at his first opportunity and told never to go opening strange doors anywhere in the Hall again. This seemed to provide a clue to the extent of his activities, but one I was not about to test. Judkins was always a shadowy creature who lived somewhere in the dark recesses of the Hall's servants' wing. Observing him one day crossing the library stooped and favouring one leg over the other, I fancied him as a thinner Quasimodo with his bent back and distorted face ringing those bells with a hellish cacophony, calling the faithful to Notre Dame.

Living in the bell tower of Thoresby Hall was the painter Guy Marson. He was the artist-in-residence whose patron was the Countess, a perfectly acceptable arrangement when considering Guy's Russian pedigree, pointing to Czar Nicholas no less. Guy's blood, in fact, was several shades bluer than that of his benefactor. Guy had a roomy attic residence overlooking the deer park. His role in life was to escort Lady Manvers to events of society that she was authorised to attend and to constantly praise her watercolours and agree with its interpretation of life. Guy shrank back into his attic world, only to appear as a duty at dinner on those occasions that the hated Boston bluebloods from Lady Manvers' American family branch, the Roosevelt connection, arrived. They consisted of a matriarch and her ageing sons. It was because of one of these sons that open but silent hostility reigned during these visits. The bitchiness between gays who detest one another is a formidable force relieved only by its pathos.

Guy was an artist with talent. Marie-Louise was a painter with title. Royal Academicians thus saw them as 'somewhat equal'. Their annual sortie to Spain where Guy and the Countess worked at capturing that certain Spanish light on canvas was seen as striking the right sort of balance in the art world. Lady Manvers' paintings adorned many of the walls in the private rooms. Guy's superb renditions were out of sight. I always found Guy cheery and infinitely interesting. He had a big story to tell but the good sense not to tell it. He knew his place, which was precarious. He painted well enough at Thoresby to stimulate his benefactor, not to alienate her. He produced nothing that was excessively masterly or conceptually demanding. Such displays might be interpreted as a grave discourtesy because his host would not understand his point, and would know that he knew that.

Pa Barton was the Vicar of Perlethorpe, the main estate village. He was a very old and crusty gentleman and had a fire in his mind which would not be quenched. Pa loved long afternoon discussions with Norma, his daughter Betty and a handful of his more enlightened parishioners. This Perlethorpe Bloomsbury Set delved into philosophy and comparative religions over a hot fire and good strong Fortnum and Mason Ceylon tea.

Pa was one of Thoresby's few original thinkers. Religion had given him this freedom, and like the Monks of the Middle Ages Pa acted as the mind and soul of the estate, able to produce a discourse on the human condition, the universe and everything if asked. He was never asked, and he was never understood. The Church probably thought it convenient to park an ageing and eccentric theologian in this backwater serfdom where there was little chance of embarrassment to them, a standard reaction of all large bureaucracies to a small irritant. Pa was a great man who always had the time and interest to dispense the wisest of counsels. That was my young man's impression. I was one of those who needed his knowledge and understanding but did not ask nearly enough. Few on the estate understood the Vicar as a man. They, like so many English parishes, regarded him in an automatic way, as a figure that led them all through the same mindless ritual every Sunday morning, nothing more. Few took the trouble to inquire further, consumed by their own routines and their daily insignificance. And what if he had some answers, as was surely expressed in his Sunday sermons. These were lost in the static of daily living and Pa Barton could see, I'm sure, the waste of it.

But there were some magical times. One Christmas morning, the sun rose on a snow-swept landscape. As I walked, with my mother, to the little Perlethorpe church for the morning Christmas service there was a new and serene stillness to the air. A pale yellow sun was punching a weak path through the white lacework embroidering the ground. A finger of frost let go with a snap in the trees as clumps of snow cascaded to the ground. The stark branches were silhouetted against a blue-grey sky. Rabbits darted across the road leaving their prints and the clean country snow crunched underfoot. Through this stillness the church bell rang.

This was the Christmas that had been described to me for all of my Australian life, and now I was living it. From the moment I awoke that morning and peered out through the cold panes of glass in my bedroom I knew that this was the way Christmases were meant to look. The church was like the country, clean and tangible. The choir was rich and melodic. The Vicar's sermon, the post-service greetings in the church garden and the Christmas lunch in the Vicarage all contributed to that wonderful feeling that in all the world, this place, and these people made that perfect, unrepeatable Christmas Day.

Pa Barton may have of necessity kept some of his theological and political ideas to himself but his joy and energy at this Christmas positively radiated onto his flock. The people of Perlethorpe were indeed blessed to have as their Vicar a combination of a man of God and first-class devil's advocate.

Aristocracy Rules

In talking about the personalities and characters of the community, the talk around the common was always of the Countess herself. Marie Louise Roosevelt Pierpont, the Countess Manvers or just Lady M, a commoner from Yorkshire, had both a French and American connection. A remote arm of the Roosevelt's sometimes came to stay, a collection of gentle dandies which in earlier times would be described as fops. Theirs and Lady M's world focused on people who 'mattered'. These people fell into two groupings. The lower group was openly enthusiastic about Lady M's art and good works and was prominent in the local community in acceptable occupations such as charity administrator or church leader. This group qualified for Lady M's luncheon invitation list. The higher group had additional qualities. They were entrenched in the social hierarchy of the Home Counties; owned a country seat, preferably by inheritance; knew nobody from Yorkshire except perhaps the Duke; spoke French or at least could inject appropriate French phrases into normal conversation without appearing to be deliberate about it; and they possessed the social clout to send a message up the line about Lady Manvers' accomplishments.

This group made it to the Countess's invitation list for dinner. Exceptions were made for celebrities, eccentrics (provided they were well dressed) or social curiosities, who could act as exhibits at the table, creating much amusement for the other guests.

Since the death of her husband, the Earl Manvers, it had been an uphill task for the Lady. But art and her county seat saved her from the eternal damnation of being ignored.

I was privy to one memorable luncheon conversation with Lady Worthing, a London socialite and long-standing friend of the Countess.

"It's such a pleasure, Mary, to have you down from London, with us here, isn't it Guy?"

"Yes, quite so, Ma'am," answered Guy dutifully.

Judkins followed the party out onto the patio. "Would you wish lunch to be served out here, M'lady?"

"No Judkins, we shall take lunch in the small dining room as always." Marie Louise sniffed her annoyance as she turned to Mary. "Really, it is so tiresome. One really has to keep telling them the same things. Shall we adjourn to the dining room now?"

She rose from her patio seat, clutching the shiny patent leather handbag that was her customary appendage wherever she went. Mary and Guy followed her lead.

"It must be difficult for you, living here. I suppose the right people are just not available," said Mary sympathetically.

"You know, I really don't think the servants liked it when I opened the Hall to visitors. And really, that was such a bother too. When we decided we had to do it I thought we could make a good start with the newspapers by having that American boxer Cassius Clay come and fight one of our lads. You know that attic, up near the bell tower, next to Guy's rooms. Judkins and I climbed the stairs to it once. I could see immediately how useful it might be for such an event."

Mary's jaw dropped in horror. "But, Marie Louise, would such a thing attract the right people for Thoresby's opening?"

Lady M sighed. "That damn fool Tapper talked about it not being practical and even said the government wouldn't allow it. Well, I think that was too much."

There was silence around the lunch table, each person, no doubt visualising what might have been. "In any event, the whole idea was dropped and it was left to me to think of something else as an opening event."

Mary extended a soothing hand. "I sympathise with you, Marie Louise. Not only are you forced to open your house to the public, but you are also expected to think of ways to start off that awful process. So unfair."

"Thank you, Mary. You're very kind. It was a very hard time and such a bother. I had no help at all. We got in Major Robinson to run the opening and he stayed on as our manager. But I tell you…" Lady M waved her finger. "The newspapers did come, and we were even given space in some London papers, though I must say not *The Times* or *Daily Telegraph*."

"So who did you get in the end? Did you have your event after all?"

"Mary, it was sheer luck. A journalist friend of mine on the BBC was able to get Sabrina to open us."

Mary's eyes widened and the jaw dropped again. "S–s–Sabrina!"

"Yes, you know, that well-endowed buxom actress, the one that gets all those good roles. It was wonderful. So many press people, all the way from London. I think they really wanted to know more about this part of the country."

"Did you know about this girl? Did you want her type here?" Mary couldn't hide her horror.

"Yes, of course." Lady M raised her voice, losing patience for a moment. "I got no support for it, naturally. The usual things. Tapper went on again about why it shouldn't go on. I refused to listen to the fool. It seems no one around here has any initiative. But we had to soldier on if we were to start the right way and after the Cassius Clay thing I was determined to make a go of this."

I was listening to this conversation as I had some work to perform that was within earshot. I needed to remain inconspicuous, something difficult to do when doubled up in silent laughter.

"What about Sabrina? How was she?"

"Oh, she seemed very good with the press. The girl seemed so happy to be opening something."

Mining a Cemetery

Mary Worthing came to Thoresby regularly to escape, as she said, the hubbub of London life. She came alone now but in the past, her mother would always accompany her as Mary's ever-present travelling companion. Perhaps it was the grand surroundings or Marie Louise's welcome attention that prompted Mary's mother to decide that the occasion was equal to the action. Tradition dictated that as a guest of the hall at the time of her demise, Mary's mother was entitled to enjoy full burial rights in the Perlethorpe Churchyard. She was farewelled with full society honours as she wished. As a bonus, her new permanent occupancy had a stunning westerly aspect with a commanding view of the great east facade of the Hall. Mary's mother lay there until one day when a new underground shaft penetrated a little too close to the surface from Thoresby's Number two Pit, one of the new National Coal Board mines.

The pit workers laboured away in the underground gloom, with their helmet spot lights swinging around with their accustomed movements, causing stark shadows to dance on the shaft walls. There was a small group of men working the seam, intent on the black gold in front of them. They had been drilling to the west and slightly upwards for days, following the stratigraphy of the seam. Halfway through their shift the ceiling began to vibrate. A cloud of fine dust sprayed their heads. As they gazed up nervously, a skeletal hand appeared, followed by an arm bone and leg bone, then the piece de resistance: the whole ceiling collapsed and Mary's mother dropped in on the miners in her entirety, sporting expensive dental work and a sleek open coffin in an explosion of dust. As the pit workers swung their heads and lights upwards, the beam trained on new shapes and shadows appearing above them. Mary's mother, never one to be alone, was then followed Pied-Piper-like by some of her neighbours ambushing the screaming miners.

Work was called off for the rest of the day. The National Coal Board performed a re-burial in a more stable but less salubrious location near the number two pit adit, adjacent to the coal washery and well away from areas liable to subsidence. Lady Manvers was thoughtful in not telling Mary about the incident for fear of upsetting her. Whenever Mary came to Thoresby, she always gave her respects to her mother in that leafy little graveyard behind the church. Most villagers knew where Mary's mother now resided, but the village precinct was much prettier and people there respected Mary's sensitivities and her delight in the beauty of her mother's former home.

The Presence of Robin Hood

My bedroom on the third floor of the Hall was known as Sabrina's bedroom. My bed was the same narrow 19th century bed that had accommodated curvaceous model Sabrina and her massive bosom during the grand opening of Thoresby. I couldn't help fantasising that she and I were squeezed into that tiny bed together, my head pillowed on her balloon-like breasts. Sadly no evidence of her former occupation remained, the walls instead displaying paintings of departed kings and lords and an array of armour, spears and swords on parade around the walls.

Looking out from the south facade I could see across the south lawn and the cricket field to the shallow valley of the River Maun and beyond to the ancient oaks of Sherwood. It was the quintessential English country view. The horizon of oak trees framing the misty meadow, ponds and stream gave the impression that this was the world and there was no outside, the estate continuing on far beyond the forest.

The legends surrounding Robin Hood and his merry band of men were written up on signs all over the county. It was easy to imagine them roaming the forests out of sight of the King's horses and the King's men, then suddenly springing out from behind the oak trees to arrest the lawful progress of the King's coaches. It was the start of one of history's longest running legends. They robbed from the rich to give to the poor. It was also history's earliest recorded example of modern guerrilla warfare and the use of progressive social policy in the redistribution of wealth. Although many parts of the kingdom lay claim to a connection with the Robin Hood legend, here, in the heart of the Sherwood Forest is really where it all happened. Robin and Maid Marion were said to have married at the church in Edwinstowe, now an independent town, but originally an estate village. There is a record of the event in the church's register. The Major Oak, a major meeting point for Robin's men stands nearby. Its huge hollow trunk was a perfect place for the gang to store their armoury of arrows.

There were places, secret places, deep in the forest where the group supposedly lived, played and schemed. In front of the main gates to Thoresby's Great Hall is a statue of Robin, said to be on the site of another of his homes. Was it real? There were locals who said they knew some of these secret places in the forest, their trained eyes apparently able to spot the evidence of ancient occupation. I never saw these places but accepted the fact that many people who lived in the forest did believe it to be true. When walking through the forest on a misty afternoon, it was difficult not to. The idea of a chivalrous and heroic figure succeeding against the cruelty and corruption of the time was very appealing. I felt there was something 'out there' through the mist and a benign sense of good overcoming evil, a sense of security. Many times on my treks through the forest I was sure I was being watched, and not just by the animals. That was comforting rather than sinister, like having my personal but invisible fairy godmother alongside.

The struggle of good and bad ran through most English legends and there were places that felt 'bad' to me and those that felt 'good'. Sherwood was at the centre of one of my 'good' regions. Once, on a dark night, when I had lost my keys, I was forced to enter the Hall through an open window in the basement courtyard. In the dark I felt my way along the black corridors, my fingers feeling the damp and rough stonework of the old servants' quarters. Up the grand staircase I flinched as my outstretched hand contacted the cold copper arm of a giant Macedonian king thrusting a spear. This fearsome figure was one of a row of imposing Ptolemaic statues lining the staircase. I inched past walls of seventeenth century weaponry and other instruments of death, past paintings of the Dukes of Kingston, their stern faces staring out at me. I felt my way from furniture piece to furniture piece across the great voids separating the lower storeys from my bedroom on the gallery level. I didn't feel apprehensive, despite the dark, eerie atmosphere. But I have walked into other old buildings even in broad daylight and experienced a chill and a pressing need to retreat.

The Great Cannon Robbery

On one particular morning during my second summer, I awoke early and looked out from my bedroom window on a scene that seemed a little different from normal. The river, the trees, and the sculptured lawn were all there. The deer seemed to be grazing in their groups, on the cricket oval as always. But there was a distinct lack of something. I peered out for a while and then it came to me. What was different was a complete lack of cannons. On the previous day, in fact for the previous 80 years, there had been a cannon guarding the corner of every flower patch, path and gazebo. Two long-range models that secured the magnificent entrance gates were also gone. Thoresby was defenceless against the foreign devils who could now pillage at will. This concerned me as one of my jobs as assistant gardener was as a keeper of the cannons and all garden artefacts. They were now missing and I felt responsible.

The alarm rang and the bell pealed and urgent calls were placed to the local constabulary. Scotland Yard was alerted and checks were made at all the air and seaports for suspicious activity. Over 20 cannons had been lifted, each weighing over 1/4 of a ton. Camouflaged in balaclavas, black skivvies and tights, the thieves had worked quietly through the night, observed only by cuckoos and grazing deer as they hauled their booty into a waiting truck. It was a very professional job.

My colonial convict heart gladdened at the telling of the story. The lawns did look bare though without their armaments, which were not insured. Lady M appeared downcast but not particularly upset. I think she may have considered the cannons as an attraction for visitors and as a nice way to balance the Victorian design of the gardens rather than as an irreplaceable part of the family heritage.

The call went out and a nationwide cannon hunt was on. The first day and then the second passed without any clues or information coming forward. Police were at the ports, on the railway stations and on the roads. Hope was fading. It was feared that some criminal, lacking a public school education and ignorant of their antiquity and value to society might melt the cannons down for the metal. Perhaps some jet plane was already winging them to Alaska, Libya or worse still, Florida. Perhaps they would find a home guarding the Buddha at Chiang Mai or a Spanish castle at Teneriffe.

The M1 between Nottingham and Leicester is a fast track, a favourite piece of road for the patrolling police in the apprehension of speedsters. On the third day of the search, a police van patrolling this section of motorway spotted a Leyland truck heading south at high speed. They gave chase but as the police drew close, what they saw turned their faces white. Through the flapping canvas at the rear of the truck they glimpsed an armoury of cannons all pointing at them. The alarm was sounded, the siren switched on and the Leyland truck as if suddenly awakened, increased its speed. Somewhere south of Leicester, the Nottinghamshire constabulary cars were joined by their Leicestershire cousins. One became five, then five became nine. Roadblocks were set up further south. The Leyland truck, an old English lady past her prime began to overheat and slow down. Now its driver started weaving with sharp changes in direction in a desperate attempt to ward off its pursuers. The truck crossed the median strip and drove down the wrong side of the motorway. With the bumping and the shaking, one by one the cannons started spilling out of the back of the truck in a metallic stream like congealed lava.

The Motorway was thick with cannons travelling in all directions on their 18th century wooden wheels. Down the northbound lanes, up the southbound lanes, along the nature strip and down the embankments into the fields and hedgerow country, fuelled by the impetus of their moving launching pad. Motorists, terrified at the advance of Napoleon's artillery onto their positions took evasive action, colliding with motorists from the same battalion. Cars bound for Nottingham, lorries bound for Sheffield, prime movers for Leeds, all ground to a shuddering halt, overwhelmed by the sheer strength of Napoleon's right flank.

It was a miracle no one was injured, although the British side sustained some 'material damage'. The tough artillery pieces went unscathed. So many cannons spilt out in some wild desire to escape their captors that all three lanes of the northbound M1 were blocked. But the French were nowhere to be seen, obviously terrified at the sight of so many British war machines of huge size and evil intent, right down to their north country number plates. The French cannons ceased their movement and appeared abandoned. It was the end scene from Waterloo when Napoleon's army in total disarray fled the British and the Hun, leaving at their rear a jumble of cannons and the bare ground of a fresh battlefield.

The M1 was officially closed. The old Leyland truck was stopped and its occupants caught by a ring of police. They turned out to be petty criminals from London. The police later told us that one of the offenders had spent time in the army, obviously an effective and valuable educational institution where practical 'commandoes-strike-at-dawn' type skills could be learnt. They never fully realised what they had in the back of their truck.

The cannons suffered less damage than did the M1 and after a few of their number turned up in court as exhibits, they were restored to their home in the gardens of Thoresby where once again their took up their role as a silent deterrent to all who would trespass upon this ground through the dark hours.

The sun rose over the south lawn and as the mist cleared I could see the faithful iron servants in place once again with a reflective shine, in balance with the dahlias, the freshly cut grass, the deer and the geometric pathways. The cannons were back and all was right with the world.

Arrival of the Masses

Whitsun came in early June, shattering a seven-month Sherwood slumber. The season opened on this long weekend. Thoresby opened its gates to busloads of Welsh miners from Methyl Tydfil, Derbyshire farmers with their large families, young trendies displaying the latest gear straight from Liverpool and the sprawling West Riding cities. Children spilled out of the 'estate' cars of the local villagers. There were even some gentry down from the home counties in their black Daimlers, MGs and Jaguars.

Kids rode the miniature train that circled the cricket oval, families picnicked near the deer ground. Lovers embraced intimately in the soft grass by the River Maun unconcerned by the traffic negotiating the nearby bridge. Some people even paid their 2/6 to enter the Great Hall, and with their guide books (another 2/-) firmly held in hand, embarked on an hour, more or less, of peering into a life they could hardy comprehend but would staunchly defend.

On weekends, the first tourists arrived at 12:30, two hours earlier than on weekdays, a fact I forgot one memorable Saturday. My prized bathroom, the one with the long tub and the most reliable hot water plumbing, was situated at the end of the long art gallery, a 100ft-long corridor which was suspended two storeys above the Great Chamber, Thoresby's biggest internal space. Through the keyhole of the bathroom door I could see all the way down this passageway so I knew when to make a dash for the nearby bedroom without being seen.

I was luxuriating in a hot bath, trying to work up a lather in the hard limestone water when the hall's big bell struck one. I heard voices, but thought them to be some of the retainers. I immersed myself in the warmth of the water and the voices became louder. In a moment of revelation my head shot out of the water and my body tensed. Saturday! Thoresby had been open for business for over half an hour!

I jumped out of the bath, rotated the keyhole cover and peeked through the keyhole. A great mass of people was closing in on me, family groups with their children running up and down the gallery corridor. I scampered back into the warm bath and submerged myself in a pathetic attempt at retreat. The world seemed so warm and secure at the bottom of the tub. But I could still hear voices, muffled but strong. I came to periscope depth with my ears out of the water. The voices were right outside the bathroom door. "This doesn't seem to lead anywhere… Do we have to turn around? What page are we on? Why can't they make the print of the guidebook bigger… It's so damn dark up here."

I knew the scene. Clutching their guide books, they combed the scene for artefacts that coincided with the pictures in the guide book. Suddenly, the doorknob turned. I stared at it, helpless. The door was pushed but didn't move. Mercifully, it was locked after all.

I sank back into the rapidly cooling water. As the chill seeped into my bones, it dawned on me that I was trapped. The waiting game began. Periodically I looked through the keyhole, hoping for a gap in the traffic, a gap large enough for an undetected streak to the bedroom. I needed a clear corridor. Just after the bell struck two there was a moment when the only group on the gallery turned to descend the stairs, but just then a child ran up the stairs well ahead of its parents, plugging the gap. The bathwater was frigid by now, but I dared not run the hot water. Shivering, I covered a portion of my goosebumped body in an inadequate towel.

Three o'clock chimed. Mrs Vart's scones down in the basement must have been working their charms. The sounds had receded and my keyhole inspection disclosed an empty gallery. Not a second to lose! I dropped the key, fumbled picking it up and in my shaky state, completely missed the keyhole. It took ages to engage the lock.

The door flung open and, almost slipping on the soap, my partially towelled form darted down the corridor and up to my bedroom door. But where was the key to the bedroom? I shook the towel, exposing my naked body, and the key fell out – just as a visitor appeared at the top of the stairs. Fortunately, he was momentarily looking the wrong way. The lock engaged, the door opened. I was inside my safe haven! I slammed the door, turned the key and dived onto the carpet, sprawling out in a delicious, gleeful expression of freedom. I had done it.

I eventually dressed and mingled with the throng, amusing myself with their chatter as we all moved towards the closed door at the end of the gallery. "This is all so grand…so many big rooms…fancy living like this, like kings and queens!"

What seemed important to visitors was that, despite the excesses of the upper classes, the privilege and the waste, all on display, Thoresby and all the other stately homes, were after all, British, part of their country, their heritage, their culture. It was part of a system for which so many had given their lives over the centuries, and yet with so few gaining even a fleeting admittance to the privilege of the class. During my time there, the exciting and optimistic 60's, the monarchical system remained very popular with the people, and it showed. They seemed proud of it and proud of its opulence. Hundreds of thousands filed through Thoresby, past the Blue Salon, the priceless Boulle cabinets with tortoise shell, the 18th century timepiece by Ageron of Paris in the Sevres case, the complete set of first edition Victor Hugo, marked by the author, the 12th century Chinese porcelain resting on the 18th century French table. Nothing was ever secured. Treasures were simply roped off, yet nothing was ever taken. It seemed a uniquely British paradox where the citizenry were prepared at any time to defend a system that would shun them as individuals while they remained deeply respectful of its power, tolerant of its inequity and proud of its tradition.

There are none so conservative as the lowliest pit worker. His life was bounded by neatly segmented social units. Order prevailed and the system endured. He was poor and unprivileged, slowly choked to death by the dust in the mine. But his labour and his politics propped up the conveyor belt of counts, dukes and earls.

Class puts people in their place, a very secure place, the security for their future and the future of their children. It is the sense of knowing one's path and identity in life, solid and unchanging for both the person and the nation.

In true upstairs-downstairs fashion, Lady Manvers thought that as the fineries gilded all of the ground and upper floors, the basement passages could be given over to less grand themes. So, with Norma's influence, the 1966 season opened with an Australian flavour in these subterranean caverns. By arrangement with the Australian High Commission, Norma set up an Australiana exhibition.

Most of the public came down to the basement for tea after overdosing on kingly portraits and medieval armour. Descending the stairs, the culture-dazed guests were jolted by entirely new confrontations of stuffed wombats, grinning koalas and swamp wallabies as they navigated their way to the baked scones and Billy Tea. Set amongst the taxidermy were pictures of Australian life, the bronzed Aussie surfer with the Chesty Bond jaw line, the Drizabone stockman with red dust in his akubra standing tall in the saddle, flocks of fat, fleecy merinos pictured against a heat-hazed horizon with a few tired acacias dotting the plains and country kids billycarting down back lanes under an intensely blue sky.

What did it all mean to a family in from the Derbyshire Dales where a farm plot providing the living would only cover the ground taken up by a homestead and a few sheds on a 'station' in Oz? What did it all mean to the old-time village shopkeeper whose father and grandfather before him kept the same shop, the country types down from their Berkshire seat complete with driving gloves and plus-fours, the pit workers with shadows on their lungs and coal-etched wrinkles, the high-tea set with social positions to maintain?

To these locals, Australian people seemed as weird as the spiny anteaters and platypus. Even Lady Manvers regarded Norma and myself as curiosities, eccentrics outside the English class system. It was as if we were on exhibition alongside our stuffed fauna.

As an assistant gardener, Lady M would not normally have talked to me, but because I was the son of Norma, her in-house Australian promoter, she continually complimented Mr Macskimming, the head gardener, on my work (and possibly my apparent gardening prowess helped too). I was paid several pounds a week for my efforts. Norma was in two minds about my small income. We needed the money, but accepting it lowered our station in life to that of mere employees or even servants. Norma wanted to occupy a niche in a much higher social strata, where money was a distasteful subject and of no real concern. My small income was undermining this aspiration.

A Side Job – A Cherry Ripe Importer

I was thinking of ways to supplement my meagre income and perhaps, as Norma wanted, to replace it altogether. I had an idea that in the end made more money for the organisation than for me. I was working in the Thoresby ticket office where the throngs paid for their admission. The ticket office displayed, rather pathetically, a few soft drinks, packets of boiled lollies and sticks of liquorice. I could see a potential for greater profits by expanding the range of stock. I had a brainwave. In keeping with the Australiana exhibition currently on display in the Thoresby Hall basement, I wanted to sell an Aussie icon in the ticket office, my all-time favourite, Cherry Ripe bars, dark chocolate covering a core of cherry paste. But could I obtain them? I had never seen them in any British shop.

I contacted the Australian High Commission's commercial section. They were most helpful with providing me an import license, manufacturer contact and customs clearance forms as well as trade discounts and a government subsidy for being an Australian exporter.

It only took two weeks for them to organise air freight as part of their export drive promotion. A large truck appeared one Friday morning and stopped right outside the ticket office. The truck's back shutter opened, displaying the hidden treasure: 24 cartons of Cherry Ripe bars, the only ones in all England, I had been informed. I was the proud retailer of 2400 Cherry Ripes. It was a challenge to store them and show off the display modules that came with the shipment in the tiny ticket office. The retail price set gave the Thoresby Hall organisation a large profit if all were sold. Norma was shocked at my burst of entrepreneurialism, saying I hadn't cleared it with Pink Gin. Thoresby soon had the proceeds of all 24 cartons. These tempting chocolate, cherry and coconut confections proved popular with Thoresby's visitors, though I was by far the biggest customer of my stock. My business as Britain's sole Cherry Ripe importer was a delicious experience.

The Cricket Match

As an Australian I was encouraged by Pa Barton, Mr Bollands and the Perlethorpe pub chaps to join the Perlethorpe cricket club. I was seen as quite an acquisition to them, carrying all the glory of Australian cricket achievement on my shoulders. There was not a moment's doubt that I came from the same mould as Bradman, Harvey and all the others. Did not all Australians? And the Perlethorpe chaps campaigned hard. At every contact it was, "Well, are you playing, are you coming in with us, lad?" I was nervous and felt exposed. I had successfully avoided competitive sports for many long years at school. What if I let them down?

They had put me in as opening batsman against a fearsome fast bowler. This bloke had plundered the Perlethorpe team for years. No longer. Today he would have the shock of his life because the little Perlethorpe team, the down-and-outers of the competition, had an Australian amongst their ranks. All eyes were on me. They were betting on how long it would take for me to reach the half century, and beyond that, the ton.

The fast bowler starts his run. My palms are wet with sweat. This huge lanky fellow arrives at his crease all too soon. The ball rockets towards my unguarded stumps. I freeze, helpless to prevent the ball looping around my puny bat and excavating my middle stump from its home. The awful scene is frozen in my mind and then replayed over and over. The shame is unbearable. I sit apart from the others, the camaraderie gone, gone forever. I live the rest of my time at Thoresby in reclusion avoiding all eye contact with the team, the villagers and the whole estate population.

"Roger, you look so serious, what is it boy?" Pa Barton had his reassuring hand on my shoulder.

"They've asked me to join their cricket team. I just wouldn't know how I'd go." I could always talk to Pa without reservation. We didn't speak often, yet he knew me well.

"Listen to me. They want you, you know. Not just your cricket. You're a villager now and that's an honour. Take them on, lad. There's no one in this village that would disagree. You're for the team and it doesn't matter what happens in the game, you're representing us when you play. Isn't that enough?"

I was overcome. How could I even contemplate turning down such an honour? To be part of a team. That was important. To be out on the field with these new friends. A new sense of belonging took over from self-doubt. "I'll play, father."

"Good, good." Pa smiled. "Now tell me – just how good are you?"

The big day came. Perlethorpe C.C. was to play Cutthorpe C.C. away. Cutthorpe was a small collection of Derbyshire slate houses on the moors above Chesterfield, on the Pennines. Their team was called the Mountain Devils and for good reason. All shepherds, tending their flocks during the week, they transformed themselves into huge muscle-bound competitors on Saturday afternoons. The moors were their training ground. Working in the open, herding their sheep day and night, in the grimmest Arctic weather of winter, their bodies toughened into steel, and their muscles into mini power stations by the start of the cricket season. By seasons end there were usually very few teams ahead of them in the competition.

Their big gun was a fast bowler called Bert, short, I was told, for Ethelbert. I was warned not to say the word out loud. Bert was also known as The Mincer because of his capacity for making mincemeat of the hapless batsmen he faced. Burt hated all batsmen, like all true fast bowlers do.

I tried to convince my teammates that my cricketing past was dubious. I did mention, though, that my father, who was in fact a great all-round sportsman, was once a reserve, so I was told, for the Australian Eleven. I kicked myself later for bringing this up as this was seen as an immediate qualification for installing me into the critical number three batting order known as the first drop, the person who had to build the innings for his team after the expected failure of the opening partnership.

Like Ethelbert for his team, I was billed as the secret weapon, for our side. Perlethorpe was considered a lowly team, an easy beat, one with little to lose. But I thought there was more to lose than they could imagine if their 'secret weapon' became the season's greatest dud. They'd be laughed out of the competition. That old fear returned, the fear of failure. Why did I listen to the Minister?

I had scarcely padded up when Clive, our number one was bowled through his legs. John, Bill, Jack and some others slapped me on the back and sent me on my way. 'Get them, son!' and 'watch his low inswinger' were words of advice shouted to me as I walked the long walk out to the centre of the field, to take my place at the wicket and face the dreaded Cutthorpe fast bowler.

They were in no mood to be defensive to Pearlethorps's secret weapon as they immediately set an attacking field with three men stationed behind me at slips ready to catch me out from an edge off the bat and at Silly Point for any clumsy scoop off a full pitch.

I never saw the first ball Bert bowled but heard the rush of air making way for it as the ballistic missile shaved my right ear and arrived in the wicket keeper's hands a millisecond later. Hissing sounds came from all the Cutthorpe boys to indicate a near miss. This was a well-used ploy designed to unnerve me. It was not necessary. I was doing a good enough job of that on myself.

Bert glared at me as if to expect my apology for surviving his first delivery. He slowly walked out to his starting point, turned and lumbered in. The second ball I saw at the last moment. Somehow I grounded my bat at the same instant that the ball was digging a furrow through to the stumps on what was a magnificent yorker. More hisses and whispers of 'bloody lucky'. When Bert was given the ball back he just stood there, tossing the ball from hand to hand, sizing me up. I knew what he was thinking. It was time for something special. Shouts of encouragement drifted across the field from the Perlethorpe encampment. I suddenly stiffened and felt angry. This time, I was going to have a go.

He came in again and released a monster that dipped and curved. I saw this one and swung my piece of willow lustily and without style. By some miracle the ball struck the top edge of the bat and took off with added pace over the heads of all three fieldsmen at slips. The ball was still moving with conviction when it hit the boundary fence for four runs as there were no fielders in the deep.

A great cheer rose from the Perlethorpe boys and my batting partner came down the pitch to shake my hand. It was a proud moment. Bert looked sullen.

It was his fourth bowl when I came unstuck. It was a good thing that I was starting to see the ball because this beast of a bowl was aimed at my chest. Then everything happened at once. I fell away from the line of flight and blindly swung the bat before toppling over. I felt the impact of bat on ball. As I hit the ground, I saw the ball ricochet off Burt's crutch and curve towards the man at silly point. Cries of "howzzat!" rang around the field. The umpire raised his finger to dismiss me. I was out, but so was Bert.

The Perlethorpe team spilled onto the field uttering whooping noises like a tribe of attacking Comanche. They came and carried me off the field in triumph while the Cutthorpe team tended to their wounded. Play was halted.

"The bastard's finally got his own back," John said. "You did it, the Aussie did it!"

"But I only got four runs."

"Who cares about the runs, you've stuffed the Mincer."

The cheers died and in the ensuing silence we became conscious of our callousness. I walked over to Bert, now rising unsteadily, doubled up in pain. Bert looked at me and saw that I was concerned. "You okay there?"

"Don't worry, mate. They're as tough as marbles. I wasn't after more kids anyway," Bert wheezed in a local Pennine dialect.

"It was an accident, I'm…"

"Shit, mate, I was going for yer, so fair's fair. I should've caught you." Bert's voice was clearing. "What's yer name?"

"Roger."

"Aren't you the Aussie? You showed guts, a bit of what Perlethorpe needs." The Mincer rose to his full height and shook my hand.

"Your balls alright?"

"Yeah, they should make a box for bowlers. I'll live."

Play resumed and I retired to the picnic shelter for the rest of the afternoon, watching the drama being played out of a side unused to defeat, going down. Bert had gone to lick his wounds and the house of cards came down. On the way home that evening, the talk was all about how I got the Mincer, each new version garnished with fresh hyperbole. The word spread quickly once we arrived back at the Perlethorpe pub. I felt both proud and embarrassed. John, from the team, made up an impromptu pub poem. Standing on the bar with cheers from the throng, he cleared his throat.

"Today Perlethorpe's cricket team saw
Cutthorpe's mincer of the moor.
A terrible sight, that was for sure,
The mincer of the moor."

Cheers and cries of 'more, more', encouraged John to continue his off-the-cuff arrangement. After a moment's thought, he went on.

"Today Perlethorpe's team were stuck
With the mincer out of luck.
An Aussie boy amongst us all,
Hit one off the mincer's balls."

A roar went up as the Yorkshire dark and Guinness flowed. John needed no more prompting and quickly thought up a finale. It took a while before the hubbub died down.

"Today, Cutthorpe's in a daze,
For the cricket game went our way.
All because the mincer from the moor,
Was no more, no more, no more!"

Wild cries and cheers broke out. The noise was deafening and spilt out onto the village common. "The mincer from the moor was no more, no more," was repeated everywhere after that. We were told later that we could be heard from Thoresby Hall itself, almost a mile away. What would the countess have made of it? I imagined Pa Barton sitting in The Rectory smiling to himself as the strains of the ditty penetrated his walls.

Conclusion

I felt a special bond with the people of Thoresby. Never before had I felt so much a part of a community, a sense of belonging. I grew greatly in confidence and maturity during these times.

The stream of crowds whose vanguard appeared at Whitsun finally dispersed into the October fog in convoys of buses, their occupants clutching prized plastic replicas of the Great Hall, pink figurines from the model of Titania's Palace, miniature stuffed koalas of Korean extraction and postcards depicting a beaming Countess Manvers.

Winter's advance, seemingly held up by the last weekend of activity, was now assured. A curtain of silence fell over the Hall, the deer meadow, over the forest, over everything.

And with that came our conclusion, with the many subtle signals from the Thoresby Hall Organisation and from Lady M herself that it was time for us to move on and time for me to stop marking time and actually do something that built for the future. This period of 19 months was a rite of passage for me. Its impacts on me were far-reaching. I had definitely metamorphosed but to what I didn't know. So it was into the unknown once again, but with all the experiences of Thoresby backing me up and saying to me I could do it, whatever 'it' was.

Sherwood Revisited

The trees parted ahead as I motored along a narrow country lane in my little Honda Civic and turned in at the gatehouse. It was a warm Saturday morning promising much. I found the new car park. Already, a few buses had arrived and there was a little activity around the ticket office.

"Hello," I said to a stranger selling 6-shilling Hall tickets. "You open at 12:30?"

"Sure, luv." She fiddled with a huge roll of tickets that looked like they had been borrowed from a cinema. "D'you want a guide book with your ticket? If it was me, I wouldn't go in without one. You miss so much, otherwise. You know, not knowing what you're looking at, I mean."

"No thanks, I'll just buy the ticket. I know this place, used to live here."

"You don't say! When was that?"

"About 10 years ago. I thought I'd see the place again, perhaps see some familiar faces. Is there anyone minding the desk inside the Hall?"

"Sure, old Mrs Judkins, you'll know her won't you?"

"So she's still around."

"Yes, but some of the others ain't. Look, you go on in and see her. I won't give you a ticket seeing you're a local, or were."

I thanked the ticket lady and walked in apprehensively, fearing bad news was just around the corner. From across the Great Chamber, I saw a tall but frail woman sitting next to a table full of post cards and key rings. I approached her, slowly.

"Roger! Where did you come from? I haven't seen you in… I don't know how long. It really is you?"

"Hello, Mrs Judkins. It's been a long time. How are you?"

"Still here, as you can see, but Bill's gone."

"Oh no, I'm so sorry. That's really why I'm here, to see you all again. That is bad news."

"Well then, you don't know about the others?" Mrs Judkins went on, looking almost cheerful now she had someone to talk to. "Yes, well, Mac went a few years ago now and Mrs Mac went back to Scotland to live with her sister. Of course, she had no home here once the new head gardener moved in, but he's really not much of one, not like Mac was. Remember how you got those lawns to look. They've never been like that since."

"What about the others?"

"What others?"

"Lady Manvers, Guy, the village people?"

"The poor Lady, she is here but not receiving visitors. It's her health you see. Of course the place is not hers, really. Yes, the National Coal Board owns it now. There were so many cracks appearing through everything that it was cheaper to buy the Hall than to keep paying compensation. This whole area is liable to subsidence."

I smiled. People had always used that ungrammatical term here, echoing the road signs warning the motorist that the underground mines were causing the ground to sink. All the roads seemed now to be 'liable to subsidence'.

"Where was I?" Mrs Judkins went on. "Yes, the mines are all around here now."

Mrs Judkins sat down and poured some tea from a thermos flask with a shaky hand. She sipped it slowly so as not to burn her lips. "I'm sorry, Roger. I haven't got a cup here for you." Mrs Judkins seemed to drift, her eyes focussing on the postcard scenes of Thoresby and Lady Manvers.

I felt it was time to go. I nodded and Mrs Judkins returned a faint acknowledgment. I wandered around the Great Hall and then down to the basement. I didn't go up to the gallery, the bedrooms and that bathroom. That would be too much for me.

I wandered out onto the lawns, roughly cut and unpatterned with flower beds showing strange species and conflicting designs not in Mr Mac's grand design. I walked the paths I had walked many times and imagined myself behind a Dorman model 220, state-of-the-art ride on cylindrical mower. I felt the power, heard the hum and smelt the intoxicating mixture of cut, damp grass and petrol fumes. All of my artful cutting patterns were in my mind's eye.

Returning to Thoresby was upsetting. Somehow I had hoped things would be just as they had been years ago. But so many of my friends from the past had passed on.

A few years previously, years after leaving Thoresby when Norma and I were back in Australia and Christmas was approaching, we had thought of the rector Pa

Barton and his daughter Betty. They had left Thoresby in not particularly friendly circumstances and gone north to Scotland, where they were living, or rather existing, in a cold crofter's hut somewhere in the Hebrides. I could imagine them, rugged up amid spartan surroundings without a heater, stuffing the cracks in the window panes. After many inquiries, the Church gave us their address and we despatched a David Jones Christmas food hamper full of rich fruit cake, shortbread biscuits, the finest Australian jams and preserves, smoked hams and pork, turkey and cranberry sauce and some vegemite. Months later, a letter arrived from Betty, thanking us for the hamper.

Betty wrote:

'Pa and I were having a miserable time. A bad storm had blown up and we couldn't get out of the house to reach any of our parishioners. The snow was banking up outside and we were even running short of water as the well is in the yard and I couldn't risk going out in the conditions.

'Christmas Eve arrived with no let up and we were both as miserable as we could be. We had no contact with the outside world at all, you see, with no telephone. Well, a miracle happened. We heard a bell, above the sound of the wind and it got louder. I was excited. I knew that bell. It was the bell of Charlie MacIntosh's bicycle, our postman. He had ridden all the way from the post office, through the snow to deliver your magnificent food hamper, all the way from Australia. God bless both of you. Pa and I were amazed as we opened the box and gazed at all the food. I had never seen such food before. You have done more for Pa than you could possibly imagine. He has had such a bad go of things. He has even been questioning things he never would have once. This brought him out of it. His cheer is what Christmas is about.'

The following November Norma and I sent off another hamper, this time including delicacies such as smoked duck and caviar and to top it off, a Cherry Ripe bar.

It was not until June that we received a letter from Scotland. It read:

'Dear Sir and Madam,

I am writing to you about a package addressed to the Rev Barton and Miss B Barton which arrived at the post office here in Stornoway last December. I have to tell you that both the Reverend Barton and his daughter are deceased. The Reverend passed away last November from pneumonia. Betty also had pneumonia and died in December. I was a friend of theirs and it caused us all a great amount of grief and sorrow here in our small community. Indeed, everybody spent a very low Christmas without them here with us, and without a Reverend to guide them.

'I believe that their house the church gave them was too cold and damp for the good of their health and last Christmas was a particularly hard one, with heavy snow and high winds almost every day from November on. They often told me of their friends in Australia. I've often wondered what it is like there with all your beaches. I was saddened that your generous gift did not reach them in time. We

took it upon ourselves to distribute the contents of your food hamper to the needy in our community.

'I am sorry that our news is so bad. We can say though that both the Reverend and Betty were always in high spirits. Thank you for your kindnesses.

Yours faithfully,

C. MacIntosh, Postman.'

Thoresby wasn't the same without my old friends. Wistfully wishing the past was still present and feeling despondent, I left Thoresby and motored out of Nottinghamshire to the Pennine hills. Cutthorpe village was drab and deserted, coated in uniform grey, the county colours of Derbyshire. The post office was behind a red door off the village green signified by a Walls Ice Cream sign swinging from a window frame.

I walked through the door, announcing: "I'm looking for a bloke I used to play cricket with. He played for the Cutthorpe team in the mid-sixties."

The postman looked up and observed me closely. "Christ mate! That sounds like a tall order. I've had people coming in here asking for all types of things but this takes the cake, I'm sure."

"I only know his name was Bert, short for Ethelbert." I suddenly remembered the old taboo in place about uttering that name. Would that now kill my chances of meeting the great fast bowler again?

"Haven't heard of an Ethelbert. That's not a name common around here. We are just a village and if there was an Ethelbert we'd know about it. Who are you, anyway? What's your business here?"

"I played against Bert back in 1966. I was with the Perlethorpe team. That's a small village in North Notts. I thought it would be nice to see him again, you know, old acquaintances."

The postman stared at me. I felt uncomfortable and reluctant to say any more in case it damaged my chances even further.

"You wouldn't be Roger Treagus would you?"

I nodded, shocked.

"Hey, Liz, he's here, he's here! Get everybody together! Get May! Get Bert!"

The postman, grinning, held out his hand. "I wanted to be sure it was you. When you said Perlethorpe, that did it. But, Christ, don't say Ethelbert again, only a few of us know that secret."

"How do you know?"

"Well, we knew you were coming. Mrs Judkins rang from the hall. She said you were asking after everybody. We guessed it. We hoped you would come."

"But, how did you know?" I repeated, astonished.

"Christ, Bert's talked about little else all these years. It's a legend, one of our local stories. D'you know you were the only batsman ever to king hit the Mincer. You did him a favour, his balls got quite active after that time and he fathered two more kids. My name's Bill. Congratulations."

People started filing in through the narrow front door and from the back of the shop. The tiny serving area was soon full to capacity. People were shaking my hand. "So you're the Perlethorpe boy. We called you the Stinger, did you know that? It's good of you to come all this way."

"Does Burt know I'm here?"

"Sure he does. We all knew you were down at the hall but we told Bert not to get his hopes up. He's always wanted to meet you again."

"I still don't understand, why the fuss? I only played a few games, and not too well, and I remember hurting the poor guy. I just thought it would be nice to see him again."

"You don't get it, do you and I'm not the one to tell you? Come over to the pub, and you'll see."

It seemed the whole village moved from the sardine-like conditions of the post office to the pub. As I walked in, a tall, lanky man stepped forward from the bar wearing an ear-to-ear grin.

"I've wanted to shake your hand for years. It's just great to see you here, in Cutthorpe, enemy territory." He laughed loudly.

"It's great to see you too. But I don't understand why all the fuss, why all this?"

"Well, Roger, I suppose I'm to blame. The boys here don't get to celebrate very often, what with the mines closing and the unemployment. But I've been talking about that game for years and about what you did after that game and with all your Christmas cards arriving, regular as clockwork, every year. You know, when a letter with an Australian postmark hits the post office the village knows about it pretty soon after." Bert looked at me and laughed again. "I suppose the whole thing has sort of blown out into a sort of legend."

"I remember that game so well," I said. "When I came on, that first time you looked so fearsome, intimidating. It was a sheer fluke what happened. I was defending myself with that shot that got you."

"Bull's arse! I gave you my best leg cutter. No Perlethorpe batsman has ever read it and I'd been playing a few years by then. I swear you saw it coming and you got in position. And the way you swung into it. It had me mesmerised. I just didn't get out of the way in time. It was really a caught and bowl chance gone begging if I'd been a 10 times better fieldsman, like Dexter or your boy, Harvey.

"You really want to be let in to a secret. Those bastards at Perlethorpe kept telling us that they had got themselves an Australian star, who used to play at the top level, your Sheffield Shield, isn't it? We just didn't believe it at first but a little news got through about your game when Perlethorpe played other clubs. We had to reconsider. So by the time you walked onto that field looking the part we were psyched out. And you thought I was intimidating."

"That's funny. I never thought I played well. I never believed what people said. I don't quite believe this reception."

"Roger." Bert looked a bit exasperated. "You haven't changed. We are all here to thank you. Look, we've got our village councillor with a little speech. I think you'd do best to listen to him. Like another black and tan?" With that Bert turned to the publican and ordered two more pints. He gestured to the Councillor to start. "Now, you just listen."

The Councillor, George Gear, cleared his throat and tapped a spoon to a beer jug. The pub quietened. "Friends and residents of Cutthorpe and the team of 1966, I think most of them are here this afternoon. We are gathered here today to…"

"Sounds like a bloody wedding!"

A roar of laughter went up raising the roof. More beer was ordered.

George shuffled the papers in front of him. "Shit, I don't need to read all this." He paused. "I know well enough what we are all here for without going to a prepared speech." George looked at me. "Roger here has come all the way from Australia to be with us this afternoon. We never thought much of Perlethorpe or Australia before his time. But, you know, our village Cutthorpe is a bit of a wretched place. We had the mine disaster, the closures, the mill closing and the tannery. They took our train away and then we had five bad seasons and our stock losses. There's not been much to cheer about, for a long time. And there are many here today who thought the village would die, a few years ago.

"You teaching history again, George?" More laughter.

"I'm coming to the point." George dried his forehead of sweat with a handkerchief. "I'm just setting the scene for our friend here. Well, as I was saying things have been bad. But a big bright spot has been Roger, here." George raised his voice. "He did three things for one of our lads. And he's here."

The councillor looked at Burt. "Jugs up for the Mincer!" A roar erupted. Bert accepted the accolade. "When Bert got hit by that screamer, Roger here was the first to him, helped him back to the clubhouse and looked after him. I remember some of our team at the time saying that they'd never seen the likes of it. Those Perlethorpe boys never did that. But that's not all. He then, for years, sent cards each Christmas to Burt, just checking to see if he was OK. You'll all tell me if I'm wrong but I don't recollect any outsider ever showing that kindness towards a Cutthorpe man."

George turned to me. "Roger, we are here today saying thank you for all of your kindnesses. And yes, that's the third thing. Roger's here today. It's great that he made the effort to come. It's not often that outsiders can even find this place. Altogether, raise your jugs, jugs up for the Stinger!"

There was a final, deafening roar followed by minutes of handshaking and backslapping. This was the England I knew, the place where I really grew up. Each day, week, month that I was here was momentous. It will always be so.

The trees of Sherwood sped past me as I pointed my little car up the Nottingham Road and cruised in top gear. It was late afternoon and a moon was rising in a clear sky. After clearing my third town, the trees started to thin as cleared paddocks came into view with small farmhouses dotting the landscape. I looked into my rear vision mirror at the receding forest and then ahead at an empty road disappearing over a bare hill. I accelerated up the hill, singing to myself. The moon's light grew stronger in the fading light of day. The North Star shone from behind me pointing the way south.

The Big Blue Bus – Photo Journalist

It was now September 1967. I had finished school four years earlier, scraping through with the barest Leaving Certificate pass after two attempts over two years. I had also had a go at getting 'A' levels – the equivalent of the Australian Leaving Certificate – in Britain by going back to school at the Worksop College near Thoresby. I failed dismally. My problem was that life was too full, too exciting, too distracting to sit down and endure long hours of study. Even when I tried to study, I just couldn't focus. My mind was off on a sightseeing trip of the Swiss Alps or walking along the towpath of the Shropshire Union Canal or selling Cherry Ripe bars at the Thoresby Kiosk. It was not on Euclidian Geometry, the War of the Roses, inorganic chemistry or Macbeth.

I was leaving the stately home scene heading south towards London with no qualifications and little prospect of a good job. Back in Australia things had not gone well for the family. My grandmother was ailing and my uncle had been forced to sell the family home as the bank was threatening foreclosure for a delinquent mortgage hanging over the house. My uncle, never on good terms with his sister, was threatening to take all Norma's possessions in the house to the tip.

London no longer held any great attraction. There was no job offer and our funds were rapidly diminishing. Norma pondered over this for long periods. I toyed with the notion of rejoining Selfridges but after all the experiences of the last 19 months that seemed a soul-destroying prospect. As well, the threat of Vietnam had passed for me. My birthday had never been drawn out of the hat although some of my friends' birthdays had. For one who wanted to become a pilot, having his birthday picked was like winning the lottery as not only was he able to become an air cadet with taxpayers funding his flying training for the two years of his conscription, but he never had to leave the comforts of Sydney.

So my plan was to go home, back to the Antipodes and the family. However, there was an immediate and simple problem: Once again we had no money for the fare. Thoresby had been an experience but not an income. We left with only enough money for food and basic necessities for a few weeks. What was our next step? Norma had an idea. We got to England thanks to a contra deal with Chandris Lines so why couldn't we do the same going back?

As soon as we hit London and settled into cramped quarters in Bayswater, Norma was scouring the shipping lines. But all had heard of our deal with Chandris; they all knew that Norma was to include their name in a new book she was to write with photos but that book was not yet written. Without a guarantee of publication no shipping line would touch us. So what else was there? Cargo vessels were not taking passengers at cut rates and airlines didn't need the publicity. So it was back to our indirect benefactor, Constance Paul, Norma's BBC friend, for new contacts.

"Why didn't you ask Marie-Louise for a higher remuneration?" she asked Norma. "Surely you were worth it for what you did there, except for that ghastly Australiana exhibition you imposed on her."

Norma pursed her lips, stung by the criticism. "I was not a mere employee, Constance, it wasn't like that. I just couldn't ask for more money."

"You ought to come on my marvellous film trip to Egypt, you'd absolutely love that, Norma," continued Connie, gesturing theatrically. "They came to Comombo. That's the title. Do you like it? It's about desert tribes returning to a village on the Nile."

"How does that help, Connie?"

"Well it gets you out of expensive London for a while on an exciting free jaunt."

"What about Roger?"

"What about him? Get a job, Roger."

Norma raised her eyebrow at me, then shook her head. "Thanks Connie, but we really have to get back to Australia."

Connie walked over to her coffee table and thumbed through a magazine. "I thought I saw an ad in here – yes, here it is – Penn."

"What's that?"

"Penn. I have a friend who works for them. I can try to set up a meeting for you."

Norma grabbed the magazine. "Who are they?"

"They're a bus company. They do overland trips. You could both go with them on one of their trips. You could write the story for their promotions and Roger could take the photos," she declared.

I looked at the advertisement. It showed a fleet of buses, emphasised how modern and comfortable they were and how professional the tours were; there were images of smiling bus drivers in smart uniforms, but no indication of any destination.

"But we want to get back to Australia," I protested.

"You can, my boy. These buses go part of the way. I know that."

"So where do they go?"

"Calcutta." Norma looked bemused. "You see, from there you can get a boat or something to Singapore and another boat to Australia or even fly perhaps. It's simple.

"So I'll get hold of my friend Elizabeth who works for Penn and put you in the PR chap's diary for a meeting. Give me a day or so and I'll ring you about it at your club. You did say you were staying there?"

"Sort of."

"Well, I'll leave a message."

Two days later a message was left at the reception of the Overseas Visitors Club for Norma to meet with a John Ford at Penn International. That meeting turned out to be very successful. They were a young company keen to establish a market and become known very quickly. Norma's impeccable journalist qualifications and experience, set out in the glowing reference Constance had provided, carried the day. My slightly less impeccable press photography certificate helped seal the deal. We were to travel on a Penn bus free of charge all the way to Calcutta. Norma was to write the story for the London and Sydney papers and I was to take the accompanying photographs.

Penn Overland pioneered overland bus travel between the UK and the Indian sub-continent. By 1967 they had established several overland routes: one through Lebanon, Israel, Jordan and Iraq; another through Syria and Iraq; and a northern route through Turkey and Iran. All routes joined up in Iran to then forge through Pakistan, Afghanistan and finally India with terminuses in Bombay and Calcutta. Our route was to be the central route through Syria and Iraq, taking in the ancient cities of Damascus and Baghdad. Our departure was set for the following week, so little time to say goodbye to a country I had called home. The bus trip was to take 6 weeks, then there was the uncertainty as to how we were to proceed past Calcutta, so it could still be months before Australia showed up on the horizon.

My job was to capture images of happy passengers with the bus and exotic scenes in the background. I had to be very conservative in my use of film as I was limited to about eight rolls due to space restrictions and there was no guarantee of buying reliable film beyond Europe. For a 6-week trip that meant less than seven pictures a day. I just had to know my exposures, composition and subject selection was right for every shot. By now experience had given me confidence. It would be so much easier to have subjects pose for me than to capture sneaking fleeting images of conveyor belts of bottles snapped through foggy windows.

Victoria Coach Station to Venice

The sun rose weakly over Victoria Coach Station on our departure day. Lugging two heavy suitcases and a back pack, I searched for our coach. There were coaches to Bournemouth, coaches to Coventry and coaches to Ipswich but no destination sign that said 'Calcutta'. Norma appeared from the coach station office with an agitated man busily pointing. It was the Penn representative.

"That's your bus. Over there!" He pointed to a nondescript grey bus that didn't look like it was capable of going beyond Surrey let alone travelling to Calcutta. Its destination sign read 'Dover'. Several confused passengers were gathering around the bus.

"Don't worry, your other bus will be waiting for you in France."

We all clambered on board and I started to take pictures as the bus moved off onto Buckingham Palace Road, as this was a significant moment in our journey to the Indian sub-continent.

"Stop! Don't waste film! This is not the image that Penn wants." Norma held up her hand to make sure the message got through to me. I knew I could be assured of quality film supplies while in Europe, and wondered whether my mother was going to be hovering over me as my director all the long way to the Bay of Bengal. Hadn't I proved myself already as an independent and capable photographer?

On French soil and off a rocky boat, all of us Penn passengers were fast becoming a group as we had the same task, to search for our shiny new coach in the terminal car park. We searched in vain. The only buses in sight were destined for local towns.

"Penn, Penn, Penn ici!" Penn, Penn, Penn!" The loud mantra emanated from the driver of a vehicle even less impressive that the English bus. "Penn, Penn, Penn!" seemed to be the limit of his foreign language skills. He motioned to us to get aboard leaving all our luggage in a pile on the asphalt.

"Oh, my goodness!" Norma clutched her head with her hands. "Don't take any pictures, Roger. This is getting worse. What have we done, Roger?"

Other passengers were wondering the same thing, especially after we discovered there was nowhere to stack our luggage except the back of bus, leaving 10 less seats than there were passengers for the ride ahead. The anger level was rising.

"Ne vous inquiétez pas hôtel bientôt très bientôt," said the bus driver.

"He said hotel, I heard that," said one of the passengers.

"In fact he told us not to worry, we will be at our hotel soon," announced a professional-looking traveller, a woman in her 40s wearing a pith helmet, giving her an aura of great travel experience.

"You speak French?" asked an exasperated passenger.

"And many other languages."

"Do you know what's happening?"

"Relax. It's all part of the trip. I'm sure we'll find out soon enough. My name's Fiona. We'll be getting to know each other very well, no doubt."

"Hôtel ici!" shouted the driver a few minutes later. The bus halted outside a hotel and we piled out. A well-dressed Latino man greeted us in the foyer with a reassuring air of confidence.

"Hello there, Penn group, welcome to our trip to India! I'm Hubert, your courier and fairy godmother right the way through to Calcutta." Relief, finally someone was looking after us.

"Sorry for the rough time. We've had trouble with buses, but the good news is we take delivery of a brand new Italian coach in Venice." Hubert was a young capable-looking Belgium with a constant and reassuring smile giving an impression that all problems could be fixed.

Just then hotel staff wheeled in some canapés and aperitifs and suddenly the mood of the room changed. Hubert was definitely on the ball. He knew what a little hospitality could do.

"Very glad to have you both aboard," Hubert said smiling even more broadly, towards Norma and me. "I was meant to look out for you."

"Did Penn tell you why we are here?"

"You're doing a story on us, aren't you?"

"Yes, I'm promoting you in a book I am writing. That's the deal." Norma smiled.

"Yes, and I believe Roger here is doing the photos."

"Yes, that's right," Norma interrupted. "And I'll be telling him what to shoot."

"No need for that. Roger obviously knows what to do," Hubert countered. I was warming to our courier very quickly. "Just hold off till we get our new bus. After Venice, with more exotic backgrounds, go for it! Just tell our bus driver where you want him to stop if you see something you like, OK?" I nodded and Norma managed a smile.

Over the next few days, Europe flashed past the bus windows. France, Germany and Austria passed under perpetually grey skies, but once over the Brenner Pass we emerged into brilliant Italian sunshine. Bright skies continued during our two days in Venice, as we soaked in the panorama from our hotel window on the Grand Canal.

Our Blue Italian Coach

On the third morning, we left our glorious hotel to behold the equally glorious sight of a brand new, gleaming blue Italian coach. It was so spacious, with padded tilting seats with back pockets, a toilet, air conditioning and even a small fridge. And here was my first photo op with a collection of happy passengers standing outside the door. The background was the Venice multi-storey car park, no canal in sight, but it was a start.

We had now been on the road for a week and the group of 32 had got to know each other. I divided them into single or married, and travellers or tourists. The singles were all young and the one married couple was old – at least 40 years old, I estimated. Of the singles, there was the young, curious well-travelled set, the slightly older even better travelled set and the group that thought they had made a mistake in coming on this bus at all and should have travelled on P&O. They were the tourists. Half were returning Australians and most of the rest were young British. This left two people who didn't fit into those categories: Norma and Mother Africa. Norma was seen as a mother figure for the young singles who clustered around her most of the time. She gave out the unstated message that she was a font of wisdom, especially when it came to travel and the observance of cultural mores. She dispensed advice on all subjects with a tone of authority. Mother Africa was a middle-aged single from South Africa who had been everywhere, done everything, was an international teacher on a variety of subjects, spoke many languages, wore African game park khaki with a pith helmet and was using the bus as public transport to get to her new teaching post in Nepal. Mother Africa was too aloof a figure for the young set to be drawn to so they continued to follow after the more approachable Norma. As the trip wore on Mother Africa mellowed, lost some of her reserve and was more like one of us.

Knowing the passenger cliques meant selection for promo photos became easier with my favourite smilers posing in front of the bus at photo stops. Our new bus driver was Wilfried, a Belgian. He wasn't informed he was driving us all the way to Calcutta, not just to Istanbul, until after we had arrived in Turkey. Then his father died as he was driving across the Anatolian Plains but he didn't find out about that until we arrived in Teheran, too late to make the funeral and get a replacement driver. Wilfried suffered for most of the journey after Turkey and occasionally took his anger out on his driving.

The Israeli-Egyptian Six Day War prevented us from transiting Syria and Iraq. We switched to Plan B, the direct route to Iran through Turkey. The drill was to be on the lookout for good shots, tell Wilfried to stop the bus at the right point in the road and select some well-dressed and happy subjects to stand next to the bus while taking my shot with the iconic scene behind. This happened every few hours initially in Yugoslavia, Greece and Turkey but trailed off as we entered the Iranian desert where all blue mosque backgrounds looked the same in photographs and the standard of passenger dress and demeanour deteriorated. Our coach was also deteriorating as we bumped along potholed desert roads, which took their toll on the springs and shock absorbers and our backsides. The toilet, air conditioner and fridge stopped working, so did the low-range gears. This was a lovely modern Italian bus designed for Italian roads, not unsealed tracks where the bitumen ran out at the town limits. Whenever we arrived in any town east of Ankara the bus was mobbed as evidently the locals had not seen a vehicle like it before. That told us something.

My background scenes in my promo photos told the story of our route: the earthquake devastation in Skopje with barely a house standing in the worst districts, the vivid white and blue colour combination of Macedonia, Delphi and the Bay of Corinth, the busy fishing towns on the Aegean coast, the great mosques of Istanbul, the 'fairy chimneys' of Cappadocia, Turkey, the cloud shrouded Mount Ararat, and the Persian carpets of Tabriz. Then followed the Caspian Sea, the Ezberg Mountains behind Teheran, Persepolis and the many blue mosques in places like Shiraz, Isfahan and Kerman. Iran was a nation of vivid blue, from the sky to the buildings to the lakes.

We had been on the road for a month. Tensions were rising. It wasn't just the constant thumping of the corrugations jackhammering throughout the springless bus. The coach's water was hot; toilet stops had to be outside (girls on one side of the bus and boys on the other, with no vegetation, so no privacy). Heat and dust permeated everything. Hubert was having difficulty in keeping people calm, constantly promising the bus would be fixed at the next large town.

The Balochi Takeover

We had entered what was known as the Balochistan Empty Quarter on some maps, close to the Iranian Pakistan border. The scenery was desolate with bare low hills and intervening sand dunes. The fierce sun was beating down on a shadeless earth. The road had gone from an unsealed corrugated dirt strip to wheel tracks that sometimes disappeared in the sand, only to be picked up on the other side of a dune. Hubert had instructed Wilfried to turn left when he saw an Iranian flag poking out of the roof of a mud hut. It was to appear by the side of the road. But what road? Wilfried never saw it. The bus laboured on as the tyres dug into the soft sand, until inevitably, we got bogged. The modern technique for deflating the tyres to get better traction on sand was unknown to Belgian bus drivers accustomed to Western European road conditions, so we stayed where we were, stuck under a burning desert sun.

Suddenly we were confronted by an amazing sight: out from the sand dunes emerged a large group of local herdsmen, resplendent in bright red shirts, white pants and white bandanas, all riding bicycles. They charged towards the bus and dismounted, brandishing automatic weapons. There were about 20 of them, yelling and vigorously waving their hands. More tribesmen then appeared over the top of the dunes until over 50 were surrounding the bus as well as the 20 climbing on board. At last something adventurous and different to film! Furtively, I took some pictures through the window of the tribesmen standing outside, but I didn't risk showing off my camera to the group now running crazily up and down the aisle inside the bus, shouting.

Then they discovered the water container. They lifted it, shook it, then opened it up and filled their cups. Then came the spluttering and screaming abuse as they spat out the water on the bus floor and all over us.

"The water is bad, bad, baaadd," gestured Hubert, who by this time had stood up and was trying to assume some control. He shook his head and grimaced in an attempt at making them understand. "They know it's bad, Hubert," called out one of the passengers.

"Here, pass this around. Give them a donation." Hubert produced his hat. It was passed around the bus, each of us unloading Iranian coins into it and some notes as well. Hubert quickly grabbed the hat and gave it to the tribesman who looked like the leader. He grabbed it and looked inside poking the pile of coins with his fingers. "Dollar," he said as he pulled out an American greenback. "Dollars!"

"Dollars, give him dollars!" shouted Hubert. I managed a few furtive shots of the colourful scene and the leader's magnificent headgear of tightly wrapped white cotton rising to a peak higher than that of his followers. The hat was passed around a second time, this time with dollar bills being dropped inside. The leader looked pleased when he saw the collection. Hubert saw his moment to start a dialogue and spread out the map in front of the leader. "Balochistan," he said, pointing to the blank space on the map. The leader stood tall and proud.

"Balochi," he said, pointing to himself. Then he pointed to all the other tribesmen inside the bus. "Balochi," he shouted out. He then rushed to the bus door, and with his staff swinging back and forth, pointed to all of his tribesmen both inside and outside the bus, now numbering over 50. "Balochi!" he shouted even louder. A cry came from his men in reaction to his acknowledgement. The leader waited at the bus door for his men to quieten. An uneasy silence followed.

Mother Africa seized the moment. She got up out of her seat and moved towards the leader at the door. He stood his ground as she appeared at the door. She raised up her hands and faced the crowd, and cried out at the top of her voice "Balochi!" and started clapping. Two other passengers then came to the door and started clapping as well. This was picked up by some of the tribesmen and then quickly spread to everyone, Balochi and European alike. I got to the door myself to take a memorable shot of the scene capped off by the Balochi leader with a broad smile on his blackened face.

We all jumped off the bus and mixed with the tribesmen. They were our friends now, and as it turned out, our rescuers. More and more Balochis were turning up as news spread about our presence. We all shook every hand that was offered. Hubert talked in Farsi to the leader. Here is Hubert's account of what happened next.

I asked them to cycle up to the mud hut that we could see in the distance with vehicles parked outside, and ask for help. I said I would pay the leader well for doing so. They replied: "Impossible. We are tribal and those are Iranian officials. If we come anywhere near, they'll shoot!" But they were willing to lend me a bicycle to ride up there myself, which I did, after drinking plenty of water and wetting my head to cool off a bit.

Walking (or cycling) in the desert has one thing in common with snorkelling under water: you can't judge distances. I cycled and cycled and after a while the mud hut came into sight. I kept on cycling but it didn't look as if I was getting any closer to it. This went on for what seemed like an eternity, together with this tremendous urge to sit down, just for a minute. But there was also the warning signal: if you dare sit down, beware: you won't be able to get up again. The Persians have all sorts of tales about this: they talk about desert spirits (the djinns) who suck the energy out of you through the soles of your feet. You sometimes see them depicted in Persian miniature paintings.

Finally the hut was only a minute or two away. The urge to sit down became unbearable. I had no more energy. Then I did a quite smart thing: I dropped the bicycle, jumped off, started running for the open entrance door of the hut and literally dropped inside, full length: Shade! There was a clay vase with cool water next to where I fell; without looking up I took the metal cup, filled it and threw water onto my neck and head, while remaining face down, two or three times. Only then did I slowly get up, whispered "Salam!" to the 6 men seated in the room and drunk one cup, very slowly.

In fact they were awaiting me, foreseeing what was bound to happen. They offered me some tea, told me to catch my breath for a few minutes—and then showed me the rescue bus, hidden behind a clay wall, and the trunks of poplar trees to put behind the rear wheels of our vehicle for a perfect grip. The price was quickly agreed upon and half an hour later we reached the coach in the rescue bus carrying four poplar tree trunks.

Back at the bus we could all see the rescue bus approaching. We cheered and the Balochis cheered also. The leader started shouting orders. Spades and shovels suddenly appeared and a small army of diggers formed to dig a space to fit the poplar trunks under the wheels. The leader started shouting at Wilfried and pointed towards a big sand dune but Wilfried didn't understand. After being bogged, he certainly wasn't going to bog us in another dune. More shouting. Still Wilfried did not move.

"Start it up, Wilfried!" ordered Hubert. "That's what he wants. You'd better do it and quick." Wilfried spun into action. The leader shouted again with expansive hand movements, motioning the driver to move. Wilfried put the bus into gear, let out the clutch and the bus lurched forward but stopped at the base of a small sand dune as the wheels dug into the sand. Wilfried's last act was to put on the handbrake and slip the engine to neutral.

This was too much for the leader. He grabbed at Wilfried's shirt, pulled him out of his driver's seat and deposited him on the floor, much to the amusement of all his followers who laughed raucously. About 15 of his men, automatic weapons still dangling from their waist belts piled back into the bus as the leader now became the driver. The leader managed to take off the hand brake and move the gear stick to first forward. Had he ever driven a bus like this before? He seemed to know what he was doing, with a little help from his jabbering friends. The coach suddenly jerked violently forward, with the engine screaming to be let out of first gear. That never happened.

It was a surreal scene, thankfully captured on film. I took numerous shots. The Balochi leader, with his bright white bandana flapping in the wind was driving the bus, surrounded by his boisterous and well-armed guard with automatic weapons still at the ready. Hubert was anchored to his seat and Wilfried was still on the floor. They said and did nothing, but could see the raw expertise on display by our new driver. All us passengers at the back of the bus felt strangely confident at the turn of events. At least we were out of the bog and still moving. Our flamboyant Balochi leader, plainly a man of action was what was needed right now. He was the right man for the job. And he seemed to know what he was doing. Glancing out of the window all of his tribe were running or cycling and one on horseback was keeping pace with us as we moved towards the huge sand dune. More photos. This was Hollywood.

The front wheels hit the front of the dune ahead with force. Instead of digging in, the whole bus bounced and careered up the dune to the top and then down the other side without hesitation. We raced across the flat onto the next dune and repeated the manoeuvre and did the same thing again at the next. Finally, as we raced down the wall of the third dune, the bus hit the road, a real road, properly formed, no wheel tracks, instead a hard surface. With this the leader stalled the bus as he applied the brakes. We came to a silent stop on the main road to Pakistan as the leader announced "Keta, Keta," pointing the way ahead. Clearly he meant Quetta. Applause was spontaneous, firstly from us at the back of the bus, then from his men in the bus transferring to his fast arriving tribe on the ground. We had made it.

We took a hat around quickly for another 'donation' without any prompting and handed it to the leader who smiled even more broadly than before. After a round of handshakes, the Balochis mounted their bicycles and sped back into the desert, quickly disappearing into the dunes. That was the last we ever saw of them or any other desert tribesmen.

After that incident, our days reverted to predictability. Sure I had elephants nudging against the bus windscreen around Delhi; the Taj Mahal was an impressive bus backdrop; and pictures of the bus next to the Ganges funeral pyre in Benares were quite dramatic; but nothing seemed to match the spirit of a tribe of Balochis stampeding over sand dunes on bicycles and horses keeping pace with their brothers driving the bus in first gear up and down desert dunes.

First Large Coach into the Himalayas

In our first Pakistani town, Quetta, Hubert sat us down after breakfast to make an announcement. "As you know, the Middle Eastern War [the Arab-Israeli War] made Penn shorten the route somewhat so we've got here well ahead of time. So we are off to Kandahar tomorrow and then Kabul and this diversion should use up the time a bit, but there is still close to a week we have extra after that. So the London Office asked us to choose now which of two routes you want." Hubert produced a giant map of the Indian sub-continent and spread it out on the floor of the meeting room. He pointed to the two routes. "We can either go south or north. South to Kerala and Madras or north to Kathmandu. Which way do you want?"

"Wow, Kathmandu!" several people spontaneously piped up.

"Anyone for Kerala?" Silence. "It has some lovely waterways and Madras is a fascinating city."

"Sounds like you want us to go there," said Mother Africa.

"Look, it's up to you," said Hubert. "But I should tell you something first. The office gave it as a tentative route only because no one has ever got a bus our size up that road. You see, Kathmandu was isolated until 11 years ago. There was no road up there from India until this road was built. Buses have been getting through for about five years but they are all local small buses. Nothing like our Italian monster. Wilfried and I have discussed the conditions and have had information from the consulate but we still don't know how good the road is. It may not take the bus at all and if that happens we lose out on Nepal and then won't have the time left to go south. But if we go south now there is no problem. What do you say?"

Now my imagination was working overtime; the chance to reach such a fabled remote part of the world, the real Shangri-La (as it seemed in the 1960s) and even the chance of glimpsing Mt Everest.

"As long as there's a chance we can see Everest, I vote for Kathmandu. At least we can try," said Mother Africa. The vote for Kathmandu was unanimous, so our Nepal adventure was on.

"Penn would love some really good bus scenes on that road so be sure you take them," Hubert told me. "Just tell Wilfried to stop when you want." I checked my film stocks – only three rolls left. I had to make every shot count and not stuff up my exposures with my manual camera.

Eight days later the front wheels hit the first incline to take us away from the Indian plain. Here we go: the first large European coach ever to attempt to reach Kathmandu. . We had been warned, but Captain Wilfried was not going to abandon ship. This was Nepal's new gateway, the Tribhuvan Highway, named after a recently departed king of Nepal. We climbed out of the hot and dusty Indian Plain shimmering below in the October heat. The road snaked uphill in endless switchbacks and blind corners with never a straight section. And the higher we got, the narrower the tortuous road became. The sweat streamed off Wilfried's anxious brow as he feverishly worked the steering wheel, first on one lock then the opposite lock.

I stood up to get some good action pictures through the windscreen and of the stressed driver. Hubert shook his head vigorously. "No standing, too dangerous!" he shouted out above the roar of the engine in second gear. He was right. I had to hold on to keep my balance, difficult when trying to keep the camera steady to cope with the low light, low shutter speed conditions. I then noticed how little traffic there was; just a few donkey and carts, motor cycles and minitrucks; nothing even approaching our size. We were the biggest thing on the road and had been all day.

Two new problems then emerged with the deteriorating road conditions. First the bus's turning circle was now no longer enough to negotiate the bends in one go, and secondly the length of the bus made it difficult to steer the bus around corners without the outer back wheels going close to the edge. And the airspace below the edge was now over a thousand feet straight down. The difficulties kept increasing. There was no conversation. The only noise was the engine labouring under the grade of the road and the low gear grind. Mercifully the low-range gear breakage back on the Iranian plateau had been fixed in Delhi. Then we saw what Hubert had warned us about a week earlier: a bridge. Perched precariously on a sharp bend crossing a near vertical stream, this terrifyingly narrow construction had a 'see-through' deck of parallel wooden planks separated by yawning gaps, affording a sickening view of the 1000-feet-plus plunge to the torrent below. Wilfried stopped the bus to inspect the bridge. Hubert and Wilfried argued in

Flemish but we all got the drift. The bridge was too narrow and there was no space on the approach for Wilfried to line the bus up. Five minutes later a silent, sullen, sombre Wilfried boarded the bus, alone. Hubert and all the passengers looked on. I made the most of my career moment, avidly snapping pictures of the bus and the bridge from various angles. “Travel with Penn Overland, the big adventure bus company!” I imagined the caption to read.

With the skill of a professional, Wilfried shunted the bus backwards and forwards in the tight manoeuvring space available until the bus was lined up with the bridge, a feat we had thought impossible. He then inched forwards. As soon as the front wheels mounted the bridge decking, a frightening creaking noise reverberated from the superstructure. The passengers standing close to the bridge scattered. But Wilfried kept going. The wheels on both sides were centimetres from the edge. Precise steering was vital. The bus lurched slowly forward as Hubert shouted out instructions from the front.

The back wheels mounted the wooden planks. The bridge groaned even louder and seemed to move as it took the full weight of the vehicle. But it held. Then, anxious to get across, Wilfried pushed down on the accelerator. Suddenly he was over. The front wheels were back on solid ground. Now he had to turn sharply. An embankment lay dead ahead. As he turned, the back wheels fell out of alignment with the bridge. The left back wheel moved to the extreme edge of the deck planks. Hubert screamed. We all screamed. Wilfried yanked on the handbrake, then jumped out to inspect the danger. The bus had double back tyres. It was only the outer tyre that was about to move into thin air, with no bridge deck below. With the acute bend in the road right at the end of the bridge and no manoeuvring room on the bridge, Wilfried was forced to continue dead ahead. Better than the even more dangerous option of reversing off the bridge.

Eventually Wilfried satisfied himself he could do it by driving straight into the hill ahead and then using full reverse lock on the steering for just a few feet when the back wheels had just reached firm ground. Wilfried climbed back into the driver’s seat. All was quiet apart from the engine and the continual clicking of my camera shutter. “Get the photos that show the extraordinary, not just a bus trip. OK with that?” Hubert had briefed me well. If only I didn’t have to ration my film.

Wilfried selected first gear of the eight-speed gearbox and let out the clutch. The bus inched forward until the front bumper bar hit the rocky outcrop ahead and started riding up the hill. Now full lock for the reverse. Hubert shouted directions through Wilfried’s open escape door. Everyone’s eyes fixed on the back wheel as the bus reversed, then turned sharply. The inner back wheel crossed back onto the outer edge of the bridge decking. But the outer wheel still hung in the air with solid ground more than a thousand feet below. Wilfried’s skilful manoeuvre, however, had slightly shifted our coach’s position, so he could now swing the bus around so that it missed the hill and was miraculously totally on the road again. Cheers and applause echoed off the cliffs as Wilfried applied the handbrake and wiped the sweat from his forehead. He jumped off the bus and took a bow. He had done it. After that feat, everything else seemed possible. The second challenging bridge seemed almost a pushover.

After hours of ascending into the clouds via interminable switchbacks, the road finally levelled out. We had arrived in Daman at the top of the front range at 2400m altitude on the southern flank of the Himalayas. For the first time in weeks the air was cool. As nightfall descended under a heavy cloud blanket, we found accommodation in a small village bungalow. Curious locals examined us and fussed over us, plying us with bowl after bowl of rice. Few Europeans came up the road from India and certainly never in a giant vehicle like ours, which dwarfed all the huts in the village. People kept walking around the vehicle, trying to comprehend its size. Before going to my small, hard bunk bed in the ice-cold bungalow, I checked my film usage. I had taken more photos on this day than at any other time on the journey.

Daman is famous for one thing: its unimpeded view of all of the main peaks of the Himalayas stretching 300km from Dhaulagiri and Annapurna in the west to the Everest massif in the east. As the sun rose, the clouds cleared revealing all these peaks jutting gloriously above a gleaming mantle of snow. Again the superlative view chewed up my film stock. I was running short. I hoped that Kathmandu, a capital city isolated from the rest of the world until the 1950s, less than a decade earlier, would have modernised enough to carry Kodachrome.

Soon the white peaks of Everest, Lhotze and Nuptse came into view, an amazing sight even though they were so far away. The road descended into our first Nepalese valley. The road had improved, the narrow bridges had gone. But we had become too complacent. As we rounded a bend, an obstruction appeared ahead. A landslide was completely blocking the road. Wilfried stopped, and we all piled out.

Villagers seem to be coming from all directions, emerging out of the forest to add their hands to moving the rocks. There were few tools but hundreds if not thousands of hands. We squatted next to local people in a common effort to clear the road. We smiled. They smiled back. They talked to us in Nepali. We had the road in common so it seemed easy to communicate without language. I was getting wonderful shots of cheerful, innocent faces with the bus in the background. These photos were far more pleasing and memorable to me than Everest.

After an hour, the pile of rubble had shrunk, and after two hours, our bus was bouncing over the remaining rocks and rubble while the villagers waved us goodbye. The narrow road, the switchbacks and the perilous bridges slowed our progress so much that we spent all day crossing just one valley. Nightfall saw us near exhaustion including our Belgian bus driver. As we rumbled into the dark most of us, including me, fell asleep, so what happened next I will leave to Hubert's account.

On and on it went, zigzagging up and down the mountains. Soon it was 11pm and Wilfried asked me: "You are aware of the fact that I'm a mountain driver, yes?"

"Sure," I said, "specialised in winter tours, especially the Dolomites, right?"

"OK," he continued, "I can last another hour or two at the most. Do you mind if I start speeding a bit?"

"Go ahead, you're a professional. And everybody's fast asleep."

And speeding he now did, up a steep stretch then down again, at quite a terrific speed. And then, all of a sudden, we saw what was below: a metal bridge, with one unforeseen detail: the metal sides were there alright, but in between there were only the two beams across, and no planks joining these beams!

I saw Wilfried go white in the face, half close his eyes like a sharpshooter who aims, his tongue licking his lips. Only the outer part of the front wheels could get a grip, and only the inner part of the rear wheels. Suddenly we were on it. In no time we were across it. We heard bridge metal crunching and denting the left rear of the bus as it turned sharply left to reach solid ground on the other side. But we both heaved a sigh of relief, while glancing at one another with raised eyebrows. I made a thumbs-up gesture with my right hand and shook it as if I had just burned one finger, signalling our narrow escape. No one on board had noticed a thing.

After four days in Kathmandu, we had to retrace our steps along this same, newly opened Tribhuvan Rajpath road, then turn east and head for Calcutta. It was only on the return journey, on reaching that same spot, that we had to give some explanation. The bridge had been completed by now, but the angle was so sharp it took Wilfried over half an hour to get his bus onto the bridge. So someone asked: "Wilfried, how the hell did you do that in the dark?" With a straight face he replied: "I don't know. Somehow, in the dark it looked a lot easier."

The road levelled out at the bottom of the last valley. It was wider now. There was more traffic – cows, bicycles rickshaws, carts, an occasional car. Our arrival in Kathmandu caused quite a stir. The bus slowed to walking pace in the congestion and a crowd gathered and walked alongside. They were in awe of the immense size of our bus. People were running towards us from everywhere and waving. Had we been the first big bus? Hubert was looking for the Panorama Hotel and asked several hundred locals at once. They all ran ahead of us gesticulating for us to follow. Our journey from the plains of India finally came to an end in the forecourt of the hotel. Wilfried pulled on the handbrake and stopped the engine. We were mobbed, a crush to get from the bus to the hotel foyer. People were shouting and wanting to shake our hand. It was indeed a fitting end.

Beyond all the temples and stupas festooning this mountain city Kathmandu was awakening to the western world. I knew this because the shops stocked Kodakchrome. And the film stock was not even out-of-date. I was mightily relieved as the spectacular photo opportunities of the last several days had drawn heavily on my remaining rolls, so I was down to just two rolls of 36 exposures each to see me through to Calcutta and beyond.

Towards Australia – Ship Photographer (Again)

By Day 71 of the trip we were travelling down India's Grand Trunk Road in West Bengal State, just hours out of Calcutta and the end of the bus trip from the Victoria Coach Station, now half a world away. The mountains, the people, the colour and the architecture all combined to deplete my film stock once again to almost nothing. I was quite proud of what I had achieved. At least I felt I now knew something about photography.

We were Australia-bound. However, the reality was we were in Calcutta, without any forwarding arrangements and not enough money to buy expensive plane tickets to Sydney. So once again my flamboyant, resourceful mother swung into action, attempting to set up contra deals with airlines and shipping companies. Calcutta was not a good city to do this as corporate decision makers appeared to avoid the place. They were all in Bombay, Delhi or more likely, in Europe. There was faint interest from Cathay Pacific in getting publicity for a free passage. After repeated visits to their office, they relented with a compromise of a discounted air ticket as far as Singapore. Norma grabbed the offer and for once I didn't have to take promo pictures.

The real negotiations were thus moved to Singapore, where a deal was struck after several weeks of lobbying with the Austasia Shipping Line, a cargo vessel outfit plying the trade routes between Singapore and Australia. As before, my photography was a selling point for Norma to offer. Our vessel was *Malaysia*, a 10000-ton cargo boat which took passengers. Curiously for such a small ship it had both first and second class. First class was up the front, naturally, and the ship's cargo hold formed the barrier between first and second class, which were at the stern. Norma and I were first class of course, and we physically looked down on the steerage stuck there on their island above the hold cover. We only ever mixed when the crew constructed a temporary canvas swimming pool on the hold accessible to both classes. Promo photos were easy. The rules were: shots of the Captain, the Captain's table, the Captain's feast, dancing with the Captain and the Captain on the bridge. Forbidden were shots of the mainly Korean crew, the ship's cargo, poorly dressed passengers and any photos of passengers from second class.

On the 15th of October 1967, we sailed into Sydney Harbour with my final shots being the Sydney Harbour Bridge (ship in foreground) and an under construction Sydney Opera House (ship in foreground again). I arrived as I had left, being a ship's photographer. My photo-journalist career was over for now.

Inside the Weather Bureau – Weather Observer

When I was born I was aware more or less immediately that I knew very little. The old Goon Show joke definitely applied to me because 22 years after my birth that realisation was still true. Right through my childhood and teenage years I was fascinated by the ever-changing moods of the weather. I operated a weather station in my back yard, kept a bulletin board with current weather observations and forecasts and I also read books about meteorology. Coming a near second to my ambition to being a Qantas pilot, the fall-back was being a weather forecaster. I was too old to become a Qantas pilot cadet, and I knew too little to become a weather forecaster; with no entry qualifications into a university science or maths faculty, which I needed for this job.

I did hold a pass in the Leaving Certificate, the barest of passes but still a pass. It did unlock a few small doors and one notable door into the weather bureau, not as a forecaster, but as a weather observer. Now that was something in the right direction. And right now in December 1967, *The Sydney Morning Herald* carried advertisements inviting interested people to apply to become trainee weather observers. I figured that once I had a toe in the weather bureau's door I might become a forecaster the back way, perhaps without university qualifications.

Three weeks after I had sent off my neatly completed application form using the best ballpoint pen I possessed, I was on a plane to Melbourne occupying a first-class seat. In those days, all public servants and even those merely seeking that status travelled first class. It was a very British culture carried over from a time when British public servants were only a rank or two below the aristocracy in stature. This mode of transport was a far cry from bumping along a corrugated desert road in central Iran on a hard bus seat.

What Cloud Is That?

The training course for weather observers was 10 weeks long. It was conducted on the top floor of an old warehouse at the Carlton brewery end of Swanson Street, Melbourne. The course taught us to understand cloud types and weather types, how to understand weather report message codes, how to make hydrogen for the balloons, how to run a balloon flight and how to plot the weather codes on a map so that the meteorologist could draw the weather map with isobars. There was a lot to learn. After completing the course, each of us was to be posted to a weather station, any weather station.

Right from the first day I felt I had finally started my career. This was it; not a 'fill-in' job but the start of a real career path. I had always wanted to work in the weather bureau. I was disappointed it wasn't as a meteorologist, but this was close. I boarded the St Kilda Road tram trundling north into the city to the strains of Aretha Franklin singing *I say a Little Prayer for you* on someone's transistor. Brewery smells from the Carlton factory across Exhibition Street greeted me as I alighted the tram at the top of the Swanson Street hill outside the Weather Bureau's training building.

We had two teachers, Ken and Bill, both diminutive Englishmen. They knew their stuff. Before we had even sat down on that first morning Ken said, "Righto, you chaps, no resting, up to the roof and get some fresh air."

The course was on the top floor, with easy access to the rooftop weather instruments. Ken pointed to a streak of white cloud on an otherwise clear Melbourne sky. "What cloud is that, chaps?"

"Cirrus!" I exclaimed proudly. I knew clouds. I had run my own little unofficial weather station for years as a kid.

Ken smiled. "Looks like we have someone in this class who knows something. You get 6 out of 10 for that effort."

I was taken aback. I was sure I was right.

"You will all learn cloud types," Ken continued. "They are fundamental to your job. There are three types of high cloud and that is one of them. Roger was close. Can anyone tell me what it is?"

"Cirrostratus," answered another student.

"Correct!" shouted Ken." There are 10 main types forming at three main levels. You will learn them and learn them and learn them until you are mistake-proof. Understand? If you get them wrong, your weather report is stuffed. Get it! They are all Latin names but don't blame the Romans for that. It was an English chemist by the name of Luke Howard who proposed them in 1802."

Being a weather observer meant more than just identifying clouds and measuring the temperature and wind. We had to learn the codes sent in by teletype from all the weather stations around the country. These codes constituted a complete weather report with barometric pressure, wind direction and speed and cloud types and coverage as the most important parts. We plotted these coded messages on a big map of Australia which the meteorologist would then use to draw the isobars of the weather map, then used as a vital tool in forecasting the weather.

As well, we had to learn how to prepare a weather balloon, set it flying and then track it with a weather theodolite so that the upper atmosphere winds would be calculated from the drift of the balloon. In the 1960s, lighter than air helium was not available so we had to use potentially explosive hydrogen instead. The weather bureau didn't have the funds to buy industrial hydrogen. We were expected to make our own. We were also required to maintain our instruments and keep weather records.

The Hydrogen Incident

Bill pointed to the two piles of inoffensive-looking powder: one was ferro-silicate and the other, sodium hydroxide. "These are the proportions you will need for a gas cylinder this size. It is in your hydrogen handbook, so always look at it even if you think you know it, because Christ, don't get it wrong otherwise you will hear this." Bill pivoted on his heels and pushed a button behind him.

Boooooom! The room shook as if hit by a violent earthquake. Two students fell from their chairs in fright. Bill chuckled. "I love this part of the course," he said. "That's what you'll hear – if you're still conscious." He surveyed the room. He had everyone's undivided attention now. "So, be careful!"

Now he emptied the two piles of powder into the cylinder. "What's missing?"

"Water," answered someone.

"How much?"

"Err, four pints," the student replied. With that, Bill swivelled again and pushed the button. Booom!

The classroom shook for a second time.

"C'mon chaps, get this right for Christ's sake. Look in your blasted handbook. It's all there."

After a long pause, Bill poured in the correct quantity of water and quickly screwed back the cylinder cap.

"Come up here and see this, quickly!" We all dashed to the cylinder, now with its cap well and truly screwed down. The gas pressure gauge needle was advancing indicating the gas pressure inside the cylinder was building. The needle moved slowly at first, then quickened. "Very exothermic, very," said Bill. A thousand pounds per square inch, 2000psi, 3000psi, 4000psi.

"Hell!" shouted a student. Some backed away, fearing an almighty explosion. But the needle slowed down, finally stopping at just under 5300 pounds per square inch.

"That's it! The reaction has stopped. Why? Because we have run out of one of the reagents. So get the proportions and amounts right chaps, to stop it going too far."

"What's too far?"

"A very good question. 6000psi is the limit. The cylinder is not rated beyond that pressure, OK?"

We all got that point, very well.

Three days later we had our first excursion away from the classroom and headed out to Essendon Airport, then Melbourne's only major airport. The bus deposited us next to an old tin shed on the airport's perimeter. It housed the

Bureau's hydrogen cylinders and the chemicals for making the gas. This was our first practical and we were organised into teams of three. Only one team was allowed in the shed at a time. I was grouped with John and Barry, two keen cadets from Queensland.

"OK," said Bill. "You know what to do now. Off you go. Read your manual again before you start and agree in your team what you are doing before you do it. Right? We will have John, Roger and Barry up first. The rest of you can go getting the cloud types right, there's plenty up there today."

We filed into the shed and went through the procedure very methodically, measuring out the right proportions of ferro-silicate and sodium hydroxide, pouring them into an empty, clean gas cylinder, then measuring out the right amount of distilled water.

"OK, we are all ready. Roger, you have the cap. So John will pour the water in and then we will both hold the cylinder at the right angle for you to screw the cap on. Do it quickly." Barry was looking a bit worried.

"I'm ready," I said holding the cap ready to screw it on. John emptied the jar of water into the cylinder which caused a loud bubbling sound as the chemical reaction started.

"Get the cap on, quick!" shouted Barry. I placed the cap over the cylinder head and started screwing as quickly as I could with the pressure building inside the cylinder. The cap screwed in for several threads as I went as hard as I could. Then it stopped. It was jammed.

"Go Roger, go, go!"

"I can't. It's stuck!"

"You've got it cross-threaded. Fuck!" cried John.

We all watched the pressure gauge. The pressure was building fast as there wasn't much leaking. We all got our hands on the cap but by now the pressure was freezing the cap. It was hopeless. Three thousand, 4000, 5000; the gauge was rocketing up.

"Shit, get out of here!" Barry shouted as he let go the cylinder and raced out of the shed. John and I quickly followed and made for the trench surrounding the shed. Just as all three of us landed there was a terrific deafening bang. Half the shed's roof had moved sideways. Bits of corrugated iron rained down on us and all the trainee cloud spotters. Then all was quiet.

Eventually we left our cover. Gingerly we approached the shed door. Inside, the cylinder was still standing but the top had blown off and the roof had a cap-sized hole in it. Chemical residue was everywhere. The cap had disappeared. It was found later, 100 feet or so away from the shed, a misshapen mess.

So ended our first practical session for the weather bureau.

The Alien Attack

A week later we were out at Essendon again for another practical, which proved to be marginally more successful than the first one. This time we were there at night. The task was to track a balloon flight at night. This was made possible by lighting a candle that was hung in a wind-proof container suspended from the balloon. The idea of a naked flame near a balloon full of hydrogen may alert occupational health and safety people these days but it wasn't a consideration back in 1968.

The technical people had prepared a whole squadron of balloons so all we had to do was to tie the candle holders to the balloon, light the candle, close the little hatch door making the cradle wind proof and let the balloon go. All this went well. As the balloons started their ascent we raced to the theodolites and followed the surprisingly bright points of light in the sky as the balloons drifted over suburban Essendon and on to Moonie Ponds.

Everything was going well. Tracking at night was easier than we had thought. We enjoyed the silence and serenity, gazing up into the dark sky watching the twinkling trail made by our aerial candle lights. Over half an hour later, we had not lost any sparklers, though they were dimming with distance. Our practical was going well.

Screaming sirens suddenly slapped us out of our reverie..

"Must be a crash or something," muttered Ken who was supervising us. "Perhaps on the airfield."

The sirens were very close now. A flotilla of headlights was making a bee-line for us. Four police cars and an unmarked car screeched to a halt beside us.

A well braided police officer stepped out of the leading car and strode towards us. "Are you responsible for this?"

Ken stepped forward. "What's the matter, officer?"

"Essendon, Pascoe Vale and Moonee Ponds police have been flooded with calls from frightened residents telling us there are dozens of UFOs in the sky. I rang the airport and was told to see you here. So what the hell is going on?"

The flash of a camera went off as a reporter from Melbourne's *Herald Sun* newspaper introduced himself.

After a lengthy explanation from Ken about our training exercise, the police weren't smiling. "Next time ring us at the station so we'll know what to say to all the frightened people out there," said the heavily braided officer. "Some old crows who rang in thought they were under an alien attack."

Next morning as I boarded the early morning St Kilda Road tram for the training building the banner headline in the tabloid newspaper stands outside newsagents all along the tram route caught my eye. "Aliens over Moonie Ponds!" it proclaimed.

The Posting

After completing the 10-week course, I felt I was now a fully-fledged weather observer and it was time to be assigned a posting. Being from Sydney I hoped to be posted back there. The envelopes arrived from Head Office and destinations were read out. “Treagus to Casey.”

“Where’s Casey?” I asked.

“Down south,” came an answer.

“It’s in Antarctica,” said Ken. “Look at your map.” I was dumbfounded. I knew once you got there you were stuck for a year before the rescue ship arrived and as well I had to have a mandatory appendicectomy prior to departure. I decided then it just wasn’t going to happen. And it didn’t, after days of protests, camping outside the personnel section of Head Office. Later I very much regretted that decision and the experiences, the adventures I missed out on.

Instead I was posted to the busiest met. office in the country: Sydney Airport or KSA, Sir Charles Kingsford-Smith Airport.

The office at KSA was a ramshackle, weather-beaten, wooden building opposite the TAA terminal. Both buildings dated back to the 1930s when the place was just a landing field and part-time cow paddock. The weather office was a hive of activity from 4:30am to 9pm, filled with observers, briefing officers, meteorologists, typists and pilots. But outside of this busy period when pilots were briefed on weather conditions, it was mostly pretty dead, owing to the airport’s night-time curfew between 11pm and 6am.

In the first few weeks in the office I discovered what normally sane, educated meteorologists do in the wee small hours of the ‘doggo’ shift when there is nothing to do. They revert to childhood. I readily accepted the culture of the office and joined in the fun with rubber band wars, indoor cricket, fancy dress parties, paper aeroplane competitions and mouth organ recitals. On one night, the revelry got out of hand and an indoor cricket shot hit the mercurial barometer in the OIC’s office, spilling the precious and poisonous liquid metal all over the boss’s floor. We spent many hours scooping up the liquid, a slow process because of its poisonous nature. By 8am the emergency housekeeping had been completed and the barometer damage was explained to our OIC as metal fatigue.

The busiest time in the office was 9am. This was when all the weather stations across Australia teletyped in their report. Most were post offices in small towns where the postmaster or mistress and their family did the observations: temperature, dew point, pressure, wind, rain and cloud. Occasionally there were slip-ups, such as the time the postmistress in Oodnadatta went on holidays, leaving instructions for the temporary staff to send off her observations, which she had conveniently written down for them in advance, on the day they were due. Somehow the temporary staff must have been confused because we, and all other official stations, received all of Oodnadatta’s observations for each day of the next month in one go. The weather doesn’t change much from one day to the next in Oodnadatta, but this was just too much for the Bureau’s managers. A stern letter was sent to the South Australian postmaster requesting that the lady in question be pulled into line. There was no talk of sacking her as there was no one else in this little outback town qualified to 'do' the weather.

The OIC

Pat, the Officer in Charge of the airport weather bureau, was a loud larrikin Irishman on a permanent short fuse. When he didn't like something, which was often, everyone in the office including the pilots being briefed knew about it. He often threw objects in a fit of temper. Once his favourite paperweight came sailing through his open door, colliding with our newfangled fax machine, rendering it inoperable. Many men emerged from his office cowering and shaking after a very loud dressing-down. On one occasion, the forecasters got the morning's forecast entirely wrong and were slow to amend it. They forecast 'fine' when in fact it was pouring outside.

Pat thundered into the office earlier than usual. "Who's fucked this one up? Own up, you idiot!" Silence. We knew this was coming and had agreed to close ranks. No one stepped forward.

Pat looked everyone in the eye with a steely look. "So, a no-show, eh? You're all a mob of pathetic cowards, a mob of morons!" he boomed. He strode over to a window and thumped the pane. "See this? It's a fuck'n window. Try looking through it sometime! See what's going on outside! Good for improving your useless forecasts." And with that he violently pulled on the latch to open the window. The hinge broke, jettisoning the glass sheet out of its frame. It smashed onto the footpath outside the building, narrowly missing a passer-by.

One day some of the office workers had had enough. Pat was scheduled to leave the office at 3pm. His car was always parked in its own special bay outside the back entrance. A clandestine group managed to tie the snout of a deflated weather balloon to the exhaust pipe of Pat's car during lunchtime. The whole office knew about it, and as Pat left and drove off, everyone raced to the back door to view the results. As Pat's car moved off along Keith Smith Avenue the exhaust gases started to fill the weather balloon, which grew and grew as the car proceeded. The balloon was as big as the car by the time it had gone halfway down the straight and at the bend in the road at the airport entrance, there was no car in sight, just a very large balloon disappearing around the bend. The office burst into laughter. The pilots at the briefing desk were giggling too. We were all waiting for the hot air explosion. Pat's reputation had spread far and wide.

I tried to avoid Pat. When he got out of his executive chair and patrolled the office, I kept my head down and looked industrious. My low-profile policy was shot to ribbons one day when I made an error which was off-the-scale for the airport.

I had been stationed out at the old control tower because some of our instruments were located there. Control towers need to be where there is uninterrupted visibility of airport operations and this one was near the east-west runway. To get there and back, I needed to drive across two major taxiways. In those days security was a bit laidback and I simply had to check the path was clear before driving across the taxiways. I needed no air traffic control clearance or even a special license. On the way back to the office on the fateful day, somehow, I missed seeing a propeller-driven Fokker F27 Friendship taxiing towards the runway for take-off. I drove onto the taxiway right into the aircraft's path, heading towards the propellers, which were rapidly filling my view. I slammed on the brakes as the pilot cut his engines and killed his power. I stopped in the taxiway, shocked, stunned. The pilot glared at me through the cockpit window and shook his fist. I screeched into reverse, then sped off the taxiway like a criminal making a getaway, and drove shakily back to the office.

Storm clouds loomed large as I entered the back door. "Treagus! In here!" thundered Pat. "What the hell were you doing?" He thumped his desk so hard his paperweight fell off its stand. "What were you thinking, you fool, you absolute idiot!" He narrowed his eyes and clenched his fist. "The pilot is ropable. Do you know what they had to do?"

"No," I replied meekly, trembling.

"They had to tow the plane back to the gate and get a compressor to restart the engines again, throwing out their entire fuck'n schedule."

I tried to say something about not seeing the aircraft but Pat cut me off immediately. "Get out! Get out of my office! If the pilot comes over, which he said he would, you'll have to explain yourself. Get out!"

The pilot never showed. I never transgressed with Pat again, but that was the last time I ever worked out at the old tower across all those taxiways.

Balloons

One of the most important tasks I had was conducting the 9am weather balloon flight.

Thankfully KSA was one of a handful of stations not required to make hydrogen. It was supplied to me already in cylinders. After inflation to a prescribed negative weight (so that I could assume a set rate of ascent) I had to run up the stairs of an old wooden tower. At the top I had my observation book, a big and unwieldy slide rule and the weather theodolite to track the balloon. This was a true case of multitasking. On releasing the balloon, I had to quickly orient the theodolite so that I had the balloon right on the crosshairs in the eyepiece. This was hard at first as the balloon was rapidly changing position, but higher up its increasing distance meant its apparent movement was less, so it was easier to track.

Every two minutes I had to write down on my observation sheet the balloon's coordinates. Then, knowing the rate of ascent, I used the metre-long slide rule to calculate the wind speed at the assumed height for that reading. I had to complete the slide rule machinations and write down the results before the next two minute reading so as to keep pace with the observations, all the time keeping the balloon on or near the theodolite cross-hairs.

Eventually the balloon reached a height when, due to expansion, the membrane became too thin and the balloon popped. This might be as high as 30,000 feet and take over an hour. Observers had to give a reason for termination, such as ‘high flying eagles’.

After many weeks of this, I found I had no problem in keeping up. We also sometimes did an afternoon flight. Eventually the task became somewhat boring, so one day for a bit of entertainment I partially filled a balloon so it was neutral in buoyancy, going neither up nor down, just floating along at the same height.

On top of the tower, I released it and was curious to see where it went. It was a calm afternoon so any breeze was affected by the local buildings. To my concern the balloon drifted towards the international tarmac which at the time was thankfully vacant of aircraft. Qantas maintenance people were darting around the apron in their people movers and one such person was driving towards the Qantas maintenance hangar which housed the brand new jumbo jets that had just arrived at KSA for the first time. Driving across the flat apron caused a slipstream effect in which, to my horror, the balloon was captured. The maintenance man kept driving, oblivious to the fact that a rather large black balloon full of hydrogen was right behind him, following the vehicle’s every move like a faithful dog. Miraculously, no one else seemed to notice. Finally the maintenance man made it across the concrete plain of the apron and drove into the narrow slot between the gigantic double doors of the hangar. His faithful balloon tailed behind. They disappeared from sight in the bowels of the hangar. What happened after that remains a mystery. I never heard a thing.

JACMAS – Flight Path Storm Spotter

On the night of 30 November 1961, a Vickers Viscount aircraft, Ansett-ANA flight 325, departed from Sydney bound for Canberra. It entered a thunderstorm cell just a few kilometres after take-off. The severe updrafts and downdrafts inside the storm cell ripped the right wing apart and the aircraft crashed, killing all on board. From the inquiry into the crash it became evident that the disaster could have been avoided if the pilot had known the location of the storm cells and flown a track that avoided them. The disaster shocked the nation unused to aviation accidents and there was pressure to devise a system that might prevent this sort of accident happening again.

At the time, weather radar was in its infancy and not considered as a serious mainstream tool for weather forecasting. Pat and his colleagues saw things differently. They saw this type of radar as the key, having a vital role in identifying destructive storm cells and improving aviation safety.

Aviation people and Pat's team worked on developing a pilot warning system. It took them eight years to get to the trial stage. The first trials were conducted at Sydney in 1969. I was one of the first operators of this system, a world-first that the Americans came out to see and later copy.

When storms were current near the airport, a JACMAS (Joint Approach Control Meteorological Advisory Service) was declared. Extra weather observers were called in to operate the system. I sat in front of a screen, part of the latest cutting-edge technology of weather radar. When storms were current I placed a Perspex sheet in front of the screen as an overlay, locked its position and traced out the storm echoes from the radar screen onto the overlay, preserving their relative screen positions. Once all the cells had been traced, the Perspex screen was taken out and slotted into position in front of a closed-circuit TV camera. The picture was displayed on screens in front of air traffic controllers who could then direct air traffic around the cells. Every 6 minutes a new Perspex screen overlay was drawn to update the positions of the cells indicating their movement over the previous 6 minutes.

All the time I was working at the screen I was conscious of the responsibility I had. If I got the cell positions wrong, a plane-load of people could be flying into a dangerous storm cell instead of out of one. I had to make sure, damned sure, that my marker pen trace on the overlay coincided exactly with the radar echoes. The developers recognised the weakness in this system and designed a lighting arrangement that had the effect of projecting the marker pen position onto the screen so I could see my positioning was accurate, overcoming parallax errors and any guesswork. Even so I made mistakes, but quickly corrected them because of this fail-safe feature.

JACMAS sessions were active as long as thunderstorm clouds (cumulonimbus) were near the airport. Occasionally this lasted many hours, sometimes during my watch they lasted all night. I came out of these sessions sweating and debilitated but deeply satisfied at the same time that I had done something very worthwhile, perhaps the most worthwhile in my motley career so far.

The Air Force – Honorary Sergeant

The powers that be thought that after two years at Sydney Airport I should expand my experience by working at a different weather station. Because I was now relatively senior I could have a say as to where I was posted. With my mother having her own career problems at the time, I felt I should be within reach of Sydney, so I chose the air force base at Richmond on Sydney's north-west outskirts. It was mid-winter and Richmond was colder, foggier and far less busy than Kingsford-Smith. I was immediately made a sergeant so as to fit in to the command structure. It seemed that the only activity at the base was the constant landing and taking off of pilots in training on C-130 Hercules transports, the freight workhorses of the RAAF. Every three hours I drove out to the instrument enclosure to take the readings. One day I discovered a frog swimming in the evaporimeter pan, rendering that instrument inaccurate. In training school I had been taught to be resourceful and self-reliant and here was an opportunity to apply that skill. So how was I to report an accurate rate of evaporation for the station? It was simple. Catch the frog and hang it by its back legs and rub its tummy till it regurgitates its water into the evaporimeter pan. It worked, except some other contents of its stomach saw the light of day as well. After scooping out the foreign material, I felt I had achieved an accurate water level for the pan and therefore a true measure of water evaporated.

After just two months at Richmond, I transferred to Williamtown RAAF Base. If Richmond felt like a backwater, Williamtown was Piccadilly Circus. Here was the Air Force's mirage fighter base with its constant screaming roar of jets taking off and thousands of personnel working on the base. I finally got my chance for a leg-up in the bureau's job hierarchy and started briefing pilots as well as observing the weather and also did some forecasting. Even though my duties now involved more professionalism, the Air Force still took my status to be a mere weather observer, which was assigned the rank of sergeant. I bunked in the sergeants' quarters, fraternised with sergeants and NCOs and ate in the sergeants' mess. Occasionally I had to see the meteorologists, who were officers, in the officers' mess. This was like moving from second class to first on the *Titanic*. The officers' mess had a refined air, with better appointments, better food, better décor and the patrons better dressed.

I knew my place. Just like poor Ronnie Corbett did in the great comedy skit with Ronnie Barker and John Cleese about the three classes which first appeared on the David Frost Show in 1966 on BBC1. The officers seemed very British even here on an Australian base just outside of Newcastle. The sergeants' mess brought home to me that I was not on the right career track. If I was going to be something and do something important, I needed qualifications more than experience. I could observe clouds all my life and all it would give me was an occupation, not a profession. I knew what I needed to gain access to the inner portals of the officers' mess: a science degree in maths and physics. Mathematics was the main stumbling block. I had failed Leaving Certificate maths. Throughout my high school years, the logic of many mathematical arguments had eluded me, no matter how hard I had tried to understand. But I needed it as it was a prerequisite to becoming a meteorologist.

Standing outside the inviting officers' mess, I had an epiphany: I had to get a university degree. This meant firstly sitting for the Higher School Certificate to matriculate. That became my aim now: to get a science degree, so I could eventually front up and say to the Weather Bureau, here I am, accept me as a more important person and give me a more important job as a weather forecaster not just a lowly observer and allow me to eat the superior food on offer in the Officers' mess.

One thing was now clear. Working on a 24-hour rotating roster wasn't going to give me the time to complete a part-time, evening course to pass the Higher School Certificate, my entrée to university. I needed a day job, nine to five, so I had my evenings free to attend classes. I needed to see Personnel to sort it out. I needed to change jobs and end my weather bureau phase.

Administering the WW2 Top Guns – Personnel Clerk

Working for the government made it easy to change employers. It was just a matter of changing Departments. The public service personnel officer (no 'human resources' in those days) asked me which department I wanted to transfer to. "Aviation," I eagerly replied.

The very next day, I fronted up to my new job as a personnel clerk with the Department of Civil Aviation, the DCA, housed in a series of flimsy World War two Quonset huts on a headland overlooking Sydney Harbour.

The WW2 huts seemed an appropriate domain for the officers in command of the DCA. It was like stepping back to wartime. It was immediately clear that the place was run along air force military lines. Although most employees were civilians, the bosses were all ex-military. But more than that, they were mostly WW2 flying aces, top guns of their era.

I was settling down to my first morning on the job sorting through leave files as a new Leave Officer, when a pathfinder raced into the room. "The RD is coming!" RD? "The regional director!"

Everyone rose from their seats as Arthur Doubleday entered the room, like a military parade standing to attention. Even the tea lady halted her clinking teacups trolley. Silence prevailed.

Wing Commander Doubleday DSO DFC had been a leading bomber pilot flying 53 missions over the enemy in Europe flying Wellingtons and Lancasters and was the only Australian to command an RAF Bomber Squadron. Whenever Arthur Doubleday entered a room everybody stood up and some saluted. He was addressed as 'sir' by everyone, from lowest clerk up to senior manager.

The scene reminded me of those war movies depicting the early morning briefing of a bomber squadron for their mission over Hamburg. The scene opens in the predawn smoke-filled briefing room when the CO enters and all the leather-jacketed pilots stand up, like Gregory Peck in *12 O'clock High*.

"Good morning sir, what can I do for you?" asked a middle manager, straightening up to attention.

"I've some along to see our new recruits."

"There's Treagus here and Jones over there. Treagus came to us from the weather bureau."

"Good show. Where were you stationed son?"

"Richmond and Williamtown RAAF bases."

"Excellent, son. There are good men keeping the fires burning in those bases. And you were amongst them then, eh?"

"Yes sir," I said. "I was the weather observer and briefed the pilots."

"Jolly good, glad to have you on board with the crew, son." The RD surveyed the room. "Carry on, lads," he ordered and with that he turned crisply and walked out with a sort of aide-de-camp following in his wake.

Doubleday ran the NSW office like his squadron, in tight formation, with a definite chain of command and well defined roles for everyone. Most of his operational managers were WW2 pilots as well. Some were exceedingly British, sporting thick moustaches and widening girths. The atmosphere in the corridors of power was a little surreal, part military, part *Goon Show*.

Working in the RHQ, everyone knew they were members of an elite band, part of the public service infrastructure on paper but culturally aloof, apart and definitely superior. The National Headquarters in Canberra was no different. The entire DCA was ruled from there by an absolute mandarin, the Director General Sir Donald Anderson. He was universally referred to as the DG. Politicians didn't summons him, he summoned them, including government ministers. Many politicians who were 'required' to front Sir Donald, walked in to his office quivering in their boots, preparing to receive a tirade about what they had done wrong. The DCA was a leftover from the days when derring-do airmen barnstormed the country as national heroes. This was a case where the tall poppies were not torn down as was customary for the national culture, but instead, eulogised. DCA was not really a government department so much as a club for WW2 flyboys, seeing themselves as an elite band of brothers understanding aviation like no one else did and running it like no one else could.

As a leave clerk, nothing exciting happened. My job was filling in little bits of cardboard with details recording the type of leave requested and taken. Boredom set in early.

There were, however, interesting diversions, like the day I helped to resupply the airport at Norfolk Island. We flew out in a Hercules, part of the DCA fleet. The DCA had several aircraft, necessary it was argued by the DG to maintain the expertise of the elite of the elite, our airworthiness inspectors and examiners of airmen. To do their job they had to maintain their own licenses to an impeccable level. There were always spare seats when the DCA fleet was active as all flights were logged as 'training'. Any DCA staff could apply to fly somewhere for free on a training flight anytime they were off-duty. I had earlier flown in a brand-new Swearingen Merlin turboprop pressurised aircraft on a day run to Cunnamulla and back with my only outlay being the bus fare to the airport. But I had never flown in a Hercules before.

Being a military plane it was not built for comfort with a row of hard seats on either side. There was no soundproofing and the standard-issue earmuffs were ineffective. I walked around the aircraft looking for a quiet corner and found the perfect spot, a Holden Kingswood. The doors were unlocked so I climbed into a really comfortable driver's seat and closed the door.

On arrival at Norfolk Island, we unloaded quickly, had a cup of coffee in the tiny terminal and within 30 minutes we were back in the air on our way 'back to Australia'. After a very cursory check with the RAAF customs officer welcoming us to Australia, we repaired to the local pub for a drink. Just another day in the office at the DCA.

After several months of processing leave applications, I was ready to leave my leave officer job. When a vacancy came along for an auditor, I applied in spite of my belief that an auditor was on par with an accountant as the world's most uninspiring, boring occupation.

Bean Counter for All Seasons – Systems Auditor

"Don't do it, Roger," my workmates would say. "It's a shitty job. All you do is to dob in on your mates. You'll be considered scunge. We won't talk to yer. Why d' you think the job's not filled? 'Cause no one wants it."

My choice was clear; getting the shitty job was better than being stuck in this dead end, I thought. My application was good enough to be granted a job interview, which wasn't hard as the field was limited to two applicants, attesting to its unpopularity. I had no training; I didn't understand accounting, bookkeeping, records, procedures, systems or anything about auditing principles and practices. I knew precisely nothing. However, as the only other person applying for the position was even less suitable than me, I was told, I got the job.

This was a pivotal moment in my career path, only recognised as such in hindsight as it directed my job path for the next 15 years.

I moved into the little four-desk office of the Internal Audit Section, the 'dob in' section no one talked to. There was the Senior Internal Auditor, Charlie Ferguson who wore a badly-fitting toupee, an Internal Auditor, Jim Holihan, an old warhorse from WW2, and myself. These two dinosaurs debated trivial points of process and procedure endlessly.

"Read this!" Charlie threw me a small green ring-bound manual. "Everything you need to know is in this Internal Audit Handbook. Give yourself a day to take it in. We'll have you auditing by Friday."

I expected the book to be dead boring and shrouded in bureaucratic jargon. I equated auditing to accounting, the most boring, useless subject ever invented, an impression promoted by accounting concepts written in double-dutch to mystify the reader into thinking the subject was highly technical instead of just being esoteric bullshit. However, I was surprised to find it was written in everyday English describing easy-to-understand concepts, giving a clear, step-by-step guide to auditing, and it was almost entertaining. Three golden rules shone out from the text.

Rule 1: Always check from the most basic document to a derived document, never the other way around.

Rule 2: Understand the system as well as the mistake to uncover the cause.

Rule 3: Use a purple pen to indicate document has been internally audited.

No one else in the whole organisation was allowed to use a purple pen. I suddenly felt important.

After half a day, I thought to myself, *I can do this job*. And I did. My first port of call was the Receiver of Public Money; the RPM. I had to count his money, reconcile the totals with the cash register and check the procedure for hold-ups.

"So what do you do if you are held up?" I asked.

"Give them the money."

"But they haven't asked for money yet."

"I'm assuming they will. They're bandits."

"How do you know that?"

"Look, it's simple. I would say to a suspicious character, 'Are you a bandit?' And if they said 'No' I would say, 'Well you don't get the money then.' OK, get it?" The RPM glared at me.

"Well, OK, assuming they do tell you, what do you do next?"

"I note their appearance, voice, manner and any identifying physical feature. I then get out the bandit description form."

The RPM handed me a form with a list of questions covering the time and date the bandit arrived, description of the bandit, name and address of bandit (if applicable), phone number if given, amount taken, weapons produced, getaway vehicle registration, model and colour and witnesses. At the bottom of the form was an instruction that stood out in bold underlined capitals: "**IMPORTANT: USE A SEPARATE FORM FOR EACH BANDIT**."

"Wouldn't it be easier to ask each bandit to fill the form out him or herself?" I suggested. "We could supply the pencils."

The highlight of the week was my surprise visit to the Bundy clock at the office building entrance. With its gigantic five-foot diameter clock face, this machine, designed to record employees' start and finish times at work, resembled my impression of HG Wells' time machine. Staff pushed their individual cards into a slot in the machine and it printed the current time unless it was out of ink, which was often. I had to check staff punctuality, which wasn't helped by the inability of the clunky machines to keep up with demand in the morning with a slow-moving queue forming for half an hour either side of start time. I had to work out whether lateness was caused by the employee or the time machine.

My job involved not just book-keeping checks but also detective work investigating the cause of systems failures, how processes could be faulty or badly run so that proper delivery failed. Often the operators are too close to the action to see the faults and it takes someone to come in from the outside to get a clear picture about why things are going wrong. I got the hang of this type of investigation when I audited my first airport.

I arrived at Coffs Harbour, a regional airport run by the local council. I looked at revenues from business collections such as shops in the terminal and rent payments from local businesses and the aero club. Then there were outgoings such as power, equipment purchases plus the cost of contractors such as the gardener.

It all seemed fairly simple so I was surprised that with almost every airport visit I discovered major failures, like the airport administration forgetting to register businesses or lessees and to collect the rent, which meant that on paper they didn't exist even though they were 'in your face' the moment you walked out of the Airport Manager's office. What they needed was to institute a procedure where all of these records were given a periodic 'reality check'.

Discovery on Norfolk Island

Each time I returned from an audit trip to an airport with a thick report I proved to Charlie Ferguson I was capable. "OK Roger, I think you're ready for the big one now," he announced one day. "Norfolk Island."

A small 8km x 5km speck in the Pacific Ocean, 1760km north-east of Sydney, Norfolk is one of Australia's external territories. "I've already been there on a Herc supply flight," I said. "Up and back in a day."

"This time it's different," said Charlie. "There's a lot to do, especially seeing it's an international airport. I'll give you a week, probably not long enough considering the workload, but that's all we can afford with our travel budget."

So this time I travelled in a much quieter Fokker Friendship with much better on-board catering, flying right over that jewel of the Pacific, Lord Howe Island and then on to Norfolk. This was no surprise visit. The Officer in Charge of the airport, John Henry knew I was coming and greeted me on arrival.

"Sure I knew you were coming," John said. "As soon as you were booked into the Paradise the whole island knew. Welcome to Norfolk. You'll get to love the place like we all do." John seemed genuinely happy to see me. "The last auditor they sent here must have been about 6 years ago. He found nothing. We run a tight ship here."

We settled into his office and chatted over a cup of tea. "So, what's on the agenda?"

"The usual things we do. Checking cash advances, equipment purchases, lessees rents, business concession payments, power and utility costs, things like that."

It was true what John said. I booked into the Paradise Hotel near Burnt Pine, the island's commercial centre. They all knew I was coming. "So you're the auditor," said the hotel desk clerk. "I hope we'll pass muster."

"I'm only doing the airport, not the whole island," I said.

"But the airport is the island," came the reply. I only understood that remark later.

Norfolk Island is unique in the South Pacific with its appearance and history. It is covered in one dominant tree, the Norfolk Island pine. The place looks a little like England, not a South Pacific palm-fringed atoll. Its history is in three parts; firstly a violent convict jail whose inmates were too tough for Sydney; secondly, a second home for the Bounty mutineers when their first refuge, Pitcairn Island became untenable; and finally as a free land, independent of Australia where the descendants of the Bounty mutineers could grow up and prosper. Surnames, predominantly Adams, Quintall, Christian and Buffett, reflect this history. Consequently the local phone book identified people by either their first names or nick-names like Cane Toad, Dar Bizziebee, Lettuce Leaf, Goof, Paw Paw, Diddles, Rubber Duck, Carrots and Tarzan.

I seemed to have celebrity status. Everyone seemed to know who I was and what I was doing on the island. I was followed around by the curious locals and asked lots of questions about what I was checking.

The first two days were routine but on the third afternoon, my plan was to look at the power system for the airport. The island's electricity came from several large diesel generators. The airport also used island power but had back-up generators of its own to ensure continuity of supply.

The airport's own supply was located in a remote corner of the airport's perimeter. I had been to many airport power sheds in the past but this one looked different. There were around 100 cables snaking out of the shed housing the airport back up power generators and exiting the airport grounds under the boundary fence. Curious, I followed the cables for some distance as they headed east towards the centre of the island, sometimes out of sight underground and sometimes exposed at the surface. Eventually the cables diverged down different roads and then disappeared on private land, passing numerous houses. I had walked over halfway across Norfolk Island before finally running out of cables to follow.

Not wanting to jump to conclusions, the next morning I asked the OIC for his expenditures over the past five years. He handed me several thick box files. "By gees, you guys are thorough," John said, laughing nervously. "Let me know if you have any problems. Some of our local suppliers don't write invoices very well."

"That's OK," I reassured. "This is normal procedure."

I isolated the cost of running the airport's generators, mainly the supply of diesel fuel and maintenance. Sifting through the invoices I found that diesel consumption had doubled in two years.

"How have your airport operations gone over the past two years, any busy periods, any special activities?" I was fishing.

"Let's see. We had the Air New Zealand DC-3 forced back on a few occasions because of the weather, a few extra private operators. We have no runway lighting so they only need power during the day. Oh, there was the Bounty picnic we had for the tourists. That was fun, everybody dressed up like they were on the Bounty. But what are you looking for, Roger?"

"Just why the consumption of diesel has gone up by so much."

John scratched his head. "Has it? So much to do around here I haven't noticed. Let's check the invoices." I got the impression that John really didn't know so I decided it was time to show him the power shed cables. We drove out to the power shed.

"There, look. What are those?" I pointed to the cables. John looked at them for a long time, checking connections. We repeated part of my walk of the afternoon before. John was carefully tracing the cables and looking worried but saying nothing until the silence was broken with, "Shit, what the hell. Not good, not at all."

"Is it what I think it is?"

"Look, I think we need to work on this. When do you leave?"

"Saturday."

"I need to get a really good handle on this. We've got four days so I suggest I get Cat Eyes, I mean Kevin, on the job. He can map all these connections and test the current loads over a night. He can get on to the cable mapping now and have that plus the power usage through the cables on your desk in the morning. Then we can discuss where to go from here. OK? I want this totally resolved to your satisfaction before you leave. Right?" John glanced at me anxiously, worry lines etched into his face. "I don't want to leave anything hanging for you to report on. How's that?"

"OK, let's work out the next steps tomorrow," I replied, wondering just what the next steps might be.

By lunchtime on day five, John, Cat Eyes and I were carefully studying Cat Eyes' map. It was an extraordinary piece of work and looked more like a map of the London Underground than the wiring diagram for Norfolk. It showed all the cables coming out of the power shed and running across the island. It also showed where each cable terminated. All were houses from Kingston in the south to Cascade in the north. "Most are on load," Cat Eyes said. "The ones which aren't are because they're on holidays off Norfolk so no one's at home."

John paced the floor. "This is extraordinary. Give me an hour and then let's discuss. I am looking for a solution. OK?" I gave him two hours. By the time I walked into John's small compact office, I had a solution too, but I wanted to hear John's first.

"What you want is for DCA to be no worse off, isn't it?" John went on before I could answer. "That's the difference between what power would have cost by normal airport operations and what it actually cost. I've calculated that. You can check my figures if you like. The problem will be, where do we account for the money?"

I was on John's wavelength. "What does your budget look like for the coming year? What do you need?"

John went fishing for the budget under a mountain of paperwork on his desk. "Here it is. Yes, we need new window frames for the terminal, new ride-on mower and a replacement gen set for the power shed, as well as a few other items."

John looked up at me hopefully. "I see what you mean now." He returned to his budget and quickly drew up a plan. "These 6 items equal the increased power cost. So, how do you want to handle this?"

"Get the money and buy the items directly with the money. Don't go through DCA accounts for God's sake. Keep it on the Island. Explain to your boss the items are donated from the Island government and get the Government to endorse the donation with a reason. Make sure they understand the true situation so they know how to answer. Do this quickly and send me the invoices directly, not through the system. How is all that?"

"Sounds fine to me. This is my priority. Don't you worry," John said with a smile. "Just to let you know, the consumers themselves don't know what went on. The charges have simply gone to the incorrect accounts. We've also had outages before and a quick fix was to swap the power sheds. That's our doing to meet emergencies. Consumers wouldn't be aware of the switchover obviously. But you know it's a small community and this thing can have ramifications if you went into great detail in your report."

"Look John, all I'm interested in is that the Department gets all the money it's entitled to, no more, no less. If it does, then there's nothing to report."

"Great, just great," grinned John. "By the way, Cat Eyes is reconnecting the cables so everything will be back to normal before you leave."

"So diesel usage will be back to normal for the next account," I said. "But you will still need to explain why it went up so much."

John scratched his head. "Er, faulty gen set, yeah, that's it, faulty generator. We have to replace it, eh? You see, the problem was that it had become terribly fuel inefficient, plus there was that BBC doco on the island and then there was the New Zealand trade. Those last two caused a big, big increase in traffic over more than a year, yeah, that's it, OK?" He cleared his throat and nodded to me. "Is that enough for you?"

"I suppose it'll do," I said. "I just hope the Commonwealth Audit Office doesn't pay you a visit. I don't suppose they will. They never follow us."

Later that afternoon I received a phone call from none other than Norfolk Island's Chief Minister. "Is that Roger? John told me we had a guest on the island working with him to keep our little airport shipshape. It's not often we get a senior person from the DCA here, so we want to show you a little Norfolk Island hospitality and our appreciation. Can you come down to the golf clubhouse after work, say 5pm?"

"Thank you very much Chief Minister. Yes I would be honoured. What should I bring?"

"Just yourself. Everything is provided for."

Cows roamed freely across Norfolk Island but there was a sacred spot out of bounds to all bovines: the greens on the Royal and Ancient Norfolk Island Golf Links, accessed via a turnstile. On the vast patio of the well-endowed clubhouse, as the guest of honour, I feasted on barbecued red emperor, smoked salmon, lobster and duty-free grog. The Chief Minister and about 50 of his closest friends were on deck to greet me, shake my hand and say how much they appreciated the work I was doing in keeping the airport running. I had never been appreciated so much. The feast was followed by music and dancing. I woke up the next morning unable to recall how I got back to my hotel room. I was sad to leave the place and all my new-found friends. My report on the airport was comprehensive and thorough. That's what Charlie Ferguson thought anyhow.

"It's good to see the place is working well," he said.

"There was nothing really wrong, just some small points easily fixed," I said. And a few weeks passed before I received in a sealed letter the invoices from John. They added up well. I'd call it mission accomplished.

Educating Roger – the saga

Having my day job allowed me to have my night job. This job was harder. It was my continuing education, something I couldn't fit in working a 24-hour roster with the Weather Bureau. I studied at the Seaforth Technical College in Sydney for my Higher School Certificate as a mature age student. It was the lack of maturity that forced me here, to do better, much better than I had at school. I studied harder than I had ever done. Now I was determined. I knew that this time I had to make it if I was ever to get a 'real job'.

I knew I had broken an invisible barrier the moment I opened up the Mathematics examination paper. I scanned the questions. Amazingly, I could answer all of them. I finished the paper before time and walked out of the exam room a new person. I was sure I had finally cracked my old nemesis. Other papers also seemed fairly easy.

In those days exam results came through in the early editions of the morning newspapers. I was in my local newsagent's shop at 5am on results day. It was a relief to see I had done very well in all subjects, and I was overjoyed to find out the following day I had perfect marks in Maths and had been offered a Commonwealth Scholarship to attend university. That 'real job' now seemed a certainty. I had finally turned the corner.

Gough Whitlam - His Part in My Career Change

The advent of Labor's Whitlam Government in 1972 introduced new thinking into the Commonwealth Public Service. Old traditional organisations like the Department of Civil Aviation didn't sit well with the reformist progressive ideology of the new Government. Innovation was the key word. One manifestation of this was to amalgamate all government departments that administered transport into one mega-department. So it was that the DCA joined with the old Department of Shipping and Transport to make the new Department of Transport, much to the horror of the aviation flyboys.

For me it had benefits, as my wings expanded beyond auditing airports to all of those other organisations associated with surface transport. These were lighthouses, shipping and the regulation of motor car manufacture. Just as the prospect of visiting yet another airport was beginning to make me feel like taking off from my job and escaping into the blue yonder, the tedium lifted and I relished the opportunity to develop a more varied, exciting career path.

The Production Line

British Leyland used to be a major car manufacturer in Australia and in the early 1970s it produced the Austin Tasman and Kimberley, which were rebadged as the Austin 1800 and later as the ill-fated P76, a lemon of a car if ever there was one. All new cars manufactured had to comply with a number of design rules identified by numbers stamped onto a compliance plate fixed to the vehicle's firewall. My job was to inspect a random sample of vehicles on the production line for their compliance plate and check that all design rule numbers meant to be listed were actually there. British Leyland top management in Australia was concerned at my visit because if I found an irregularity the whole production line could be halted, costing the company millions of dollars.

On my arrival at British Leyland's Sydney plant, I was greeted by an immaculately suited young executive with a bone-crushing handshake. He led me past the huge, cacophonous production floor, throbbing with hundreds of machines, then up a steep flight of stairs into another world of ornate, soundproofed conference rooms and offices breathing opulence and serious money.

"Well Roger, it's nice to have you," said Ron, the Managing Director, pointing to the finger food. "Please, help yourself." There were rolls stuffed with smoked salmon and capers, croissants with ginger jam, cheeseboards, eggs, bacon and several nationalities of sausages. A waitress asked what type of coffee or tea I wished to order.

"We'll get George, our chief floor supervisor to go along with you and iron out any aspects you may not understand. He knows everything," continued Ron, smiling at the supervisor. "Then, once you are done we'll all meet back here for lunch where you can meet the rest of the team."

Licking the delicious ginger jam from the corner of my mouth, I nodded and smiled in approval, wondering after such a sumptuous breakfast what lunch might be like.

Jam-full of croissants, I clambered down the gantry onto the production line floor feeling distinctly overdressed. George and I walked slowly along the floor passing numerous car bodies. All the workers looked very industrious and well kitted and presented an air of somewhat artificial cheerfulness. They appeared as if they were from Rent a Crowd, with the whole set-up staged to give me a good impression – like those Hollywood film scenes of German prisoner-of-war camps made to look more like holiday camps when Red Cross officials arrived.

I searched for the compliance plates on vehicles, but couldn't find them. George couldn't find them either. He immediately shouted to a nearby worker in some Eastern European language. In a flash a scrum of managers was loudly discussing the issue. Fingers pointed to a different production line queue.

"Hmm, sorry Roger, I led you astray," said George, rubbing his chin. "Add-ons such as compliance plates are further down the line over there." The posse dispersed and we moved to the 'advanced' line where the compliance plates were certainly in place.

The smiles resumed – until I came across a couple of plates with different numbers from those that the model was supposed to have.

"George, this one has got 2, 5, 11, 22A and 25. The model is meant to have 2, 5, 22, 24 and 25." George stared at the plate. His face darkened. The shouting started again. This time an alarm sounded and the conveyor shuddered to a halt. A conga line of managers descended the gantry and floor workers stood away from the line, looking confused. A new managerial scrum formed with various lower-order workers being drawn in and then rejected. I tried to keep a straight and serious face, but it was like a scene from Monty Python.

"It's all OK, Roger. We've got it sorted. Not a problem really. The plate stamp machine malfunctioned for a couple of stamps, but our internal check picked it up and rectified the problem, so for all stamps after that she's sweet again." George beamed at me reassuringly.

"What about the cars with the wrong stamps?"

"That would be picked up by the inspectors at the end of the line," answered George confidently. I was quickly introduced to the inspectors to confirm his story.

After the drama, the smiles returned once more on the shop floor. The stress level that accompanied breakfast was noticeably absent at lunch, with food platters and free-flowing grog for middle and senior managers. I wondered how productive their afternoon would be, but at least they were rid of me and with a clean report as well.

Ships and Hiding Places

Unlike cars, ships have been around since before the Pharaohs. The bureaucracy that goes with ships seemed about as ancient. In contrast to the go-getting culture of car manufacture, people buried in the paperwork of shipping were Dickensian characters not out of place with quill pens, eyeshades and vest pocket timepieces. There was no glamour, no enterprise, just forms and more forms.

My particular form was the Bill of Lading. My role was to check for a custom clearance and to run an unannounced independent check, meaning I boarded the ship and had a sticky-beak around the decks. I didn't like the job because it was creepy wandering around the bowels of some of the ancient cargo vessels visiting Port.

I was assigned the Port of Newcastle in the days before containerisation became a widespread practice. This meant that I checked bulk cargos stored randomly and occupying any space in the ship. Wandering around the ship looking for something described in the Bill of Lading was pointless. Even if I was shown the cargo I was needing to check, there was no way of knowing if that was all there was. I had no idea whether tons more of the same stuff was hidden several decks below or in a different hold on bulk loaders.

I soon worked out that a much better way to go was to arrive without warning, get the ship's captain to authorise me aboard, and then in the mandatory company of one of the officers or chiefs, do a walking tour around the ship to identify a good sample of the type and amount of cargo being carried.

On one particular day, I boarded an old bulk carrier and with the second in command, worked my way down into the dimly lit corners below decks near the stern. We both carried torches and in his broken English Mr Kim told me to stop near the end of one of the passageways. I could hear some rustling above the throb of the ship's generators. Suddenly a tsunami of rats swept past my feet and disappeared into the dark near the bow. Mr Kim exploded with laughter. After checking that no rats were gnawing on my legs, I explored the area they had come from and found tons of unidentified powders, possibly flour, possibly something else.

Mr Kim wasn't at all perturbed at my discovery. Back in the office no trace of this cargo was in the documentation, so it was unaccounted for as well as being a health hazard. Samples of the mysterious white powder went to the chemical lab of customs, but I never heard what it was. Auditing ships was often greasy, dirty work, but I learnt a lot about shipboard life on working cargo vessels.

Captain Blood

Marine surveyors were the seafaring counterparts of aviation examiners. Like them, they knew they were the elite of the elite. These men – they were always males – established the seaworthiness of ships. They were usually retired ship captains tired of life at sea and keen to get a shore job with similar status. They were still addressed as captain and retained most of their shipboard idiosyncrasies. Ports like Sydney and Newcastle were home to many of these people. One of the most memorable of these was an autocrat whose name was Blood. But in the office on duty he was Captain Blood.

My shipping audit boss at the time did the introductions as I moved into this new realm. He led me to a tall man wearing gumboots and an ill-fitting suit topped with a gold-embroidered captain's cap, several sizes bigger than his head, so it appeared to be sitting on his nose. The hat looked like a refugee from a fancy dress shop.

"Roger, this is Captain Blood," said my boss with no hint of humour.

Captain Blood! My mind switched to the dashing, swashbuckling pirate Captain Blood, the daring and romantic adventurer played by Errol Flynn in 1935, winning battles as well as the hand and heart of Arabella played by Olivia de Havilland.

"Roger, meet Captain Blood," my boss repeated.

I snapped out of my micro reverie. I sensed the need to be formal.

"How do you do, Captain Blood," I said, politely extending my right hand.

"Welcome, boy," said the Captain, acknowledging me briefly with a nod.

Walking back to our office, my boss explained: "Captain Blood has been at sea for years and is only now getting used to an office.

"Just getting his land legs," I added innocently.

"Don't you let Captain Blood hear you say that. He's got more land than you or me. He comes to work each day from his property. He has a farm at Ten Mile Hollow, about 12 miles up an old convict-built road north of the Wisemans Ferry Punt across the Hawkesbury River. He says he likes the idea of needing to voyage on a punt to get to work here in the city."

The Lighthouse Service Family

In the early 1970s many of the Commonwealth operated lighthouses were manned, although a slow process of conversion to automatic operation was under way. In NSW these manned lighthouses included two on islands just off the mainland and seven along the coast, from Cape Byron in the north to Green Cape near the Victorian border.

The traditions and rules of the lighthouse service developed over many centuries and remained very rigid right up to the 1980s. My job was to audit all of the Commonwealth lights in NSW. I had to make sure lighthouse staff stuck to the rules. These were the 'modernised' rules as set out in the *Instructions to Lightkeepers* manual, published in 1917. These rules covered everything a lighthouse keeper had to do, ranging from maintaining the light to saving lives on ships in distress to the sleeping arrangements of guests.

Staff on each station always comprised the Head Lighthouse Keeper, who lived in a large detached house, and the Lighthouse Keeper, who lived in a small semi-detached house. All lighthouse keepers had to be married.

As with naval ships at sea, the chain of command and responsibilities was rigidly hierarchical. The biggest challenge facing the lighthouse men wasn't rescuing people from sinking ships or keeping the light going when the power failed. It was staying married. A keeper lost his job if he was divorced. Losing his job took longer if he was widowed. This meant marriages were maintained regardless of the state of the actual relationships. Rumours spread about wife-swapping between light stations. Such activity was seen within the Lighthouse Service as an inventive way of preserving marriages by increasing variety. This principle though was especially difficult to apply to island stations such as Montague due to a lack of choice. It was said that on island stations, the two families that went on to the island were not the same two families that came off at the end of their island stint.

Whether this was true or not, it had no effect on the great affection each member of the lighthouse service and their families had for one another, no matter which light they came from. This community inhabited their own special world. They were isolated but knew intimately the families of all the other lights as if they were next door neighbours. There were the occasional meetings of many of the families at some chosen location central to all of the lights covering the 1200km of exposed and hazardous coastline from Byron Bay in northern NSW to Green Cape in the south. In adversity they shared a bond, and I entered this world.

The rules stated that I had to inform the Head Lighthouse Keeper I was coming. Normally one of the main tools of trade for an auditor was the surprise visit, but not here. The official reason was that the station staff needed time to prepare my accommodation. The real reason was the need to get the light station in order, meaning an intact family and normal domestic arrangements. The wife had to be 'on station' because the rules said that visiting dignitaries, meaning me, were to be given full board as described in rule 101 of the Instructions circa 1917. In practice this meant that the lighthouse keeper's wife serviced the Government Room, where I stayed, and she was required to cook me a hearty English breakfast. I could interpret the absence of said wife as indicating family breakdown. This was looked upon seriously by the revered Regional Controller of the Lighthouse Service, Captain Taylor.

My first station was Cape Byron, the most famous light on the coast partly because it is at the most easterly point on the Australian mainland and partly because it is very accessible to the tourist town, Byron Bay. From the Cape there is a magnificent view, from the Lamington Plateau and Mt Warning to the northwest around to the town immediately west and then the broad sweep of pristine beaches fading into the distance south towards Lennox Head.

I arrived in Byron Bay from Sydney via the new Gold Coast Motor Rail Express (which sadly no longer exists). As soon as I stepped onto the platform, I was greeted by a suntanned middle-aged woman wearing a sun dress and sandals.

"Hello there. You must be Mr Treagus," she said. "I'm Valerie, John's wife up at the light."

"How did you identify me so quickly?" I asked, intrigued that she had immediately singled me out from all the other train passengers.

"Your collar and tie, your formal office clothes," she replied. "You're out of uniform here, Mr Treagus."

"Please, it's Roger. I'm more informal than I look. It's just that you are my first station, so I wasn't sure how to turn up."

"It's OK, Roger. We may look informal, but we run a pretty tight ship. You'll see."

A short drive took us barely out of town before we hit the hill leading to the lighthouse reserve. The road snaked around the Cape and delivered us quickly to the carpark adjacent to the quarters and the light. John, the Head Keeper saw us coming and was quickly on hand to greet me. After the small talk, came the surprise.

"Now I know, you auditors work to your own plan but a little bird told me this is your first, so to help you I've drawn up a task schedule for your two days here. It covers all of our operations that you need to see. I don't think I've missed anything but please tell me if you think I have."

I studied the list carefully. I couldn't fault it.

Roger's Check List of Cape Byron Light Operations

- cash advance
- budget
- cash book
- purchases
- wages
- light power
- light sequencing
- light failures
- repairs
- maintenance
- goat management
- sightseeing management
- communications
- signalling
- disaster and rescue equipment
- training schedule
- staffing
- incident reporting
- weather reporting
- electricity costs
- lightning damage
- fire drills
- bulb replacements
- vessel movement reporting
- cleaning
- security systems
- keys and locks
- manual operation exercise

John had it all, including checking the Station's goat population. I just had to work through each task and tick them off against my audit manual, a busy two days with just a little time over for a walk to the local beach for a swim.

Everything went perfectly well, including the early morning cup of tea with the inevitable eggs and bacon. I met the two families on station. Everyone seemed to be on their best behaviour, perhaps holding their tongue until I left. It all seemed too perfect. I was left with almost nothing to report, except for the goats. These animals roamed the Cape, defoliating it, and in an effort to minimise their impact, the lighthouse keepers were meant to be corralling them to a restricted area. This wasn't happening, not surprising since there were no fences. It's very hard to tell a goat to stay in a particular area when there are no fences. These were not permitted in the reserve. So thank God I did have something to report. Otherwise my boss would think I was just having a good time.

My second inspection was at Sugarloaf Point Lighthouse, perched dramatically on a headland east of Seal Rocks, at the northern end of Myall Lakes National Park. Completed in 1875, it was the first lighthouse designed by colonial architect James Barnet and one of only two towers in Australia with an external stairway.

Each lighthouse along the coast can be identified at night by the characteristic of its light flashes. Any ship passing a lighthouse flashing every 7.5 seconds would know it had to be Sugarloaf Point, while a flash every 15 seconds indicated Cape Byron.

To achieve such frequent flashes Sugarloaf's light lens had 16 separate panels, which, when the light was rotated at one revolution every two minutes, the standard rotation speed, produced the correct flash frequency. Every night the surrounding hills, valleys and cliff tops along that rugged coast were illuminated for an instant with the brilliant flashes of a kaleidoscopic display as each of those 16 rotating beams shone forth like spokes on a fairy's wheel.

I was greeted at the lighthouse reserve gate by Norm Reynolds, the Head Lighthouse Keeper. This time I was deliberately informal, having ditched the collar and tie uniform. Norm was the same. His casual style made him a friend right away.

"Ï heard what John did to you at Byron. All the keepers up and down the coast had a laugh over that. Don't worry, I'm not about to manage you. I'm sure you know what you are doing. Come up to the house to meet Grace and my daughter, Angela. She's supposed to be at school, but she's home today."

We walked up the rocky path to the stunningly white keeper's house, sitting on a small grassy plateau, the only level spot on the rugged headland. Grace and Angela greeted us at the door and ushered me inside for tea and cake.

"Grace knows more about this place than I do," Norm said. "If I lose something she knows where it is. If I'm not sure of the tools I need for a job, she does. She runs the light and fixes the machinery, something I can't do nearly as quickly or efficiently. Sometimes I think it would be better for all concerned if she was the Keeper and I just lounged around."

"So you think a lighthouse keeper's wife just lounges around?" Grace laughed. "Norm loves baiting me."

I spent the rest of the day working through my task list, the same one John had written for me. It was better and more complete than the audit manual Charlie, my boss back in the city office, had provided. Every time I walked around the station I was taken by the extreme beauty of the place and the views of rocky headlands to the north and unbroken sweeping beaches to the southwest. A fantastic outdoor office.

At 9.25pm I was settling in for the night in the Government Room when suddenly a shrill alarm pierced the howling wind. Slamming doors, agitated shouting. What was up? I looked out the window. All was dark. No light! I ran outside to see if I could help.

"The bloody power line is down again somewhere," growled George, the second in charge. "It would happen now just when the backup gen's on the blink. Norm is up top to get the light going."

"We have to use the old kero light," he explained.

"What about the acetylene light?" I said sporting the one bright spot in my meagre knowledge.

"It's on the blink too wouldn't y'know. So we're back to basics. Now I have to get the kero bottles up to Norm. He gets the kero light going and we both take turns to rotate the mount, keep the vapour pressure up and switch bottles when needed. It's a real bugger."

"Can I help?"

"Go up and see Norm."

Leaving George to sort through the station's collection of kero bottles, I raced up the outside stairway that wound around the tower, exposed to the wind and rain, until the first landing, then up the internal spiral to the lantern room. Norm had set the replacement light and was putting on the cover. He was sweating. He stood up and adjusted the ventilation.

"Good to see you, Roger. You see what we have to put up with here. This happens all too frequently. What's George doing down there?"

"He's organising the bottles. Can I help?"

"Sure you can. Help George get 6 bottles up here."

With a thumbs-up, I circled down the staircase to the bottom. Together George and I, puffing and sweating, eventually lugged 6 heavy bottles up the two-stage staircase. By then Norm had rigged up a chair, anchored to the floor, its back against the wall, so his feet had the leverage to push against the mount sufficient to rotate it.

"Men, we have a long night ahead of us," he sighed. "I'm glad you're here, Roger. With you we can divi up the shift times, OK?"

I nodded. Norm pointed to some marks he had drawn on one of the lantern room walls facing his chair. "See those marks and the numbers above them? Well, I've stuck this little French flag on the rotating mount. When it gets to the first mark, it should have taken 30 seconds. See, the mark has 30 above it. The second mark – the 60-second mark – is over there, the third with the 30 above it, marks 90 seconds and the fourth with the 60 above it marks the two minutes for the full rotation. The numbers should be the same as the second hand on the clock. Got it?"

Norm was in position, almost horizontal on the chair. With his feet he started pushing down on the edge of the circular platform of the lantern mount. He pushed and pushed, but the heavy platform barely budged. The sweat was pouring down his face. Push, push, push. Eventually it started to move, so slowly at first, but with more effort from Norm, the mount built up rotational speed, until after several minutes it had reached a speed that coincided with the timing marks.

"So, Roger, what you have to do is move the mount so it rotates at just the right speed so the flag gets to each mark at the right time, like this." Norm demonstrated what the correct speed looked like. "The big second hand on the wall clock there gives you the right timing. Is that all clear? The whole mount floats on a bath of mercury so there's little friction. Once it's going it'll tend to stay that way."

"Yes, sure," I said brightly, feeling full of doubt that I could be so accurate.

"Just make sure the flag on the rotating plate gets to the numbered mark on the wall at the same time the second hand reached the same number in seconds. I can't tell you how important it is to get this right. If it's out, our flash changes and ships may think they're out of position. I don't need to tell you what that might mean."

I nodded. I was well aware of the numerous shipwrecks there. I watched Norm's actions intently, trying to learn his technique. His movements had the fluidity of a champion cyclist.

"Now you try it." I moved in behind him as he moved forward out of the chair in a choreographed-like movement. It took quite a while to get used to the pressure I needed to apply to keep up the required revs per minute, but once the right speed was achieved, I found I could maintain the rate.

"Feels like fun," I remarked.

"Well, it won't feel much like fun after a few hours. It's eight hours till dawn. But there are three of us tonight, so it's 30 minutes on, one hour off, repeated till light. OK?"

I felt I couldn't refuse, so I just kept nodding. And so Norm, George and I kept Sugarloaf Point Lighthouse going all through that dark winter's night, as the wind whined and whipped the waves outside our shadowy sentinel. Norm was always there, chatting, making sure I wasn't too fatigued. His banter continued for several hours.

"Now you have a taste for what it's like here," he said. "A good life, but tough. Tough! If you want to know about tough, go see the Conleys on Montague. That's real isolation. But we're a family, you know. One big family that just swaps lighthouses every few years. The Chalkers are coming here next and we'll move on, but it's the same job everywhere, so when the lights call each other, we all speak the same language. You know, I wouldn't trade it for anything, not anything." Norm drifted off.

I was half-way through my first half-hour and my legs were tiring. The only noise now was the whirr of the rotation and the incessant wind and roar of the surf. Norm opened his eyes. "Goodness, I think I drifted. I'd better start talking lest you drift, eh?"

"My legs are aching. How much longer?" I asked wearily.

"Just seven minutes now, just a bit more than three revolutions. You'll make it. "Reminds me of a bit of poetry old Harry Handicott recited to us. You know him, he's a legend. Doing Smoky Cape now. Goes like this:

The man stood at the pearly gates, looking all tired and old.
He meekly asked the man of fate for admission to the fold.
"What have you done," Saint Peter asked, "to gain admission here?"
"I was in the Lighthouse Service and got leave once a year."
The gate swung open widely as Saint Peter tolled the bell.
"Come in," he said, "and take a harp. You've had enough of hell."

"Wow, that's good. Where did it come from?"

"Harry found it handwritten in an old *Instruction to Lightkeepers Manual.* Says a lot, eh?"

"But, you know the soul will go out of this light once we have to leave and it all goes automatic. Same for the other lights too. Very sad. I think we lose a lot, just for the sake of efficiency." Norm fell silent for a while.

I had forgotten all about my legs when there was a tap on my shoulder. "Time's up. Here's George." I was replaced by the second in charge and looked forward to my hour of rest. Norm continued to chat for the rest of the night, encouraging George and I to keep up the talk and energy levels, aided by the steaming cups of tea delivered intermittently by the wives. It was a team effort to keep the light going, always flashing.

Late in the morning, after grabbing some sleep, I walked up to the Head Lighthouse keeper's house for coffee. Norm walked in.

"Now that it's all over I just have one question, Norm. What's with the French Flag?" I asked.

"Ha. I wondered when you would ask that. It's a bit of a long story but a French mariner who I rescued off his sinking ship a few years ago gave it to me to remember him by. I treasure it. It seemed right as a marker last night, in a way saving other souls out there in that blackness."

I left Norm and George and Grace and the others two days later and returned to the boringly normal world outside. United in adversity, I felt a strong bond had developed and could understand what the lighthouse service family really meant.

The phone rang in my office two weeks later. The Regional Controller of Lighthouses was calling me. I was very surprised. Why would the great and revered Captain Taylor be ringing me, a lowly, bottom-rung auditor?

"That's Roger there, is it? Good. I heard all about your exploits at Sugarloaf. Very commendable. It's because I was advised of your welcome assistance on that night that I knew I needed to make this call. It is difficult for me, you see."

I wasn't sure what the Captain was getting at. He continued: "Norm Reynolds was killed this morning. Apparently he was driving his daughter to school and a truck he was following on the road lost its load and a steel pipe came right through the windscreen at him. His daughter is OK, but I'm afraid Norm got the full impact. I'm very sorry to have to make such a call but in the circumstances I feel you had a right to know before most people here."

Two months later Norm's family was forced out of their home. The accommodation had to be reserved for the incoming Head Lightkeeper and his family. It was in the rules. In the history of the Commonwealth Lighthouse Service no woman was ever considered for the job. That was in the rules too.

Airports of the Future – Information Officer

My heart went out of the audit job after Norm's death. I needed to find fresh pastures. At the time there was a move afoot to plan for a second airport for Sydney and a person was needed who could explain the planning process to the public. I went for the interview, said all the right things and got the job.

I was the Information Officer for the Major Airport Needs of Sydney (MANS) Study. I was meant to explain to the interested public what the Study was about. Anything to do with airport expansion and development had been controversial in Sydney, partly because aircraft noise was a political issue and governments had been hopeless at making any planning decisions. This inaction invited critical media attention.

The issue went back to 1947 when the idea of a second airport for Sydney was first proposed. Since that time a procession of airport development studies had come and gone with no one the wiser about what to do. The politically safe thing was to do nothing. A quarter of a century later with more and more noisy jet aircraft flying over the Sydney rooftops on their way in or out of Sydney (Kingsford Smith) Airport, or KSA for short, the issue had reached a sort of tipping point. This pushed the Commonwealth and State to join forces in a rare display of unity to produce an airport study designed to find a real solution and end the uncertainty once and for all.

"So what do I have to tell the public if they ring me or walk into the information centre?" I asked my new boss.

"Well, here are all the Study reports. We have an economic analysis, a financial analysis, a noise analysis, an access analysis, a land use analysis, an environment analysis, incidence analysis, wake turbulence analysis and passenger forecasts. All of these cover 120 potential second airport sites plus KSA coupled with four aviation sector split options."

"What's a split option?"

"'That's where we make KSA domestic and a second airport international, or the other way around, or a mix of both, or relegate regional RPT to Bankstown Airport or do something else entirely."

"RPT?"

"Oh, you'll need to know the acronyms – regular public transport."

"What about these 120 sites for a second airport?"

"You mean, how did we come up with that many? Simple. We drew a 120-kiilometre-radius circle around Sydney and split up the area into 10-square-kilometre blocks, and ran a computer model that took into account the amount of flat land in each. Then we eliminated blocks with another computer program taking into account land values. The point is, can you explain all this to the public?"

My head was spinning. "I think they will just want to know what the answer is." My boss looked a little nonplussed.

"Answer? There is no answer. There are just options. And there are hundreds. Just read all this. Get back to me if you need more and get yourself ready to respond to enquiries starting tomorrow. OK? Oh, and by the way, if anyone wants to know more just get them to ring my office assistant. She has some backup material that we can release, except for runway capacity."

"Why not runway capacity? People might want to know how much traffic KSA can handle before a second airport can be justified. I can see someone asking me that."

"Well, I hope they don't because our runway capacity guru worked out his very own computer model that predicted capacity but no one else understands what he did and he's not telling."

"Why not?"

"He says it's his intellectual property and he doesn't actually work for us, just an outside consultant. He just wants us to accept the results and believe him. Sorry can't help you with that one. It's sort of a Mexican standoff."

He stood up and slammed a weighty pile of papers on the desk. "Read these notes, they explain everything. Got to go now. Ring me if you need more, but I think you'll be alright."

And with that he was off. Off to another important appointment, I suppose, keeping the MANS Study rolling along.

I felt very alone. I struggled with the reports, not written for the public but for the writer's scientific and technical peers. The documents presented a maze of mathematical formulae, unlabelled diagrams and obscure jargon. There was no outcome, just a jumble of dense report conclusions that didn't add up. *"RPT split options may work in secondary control zones where T-Vasis approach controls are employed provided runway 25 arrival approaches do not compromise KSA primary control space."* That sort of language was never going to pass muster with the lay public. It all looked like a smokescreen, a clear case of patronising bullshit. How was I to make sense of it to the public?

The next day the new information office opened, a showcase city space with big display windows featuring a giant 3D relief map of the Sydney Basin. But not a soul visited. No-one phoned. Not surprising, I suppose, because neither the opening, nor the office address, nor the phone number had been advertised. But my relief at this respite was short-lived. On day two, the TV stations found out and an army of reporters and cameras descended on the information centre and me.

I rang my boss. "What do you want me to say to the reporters?"

"I'll be there in 10 minutes. Stall them."

I turned to one of the producers. "Look, I've arranged for one of our executives to be interviewed. He'll have all the information about this for you."

“What’s wrong with you? Aren’t you the information officer? Isn’t this your job?” demanded one producer.

“I haven’t been media trained. I’m here for the public, not the media.”

“Bloody bureaucracies,” muttered the producer. Mercifully my flustered boss arrived and guided the media throng away from me and into an isolated meeting room.

The television news on all channels that night reported the MANS Study as just another in the long line of airport studies going nowhere using phrases like ‘clueless’, ‘makes no sense’, ‘another example of bad planning’, ‘waste of taxpayers’ money’.

Over the next few months, the Study kept tumbling downhill. The Study Executive organised public meetings in a misguided attempt to regain popularity. I knew that this type of meeting was the worst option as public meetings are the least controllable way of sending a message. And by this time crowds attending these meetings were all fired up. It wasn’t helped that the people on stage addressing the locals were all Canberra senior public servants who had no empathy for the lifestyle and feelings of the local community. The locals sensed this before the meeting even got started. I cruised around the meeting hall, trying to engage individuals in the audience.

“Hi there. I’m the info officer. If there is anything that isn’t clear in what is being explained up front, I’m happy to help.”

“Too late, mate,” muttered a gruff old man in worn overalls. “I’m a farmer and I don’t take kindly to people telling me what I can or can’t do. Don’t know about you, mate, but the drongos on stage are going to get it!”

I looked closer at a cardboard box he held. It was full of eggs and ripe tomatoes.

“Hey mate,” I said. “These blokes are just doing their job. They’ve come down here because they wanted to talk to you personally and understand what your problems are. I don’t think it helps conversation if you pelt them. I’m very happy to get your views and tell Canberra what your concerns really are. I guarantee it. I really will.”

The farmer looked me in the eye. “You fair dinkum, mate?”

“Fair dinkum.”

The farmer slowly backed off. He put his box of ammunition down, hurriedly wrote a telephone number on a piece of paper and shoved it into my hand.

“You’d better be right on your word, mate. I’ll expect your call tomorrow.” And with that he walked out with his full box of eggs and tomatoes.

This situation repeated itself at other similar functions. Each meeting degenerated into a rowdy shouting match. The Canberra mob was out of their depth.

I had constant trouble in explaining the morass of Study details to anyone, so one day I decided to make up my own story.

A middle-aged couple approached my desk, eager for information.

“M’name’s Roy and this is my wife Ruby. We’ve come all this way in here from out west to find out what’s going to happen out in our little part of the world. I've been told you're a straight talker. Not like those bullshit artists from Canberra."

"Thanks for coming in. Take a seat and I'll keep it short and simple. Have you got a bus stop near your place?"

"Yes, sure. The bus goes to Penrith to the shops and train. What about it?"

"Well, what would happen if not one but 20 buses showed up. All the buses were full, and everybody wanted to get off at your stop?"

"I'd be bloody amazed. No one gets off at our stop."

"But if they did, and they did that all the time, you'd have to build a bigger bus stop, wouldn't you, and build more shops and facilities for all the passengers getting off? Right?"

"Oh, I get it. So that's what all these millions of dollars are for. Well fuck me, what a waste."

"No, we have to go through all this because in our case it's not just a bigger bus stop but a new airport that needs lots of land, lots of new roads, a railway, in fact a new city so it's a big deal, and we need to get it right so as not to waste taxpayers' money."

"OK, I see what you're getting at. That sounds clear. But why us? Why not some other poor bastards?"

"Well, we have to find the best site, so we have to look at every possible site to start with and then find the best one out of all those. Yours is just one of 100 such sites. When we get down to just a few based on flat land and distance from Sydney and other factors, we will then look at the remaining sites much more closely and then talk to the people in those sites with much more detail. But we haven't got to that stage yet, so don't worry, nothing is going to happen for a while. I'll tell you what I'll do. I will make sure you know what is happening whether I'm in this job or not, OK? I don't want you to feel left out of it."

Roy looked at Ruby and then back at me. "I think the missus and I are real glad we made the trip. It's not Double Dutch to me now. I think I can see what you are getting at. Good on you. But tell those idiots back in Canberra not to waste trees on these useless reports. No one reads them. They don't mean anything to us. Just tell 'em that."

I could see what was going to happen before it happened with the MANS Study. It grew into an unmanageable hulk of information to the point that it couldn't be effectively explained to anyone and especially the politicians. It was too complicated, and simple outcomes, if there were any, got lost in the information noise. Suspicions arose between Commonwealth and State officials, reflecting the governments they represented, which were of differing political persuasions. Eventually the whole show collapsed under its own monstrous carcass and died, and with it my job.

The Déjà Vu Airport Study – Media and Community Advisor

I spent the next three months documenting the death and filing all the papers so that lessons could be learned, that might mean the mistakes made might never be repeated. At the end I walked into an empty office, did nothing and got paid. Days passed, and then came the telephone call.

"My name is James from the Secretary's office. Can I talk to Roger please?"

It's Roger here," I said tentatively.

"We would like you to come down to Canberra to discuss a job we have for you."

I was intrigued at the mystery. They didn't want to discuss it over the phone and it was the Secretary's office no less, the Head of the department, one of the Canberra mandarins. So I flew the short hop to Canberra and on arrival was ushered into a public service office whose plushness signalled its occupant's status.

The Secretary's personal assistant, the PA, entered the office from a side door. "Ah, Roger. Thanks for coming down to the cold. I know the weather is always a shock for someone from Sydney. I'm Paul."

"Hi Paul, this is a bit of a mystery to me so I'm very curious about what you had in mind."

"Well, to cut a long story short, we all know the failures that have occurred along the way to getting some resolution on the airport issue in Sydney. Like a slow moving train wreck, not helped by the recalcitrants in the NSW Government. You'd agree, wouldn't you?"

I nodded. "The Minister still wants to score a win, and with what we already know, I think we can. The key is to keep it simple. That's one thing we have learned out of the wreckage. Keep the study simple and keep the message simple. That's where you come in, Roger."

"What's the message?" I asked.

"Which is the best second airport site, that's all, no multi-strand analyses, no complicated list of options, just a simple search for the best site for a second airport."

"That can be complicated as well," I said.

"Well, that's where you come in. We, in Canberra, have heard reports of you getting the message across to the public very well, and simplifying it for them. So when this idea surfaced we thought who better to carry the message to the affected Sydney community than you. You have the rapport with the people there. So you can get the message through and tell us back here what local support there is."

I was thinking fast. Could I really get a community's confidence, especially if they were likely to be evicted from their homes because of 'my project'?

"Thank you for your confidence. I'll do my best. The one thing that is important is to gain the community's trust and acceptance, so I need to be with them and not look like a Canberra public servant, so then I think I can find out what true level of support a second airport has in western Sydney."

A day later the telephone rang. I got the job. The following Monday I entered the Study's Sydney garage as arranged. A cheery foreman called Red greeted me.

"Jeez, we've been in a panic here, Roger, since Tuesday, and it's all about you," he said. "Canberra has been on to us every single day about this, so I'm relieved we've finished in time for your arrival."

"Look Red, I haven't a clue what this is all about. The powers that be didn't want to tell me, said it would be a surprise. So surprise me then."

"Right, come this way." Red led me into the workshop floor. There ahead of me was a bright yellow and black motor home with a huge illuminated sign stretching across the length of the vehicle on both sides proclaiming that this was the *Community Access Bus – Second Airport Study*. The Commonwealth coat of arms above the sign lent a halo of authority. Inside was an office with desks, typewriter, wall maps, a kitchen, toilet and a small sitting room that folded out into a bed.

"Welcome to your new home," said Red proudly. "Canberra wanted you to live with the communities in the west, but to also be mobile. So this is it. Your travelling office. Your home away from home."

I was more than surprised. I was shocked. Did Canberra expect me to live in this for years, for surely the study would go for that long, judging by the longevity of the predecessors. But I could also see their point. I would always be the foreign outsider if I simply drove to some temporary office near the affected areas for a few hours and then left. But I needed to have a life as well.

The Community Access Bus or Trojan Horse?

Of all the technical and infrastructure issues about establishing a new and controversial airport from scratch, the one issue that could stymie the whole project was community support. This was political and, more than anything else focused the minds of the politicians. Local unpopularity for a project as big as a major airport could cost the Federal Government a swag of seats in Western Sydney, enough to turf them out at a general election. Saving their arses was therefore an important consideration to the Federal pollies, more so than the project itself.

After the negative treatment, the media meted out for the MANS Study, the Canberra decision-makers didn't want to make the same mistake with this new incarnation. Understanding the true level of support and the real local issues was what Canberra wanted to know more than anything else. Any technical, environmental or economic problem could be dealt with by spin, but not this. Canberra knew this well and telephoned me constantly to ensure I had the message down pat.

So that was my job: to present The Study to the public and be seen as understanding, empathetic and 'genuine'.

"We want you to plant yourself out there," urged the Canberra minder. "You know, be there all the time so they get used to you. We need quality feedback from these groups."

"Do you mean I have to live on board? It's not a home, it's an office," I said, picturing myself as a sluggish snail, constricted by its 24/7 shell house. ""I don't think people will expect me to live in my office."

"But you have to show you're committed to the area. You know, talk their language, know the people, get the lay of the land," Canberra enthused.

Panic. Living in a black and yellow bus in the middle of the western suburbs was incompatible with my idyllic waterfront home life on Sydney's beautiful Pittwater. Then came an epiphany. I saw the vision.

"How about we advertise constantly in the local papers and community radio where I'll be each day," I suggested, "so everybody gets to know I'm there in their area every day. Then I get there early, before the advertised times. People will notice that. Make the Community Access Bus – the CAB – a welcoming office space, with tea and coffee on board, have all the material on hand so they can see I'm prepared, and tell them we can handle any question they have. I mean any. So any question I can't answer, I use the mobile phone we will install, dial the number of the expert and hand the phone to them so they can talk directly with the expert. I will have a list of available experts in each field and their telephone numbers. That will impress the locals. I would have the first mobile telephone most people would have ever seen. I know I can do it because there is a repeater in line of sight over most, if not all, sites I am going to. I'm lucky as it is the only repeater in western Sydney."

I paused and eyeballed Mr Canberra. "So what do you think of all that?"

Silence. Then the eruption. "Brilliant! Simply brilliant! That's the sort of thinking we like around here. Right on! We can fix up the CAB with all of that. But I'm not so sure about the phone. Mobile phones are a new concept for us, even in Canberra. I don't think we have any except for the cars used by the Prime Minister and Cabinet." A pregnant pause. "But, I do see your point. You'd be the first non-pollie I'd say to have one."

"I need one. It would be the coup de gras to any lingering doubts about my authenticity," I said confidently.

"Coup de what? You Sydney people are funny. OK, we are on to it. Thanks for that. I feel better now."

And from that conversation the new Community Access Bus was born, complete with shoebox-sized mobile phone attached to a cradle welded into the frame of the vehicle.

My new job was launched with my schedule advertised in every local rag between Parramatta and the Blue Mountains. I went on several community radio stations doing interviews. Everyone I met in Western Sydney seemed to know where I and my brightly coloured CAB would be at any given time over the next three months.

My typical day started at 5am on Lovett Bay on Pittwater, when I started up the outboard motor on my 'tinnie' and glided across the silk-smooth pre-dawn water to the commuter wharf at Church Point. I then transferred to the CAB in the adjacent car park and made the long trek out to my site for the day in western Sydney. Usually I arrived by 7am and was all set up to receive visitors in just a few minutes. My three-month schedule of CAB locations was carefully designed to cover all of the second airport sites being proposed for Sydney.

Each morning I 'dropped anchor' in villages like Leppington, Luddenham, Rossmore, Oakville, Pitt Town, Scheyville and Wallacia, and opened up my shop with welcome signs displayed. And in came the customers. They queued at the door and all spaces inside were taken up with visitors inspecting the displays, posters and books, as if I was a travelling council library visiting a remote outback town where the monthly arrival of the library van was a significant social event.

"So where's this airport going, mate?" asked a local drifting out of the nearby cake shop.

"Over there." I pointed to a flat green area behind a row of trees.

"Yeah, but how far over? How big is this damn thing? I'm Jim by the way."

I produced maps and the visitor peered at them closely. "Can you tell me this, what's this line here on the map?"

"That's the eastern boundary of this proposed site, Jim."

"Christ, I'm inside that!" Jim exclaimed, his face tensed and anger mounting in his voice. "I didn't realise that before. What do I do about it, you tell me, that's what you're here for, isn't it?"

"Well Jim, we have at least 6 sites to look at around Sydney, and this exercise is simply to identify the best one," I reassured. "So it may not be this one at all, but if it is and you are inside the area to be acquired by the government, they will buy your property at the commercial rate. So that could be very good for you."

"It's not that. Geez! You just don't know. It's Poppy and Buffy and eight others I have. My Angora breeders – my goats, mate," Jim thundered. "The animals and the business is worth a lot more than the property." Jim shook his head. "What about the business, eh? Lot of farmers around here will ask you the same. So what's the answer there, eh?"

It was a good question and I knew my literature and brochures didn't cover this. I looked up our list of experts and rang the telephone number of our agricultural economist and hoped like hell he was in his office this early. To my relief the phone was answered and after a short explanation I handed the phone to Jim. He looked startled.

"You have a phone here? Is this for me?"

"Take the phone, please." After an animated phone conversation, Jim handed the phone back to me." "Did you get your question answered?"

"I sure did. The business is covered and on my valuation. I can't tell you how impressed I am by your help in this bus. I never expected to get it. Thank you so much. I'm going to let my neighbours know about you and this bus."

He shook my hand, and was off.

Over the next week this situation was repeated many times and the number of happy visitors grew exponentially, thanks to the bush telegraph. The local community radio station, Hawkesbury Radio, started running a one-minute spot on their breakfast program entitled "Where's Roger?" and listed the locations for my CAB for the rest of the week.

I tapped into these communities and started feeling strangely that I belonged to them. Their concerns were my concerns.

"Hey, mate," a local tradie called out as he entered the CAB. "I read some stuff that the noise will kill me. How can I get it changed, tell me?"

"What's that, mate? Can you speak up?" I was parked next to the Northern Road, a main western Sydney north-south truck route and with the door open, I could hardly hear him over the roar of passing traffic.

"The fuckin' noise. It'll kill me!"

The tradie handed me a brochure from the local action group which showed the noise footprint of jet aircraft using one of the hypothetical runways at the new airport proposal, planned to start operations in about 20 years' time.

I pointed to the road. "What about the noise from the traffic?" I shouted.

"What do you mean?" I pointed again. "Oh that. That's nothing. Doesn't worry me at all. It the planes I'm worried about."

So here was a local who dismissed the deafening roar of traffic while loudly voicing his concerns about noise that may or may not occur in 20 years' time, something that would probably be a lot less disturbing than the road traffic. But he was used to this. The airport was something new. That heightened attitude towards the noise of the distant future was one of the key insights in my reports to the Minister.

Meeting the Minister

By week four, I was forming the impression that the level of support for a second airport had risen. This seemed particularly marked in the main centres like Penrith and Blacktown. My visitor numbers were way over expectation and the mobile phone was getting heavy use and for most this was a novelty. One morning while parked in a quiet village, I received a mobile call requesting that

I come to Canberra to discuss my impressions of the mood in Western Sydney towards the airport site directly with the Minister for Aviation.

My flight from Sydney touched down on a cold grey morning in Canberra. I was whisked to Parliament House, accompanied by two heavies from Central Office if not Central Casting. In the 15 minutes from the airport to Parliament House I was given a crash course on how to behave in front of the Minister. It was like a shopping list:

- Make eye contact
- Only answer questions
- Do not give unsolicited opinions
- Do not make value judgments
- Stick to the facts
- Defer to us on overall issues
- Keep to your area of knowledge, which is about your Bus activities
- Look to us if you need clarification or can't answer a question
- Let us handle all the pleasantries and intros
- Look to us for signs, such as if you are going off track.

The message I was getting was: you will probably stuff it up being so inexperienced but we will be with you all the way to ensure you don't embarrass the Department in front of the Minister.

'"We're here," announced the chauffeur. We all alighted and walked through the cramped corridors of the old Parliament House to a collection of plastic chairs in a passageway opposite a big wooden door. After a few minutes, the door opened and we were ushered into a tiny anteroom.

A few minutes later, the Minister's PA dismissed the two heavies. "I think we can dispense with your services now, thank you. Roger's fine with us."

The heavies were flummoxed. Worry lines spread across their faces. Then their protests began. The PA pulled rank. "Gentlemen, the Minister's office is not the enemy. We will ring you if we need you." And with that, the two frowning senior public servants were briskly escorted out of the room, and I was led into the office of the Hon. Kim Beazley, Minister for Aviation in the Hawke Government. A large man with a commanding but warm presence, he stood up, smiled and held out his hand.

"Sorry for the dramatics out there," he said. "I don't take kindly to sanitised messages, which I suspect is what I was going to get from those fellows. What I am interested in is the truth about what is going on with all those potentially affected communities. They all have their legitimate grievances, especially with such a long-standing issue as this. I'm thinking from your reports that we may be getting a level of support out there. That's why I've got you here. I want to know just how real that support is. What do you think?"

My nerves evaporated because I knew my subject which engendered confidence. "What's been happening is that because I'm visible in the community almost daily many people who have been to see me give me the impression that I'm accepted. Even if not actually one of them, at least I'm someone who understands them, not just an interloper from Canberra. So they are giving me their honest views and the general message I'm getting is that they will accept an airport, provided they get a fair compensation for their properties and the impacts of the development."

"Good. That's what I wanted to hear." Kim smiled. "I think we have a real opportunity here for the first time to push ahead and not get stonewalled with opposition. I'm wanting runs on the board with this issue, finally. So what I want you to do is to send me a report weekly on your activities and your impressions on the general attitude plus any emerging issues. Don't hold back. Give it to me straight, OK? No Public Service waffle. I want to see your original stuff without the so-called value-adding from the Department."

"We also want you to do a speaker's circuit, talking to groups and on radio," said the Minister's PA. He handed me a talks program which included RSL clubs, business groups, chambers of commerce and councils plus community radio. With the meeting over I was handed back to the two now sulking heavies and unceremoniously put on a plane for Sydney. Little was said.

Accidental Counselling

The next three very busy months went quickly and for a while there was a definite opportunity to build a second airport with local support. I became a fixture in a scattering of urban-rural fringe communities, someone to talk to who was independent of the little intrigues of village life. Many days went like this.

"Hello, Roger. Thought I'd see you here today," said a weather-beaten blonde lady with a gravelly voice drifting in from the local shops. "Got many customers?" She peered inside the bus. "Thought not. They all know about it now for sure."

She moved inside and got comfortable on the CAB's sofa. "Jenny's m'name. We're very close around here so I expect once you tell one person they'll all know pretty quickly. Too bloody close, if you ask me, 'cause my Fred has gone off with the old bat up our street. The scumbag's pissed off. And if you see him, you can tell him from me I'm not having him back."

I coughed nervously and shuffled some brochures. "Well, er, what do you think of the airport plans?"

She was oblivious to my question. Her eyes watered. "I'm so confused, I don't know what to do. You're the only one I can talk to. They're all against me in this fucked up place." She sniffed. Tears ran down her cheeks.

I hated seeing her so upset and stupidly felt like putting a reassuring arm around her. Instead I moved away. "I'm afraid I can't help with your relationship problems but if you've got any airport issues ..."

"It's alright. You've helped me already. I know I can talk to you and you're not going to gossip."

I became something these small settlements on the fringes of Sydney never had, a totally independent and understanding person, not part of the community and its local issues but at the same time someone who had tapped into the local community life and had status.

Kim Beazley was getting the message he wanted for months, but like all governments that had come before, this one stumbled as well. . I warned the Minister the window of opportunity was starting to close. Short-term politics trumped policy courage and the government prevaricated. New opposition came from councils responding to newspaper reports about aircraft noise and the message about a boosted local economy and more jobs got lost. The sorry second airport saga shows how bad politicians were and are at making unpopular decisions affecting their own jobs.

It had been apparent since 1947 that Sydney would need a second airport, but the decision that it was really necessary and would be located at Badgery's Creek, 50km from the Sydney CBD, was not made until 2014. And even today, in 2018, there have been no decisions made regarding how the site is to be developed and accessed. Buying the land was the easy part. The saga continues.

My job came to an end in 1983. The community consultation period had past and the issue was put on the backburner. I was out of the game, or so I thought.

The Rooftops of Sydney

The call came from Central Office early one morning. At the end of the line was a gruff, no-nonsense Aussie larrikin from German migrant parents, Karsten Groening. He was my boss's boss and had two bosses above him, such was the hierarchical structure of Canberra government departments.

"Say, Rog, it's Karsten. The media have blown up about our figures on the number of people living under the flight path and getting the noise. They're giving us hell. It makes the new airport look bad."

"You mean the people living there now with the noise they may hear in 20 years' time," I retorted.

"Yeah, that's it. Minister's gone bananas about it. We've gotta get accurate figures, and, guess what?" Karsten paused for effect. "That's where you come in."

"Me? What about your highly paid consultants? Didn't they give you good data? It's their field, isn't it?"

"Nah, we don't have a budget for it. Imagine what they'd charge for doing a house count in the huge area we have mapped as being affected."

"House count? Why that? Don't they have aerial photos and council subdivision maps or something?"

"Nah," Karsten repeated. "Photos give you roofs, not dwellings. They could be tool sheds, chook houses. It's council bull anyhow. We don't trust councils.

Nah. The only way to be damn sure a building is a dwelling is to actually see it from the street."

My jaw dropped. "What! Are you saying someone has to go up and down every street in western Sydney within the noise zone and physically count all the houses?"

"Yep. That's your job. Good, isn't it? You were saying the other day how your time has run out. Well, now it hasn't."

I didn't answer.

"Hey, don't fret. It's not just you. I'll be down every day you are onto it and help you. For the figures to be credible, we need a witness."

So for the next three months that is all we did. Up and down every single street within the line on the map that indicated significant noise from aircraft that will fly in 20 years' time, assuming all the study forecasts were accurate about aircraft noise signatures, runway orientation, traffic density, suburban population growth and suburban housing densities. So even counting all the houses accurately didn't result in an accurate figure if any of those assumptions were wrong.

The entertainment came from Karsten. Used to the bucolic Canberra countryside, he reacted badly to the real world of struggling Western Sydney.

"Christ, look at that shitheap!" he bellowed, with the windows open. Out came an irate occupant, shaking his garden rake and obviously offended.

"Keep your voice down or wind up the window!" I implored.

"You've got to admit it, Roger. Some parts around here are crap. How do people live like that?" Karsten pointed to several tin sheds with letterboxes outside. "You see now why we need to do this. Can't tell from air photos what they're like."

We drove on. Karsten kept his window down. "Look, there's another one. No one could live in that heap. Geez, it's bad. I don't care if there are squatters or what living there, I'm not counting it." Karsten just couldn't countenance the word 'dwelling' applying to some of the humpies he saw. To him they were uninhabitable.

One day we were cruising through a higher income area in a well-established market garden area and came across a very substantial house that seemed more like a small cathedral. The letter box was stuffed full, indicating the occupants were away. We stopped outside for a few minutes. A neighbour stirred and drifted over to our car.

"You blokes interested in that?" he asked.

"Yeah," Karsten answered. "It's big, isn't it?"

"An Ayatollah guy from some Arab country owns it. He's away overseas at the moment. But would you like to know a bit about it?" The neighbour was keen to spill the beans.

"The bloke's got a harem. Twelve bedrooms he has. One for each. How would you go, eh? I mean what are we doing wrong here in this country? Why can't we have what he has, eh?"

“This makes a mockery of your 2.8 people per dwelling assumption.” I muttered to Karsten.

“I wouldn’t worry. This is not typical. It balances up all those vacant places and ones that are too horrible to live in.”

After 12 weeks of counting, we drove up our last street in Rossmore.

“You little beauty!” Karsten screamed out, windows down. “That’s the last fuck’n house. Wheeee!” He rummaged around in his bag and produced a bottle of champagne and flutes.

“Don’t open that in the car Karsten, it may…”

I was too late. Karsten pushed up the cork aggressively and it shot out like a cannon ball, bouncing at high speed off the ceiling followed very shortly after by a white jet of bubbles, hitting the ceiling as well and raining down like a cloudburst onto his work sheets.

“So there are 192,457 people overall and 22,890 in the high impact zone. That’s it. Way more than the consultants are saying.”

“That’s bad.”

“Who cares? We’ve done it. I don’t have to come down here again, ever I hope.”

And he didn’t.

The period for consultation passed. After a lengthy hiatus, the Government decided on Badgery’s Creek as the site for Sydney’s second airport and the focus then shifted to a third runway at KSA. It was the start of a new project but without a clear consultation program. So in 1985 my job was over and I was feeling burnt out.

Frogs and the International Terminal Environment Officer

The Green and Golden Bell Frog has very big eyes. I was looking into a pair of them belonging to a fine specimen we had just caught as we waded around the marshes of the lower Cooks River adjacent to Sydney Airport. We were surveying frog numbers as part of the work of assessing the environmental impact of an expanded international airport terminal. These frogs (one of few frog species in the world that are active during the day) were endangered, so any habitat disturbance caused by the expanded terminal could spell big trouble for the airport developers. This turned out to be a vital part of my next job.

My interest in airports had been rapidly waning. I had started out with World War two fighter pilot aces running the shop. They had gone, and with the split of Aviation into operations and development, my bosses were now all engineers, because I was shoved into the development arm. Engineers knew how to build airports but not how to run them or manage the people in them. Not being an engineer, I was dumped into a back room and forgotten. The life had gone out of my job, the black hole of purposelessness loomed. I decided it was time to steer a new course for myself.

News of my partially completed resignation letter reached the upper echelons of the organisation. I was called into the Chief Engineer's office for a chat.

"It has come as a shock to us, Roger," said Ian, the Chief Engineer. "We can't just let you go after all you have done. Listen, I think I have something for you." Ian rummaged around in his desk drawers, eventually pulling out a file and handing it to me.

"All the engineers here thought this would be right up your alley. It's the work on assessing the environmental impact of expanding the international terminal. How would you like to be the chief author and coordinator for it? It can be your baby. We won't interfere with the work. You can run your own show and get who you need to do the technical stuff. How does that sound?"

It sounded all too convenient, and the fact that Ian had to rummage around to find the file suggested a very low order of importance from an engineer's perspective. But it was something a bit different and it seemed like I had a smidgen of autonomy. So I accepted.

I knew engineers didn't put much store in Environmental Impact Statements (EISs). Their faith lay in engineering drawings and documents. EISs were a requirement but for them it was just a case of ticking the box. So for a job they were not going to take any notice of, they weren't taking any risks giving the job to me. I didn't know till years later how important this particular job would become to me.

Feeling free to do what I wanted and fresh from a newly minted undergraduate degree in science from Macquarie University, I launched into the work and set about coordinating a team of experts in land planning, fluvial geomorphology, riparian ecosystems, aviation planning, econometrics, runway capacity modelling, air pollution and ground transport access modelling. In the back of my mind though was the thought that perhaps I was just being humoured by the engineers as a means of keeping me and was not to be taken too seriously.

In the end I produced a thick and I thought worthy document. It covered matters such as proposed gate numbers for the calculated density of air traffic, ground traffic management and a host of operational matters to gladden an engineer's heart. Ian's smile was broadening as I presented these findings to him.

"There is something else. It's environmental, not operational."

"What?" Ian seemed to prickle at the mention of the word "environmental".

"It's about the Green and Golden Bell Frog. Its numbers are declining rapidly and its main habitat in Sydney is the Cooks River. The new building will encroach on that habitat."

"What the hell! Tell me please this isn't happening?" Ian's expression was darkening. The smiles had disappeared.

"But don't worry about it. We have a solution. Our ecology people have worked it out."

"I don't care what they have worked out. I know it will cost us. Why is it, every fuck'n time we plan to build something, some colony of long-eared bunyips that must be saved just happens to be located right where we pour the concrete? Bloody hell, it always happens. I mean, geez, give us a break."

Ian thumped his desk hard. The desk bound paperweight jumped up in response to the earthquake.

"But it's good news, Ian," I said, trying to quickly insert some positives into the discussion. "The EIS give us a solution to managing them so the development and the frogs can co-exist. We donate some land we weren't going to use anyway to replace the lost habitat. It's all low cost as it's a simple rehabilitation. The local council will even chip in for free."

"Well, that's a relief. I suppose that's what these reports are good for, just as long as we have a fix and it doesn't complicate the project."

Ian picked up the EIS and thumbed through the pages, glancing at random pages as they flipped open. I waited, hoping he would discover a good news page, of which there were many peppered through the volume.

Finally Ian closed the covers and dropped it to one side on his desk.

"It's OK, Rog. I'm not blaming you for the friggin' frog. I can see there's a lot of good stuff in here. Thanks for your work. A worthy tome, isn't it, Peter?" The assistant started nodding on cue.

After the exchange of more pleasantries, I was escorted out of the opulence befitting a head engineer's office, and I headed back to my black hole office. A week ticked by, then two. I heard back nothing. Then one day travelling to work and to a job that was drifting into the ether like my lost EIS, I suddenly knew it was time to move on and complete my resignation letter. And I did.

The Voyage of the Argonauta – Photographer

The door to the flight deck of our 10-seater Piper Navajo aircraft opened. The co-pilot leaned out from his seat and handed us cheese rolls accompanied by bottles of Peruvian Pisco brandy, standard breakfast fare on this route, flying from Punta Arenas over the ice cap on Terra Del Fuego near Cape Horn. We were bound for the world's most southerly town, Puerto Williams on Navarino Island, part of the cold, windy archipelago at the bottom of South America.

South America was always on my bucket list. I was to travel solo for a trip lasting 6 months but an old friend convinced me to go with him and a group of bushwalkers on a package tour with International Park Tours to Peru and Chile. I knew the leader, Tony Groom, well. Groom was a famous name in Queensland. Tony's father established and ran the heritage-listed Binna Burra eco-lodge in the Lamington National Park in the Gold Coast hinterland where I often stayed on holidays. Tony was a committed environmentalist and a meticulous planner. His tours were bound to be something special.

On learning of my previous photographic assignments documenting my last big tour, Tony suggested I could do some work for him, doing promotional shots of the tour's new cruise through the Beagle Channel. So I was back to being a photographer again.

Puerto Williams was where my job of sorts began. The airport terminal was a tin shed. This sized up what the town was like, just a small main street, several scattered buildings and clumps of houses further out punctuating the Antarctic beech forests cladding the surrounding hills. Backed by jagged, snow-capped mountains, this remote, wind-blasted town really does feel like the end of the earth. Further south is the last island of the continent of South America, Horn Island, where at Cape Horn, the Atlantic, Pacific and Southern oceans merge. Beyond lies Antarctica.

Through this most isolated archipelago two channels connect the Atlantic to the Pacific, the broad Magellan Straits to the north and the narrow Beagle Channel to the south. The channel cuts through the Darwin Plateau, an ice cap surrounding a cluster of 7000 ft. peaks on the largest island, Tierra del Fuego. Huge chunks of this ice crash noisily into these wild waters from precipitous glaciers, creating towering icefalls and icebergs.

Chile and Argentina both lay claim to this territory. Chilean and Argentinian gunboats patrol the Channel to ensure that no wayward vessel from the opposing camp crosses the border line. Chile claims Puerto Williams is the most southerly town in the world, while Argentina argues that its Channel port city of Ushaia, which lies opposite PW, holds that title as PW is too small to be truly called a town.

Down at the port our ship *Argonauta* was waiting. Streaks of rust emanating from joints and rivets were etched into its white superstructure, adding to its down-at-heel appearance. As well as taking on passengers, it was a supply vessel for the 1500 Navarino residents and the naval base making the run to Punta Arenas and back every two weeks. Tony's small group was among passengers travelling north to Punta.

Argonauta was an ageing German passenger ferry. Local cargo ships and passenger ferries in these waters seemed to form a sort of intermediate stage in the ferry life cycle that began in the Baltic or the Mediterranean as a well fitted-out new ship in tip-top mechanical condition to meet rigorous European standards. As the vessel aged it would become uneconomic to keep it up to the standards required, so it would then be sold to a country with lower standards. As a South American ship, a second life began. No matter that the freshwater pipes were rusty or that the air conditioning didn't work or that the engine's bearings were running hot. Typically, more years would pass with problems mounting. One day a rare inspection by a maritime safety officer from the government might occur, possibly responding to complaints. He or she might have concerns as to the safety of passengers and crew and order a refit. The costs would be unacceptable to the owners already running the ship down with little maintenance and so it would now be sold to the Government of Bangladesh or Nigeria or the Philippines as a river or coastal ferry, where it would struggle through its last days unconstrained by standards.

It didn't matter to us that *Argonauta* was no luxury liner. Nor did we really mind that it was three hours after our scheduled departure time that we finally pulled out of the forlorn-looking Port area, heading for the main Beagle Channel. Adventure called.

The Channel was about 8km wide at this point. Down the middle of the channel was an imaginary line, the international boundary between Chile to the south and Argentina to the north.

These two countries had a long history of conflict over territory. In Chile all maps of the country included a big chunk of Antarctica looking like a wedge cut from a circular cake. On the walls in most Argentinian public buildings were maps of that country but with the same serving of Antarctic cake. This problem had never been resolved. There was little international meaning in it as territorial claims by any country of bits of the frozen continent lacked any official international recognition. That point was lost in the national fervour stirred up in true Latin political style for the protagonists. Remarkably their claims seem puny beside those of Australia, which believes it owns almost half the white continent.

Chile and Argentina are separated by the Andes for all of their common border except in the extreme south and the Beagle Channel. It is here that they rattle their sabres the most. As a Chilean ship we were escorted part of the way by a Chilean navy vessel from the naval base at Puerto Williams and were shadowed not very discreetly by an Argentinian counterpart a few kilometres astern.

Argonauta's captain was Alfonso Adolfus, a small but noisy man of great humour and greater emotion always on display on his ruddy, highly mobile face. With his ill-fitting uniform, very short legs and Captain's hat several sizes too small for his large head and mass of matted hair he looked like a cartoon character.

Al saw the warship tag event as an opportunity for great fun and gleefully demonstrated to those of us on the bridge how the ship reacted to be taken off autopilot. With the first officer at the helm, the ship weaved to port and starboard with continuous course corrections, tripping the light fantastic across the international border every few minutes. Every time we crossed the imaginary line into Argentina we could see some commotion on board the Argentinian frigate with sailors running back and forth gesticulating wildly. Our radio officer reported to the bridge messages that seemed to fit the sign language.

"This ees a good one, huh? I pull it every time," Alfonso wheezed. Pointing excitedly at the Chilean warship, he cackled with glee. "Ha! They never know what is going on, the fools!" He hit the horn button – the international signal to other vessels that we were going to starboard. This caused further activity aboard the frigate. With my telephoto, I could capture some of the action. The first officer and other crew on the bridge smiled. After a while, our Argentinian shadow turned for home. Perhaps they had lost interest in the game, or maybe they knew what we didn't: that a huge storm was brewing and it was time to head for the safety and comfort of Ushaia.

The westerly wind stiffened during the night with white caps all around us illuminated by a stormy moon. Spray enveloped our ship, even though we were in what the maps described as 'sheltered waters'. We were sailing into the teeth of the storm and the ship's old and tired engines laboured loudly. We had passed the harbour entrance into the Port of Ushuaia some time back and the distant city lights had passed from view as we steamed west. Now those same lights started to re-appear from behind the headlands, first one building, then the port facilities, then the whole downtown area as gradually but definitely we sailed backwards.

"Give me what's she's got, Scotty!" The Captain from TV's Star Trek was in no mood for compromise as the Klingon ship approached. There was furious activity in the engine room as Scotty was trying to connect circuits. With frustration he shouted into the intercom: "But the dylithium crystals are not completely operational after the last attack. I don't think she can take much more of this Captain."

Kirk stood up and surveyed the scene. Spock was looking intently at sensor displays. "They have their shields up, Jim." Kirk's face hardened.

"I need full warp drive now, Scotty. Push into the red zone."

"But Captain, it may fail and we then have barely enough power left for our impulse engines."

"Just do it," shouted Kirk.

"Aye Aye Capt'n." A resigned but gritty Scotty swung around to give the orders to someone off screen. The great starship shuddered as the transition to light speed was made. The engines held and once again Captain Kirk staged a miraculous escape and disappeared from the battle scene leaving the klingons dangling.

So it was with the less fashionable and lower-tech *Argonauta*. Alfonso was shouting down to the engine room imperiously in Spanish. The engineer, rather like the Enterprise's Scotty, initially responded in a pleading tone, which changed to anger. The volume of the conversation up and down the intercom pipe was ear-splitting.

One of the officers took we passengers up on the bridge aside and attempted an explanation.

"It is bad blood, the Captain and Gonzo." First officer Santos was referring to the engineer. "You see, he married the Captain's sister. Always now bad blood." He shook his bowed head and returned to his station.

We felt it best not to return to the bridge, giving the combatants their privacy. As their volcanic rumblings intensified so did the feverish vibrations from the engine. Eventually Ushuaia once again slowly disappeared from view to our stern.

The ship was still shaking angrily next morning. We were being tossed around in a narrow strait with Isla Navarino to our left and Tierra del Fuego Island on our right, with its mountainous shorelines and some of the world's biggest sea cliffs. The Tierra del Fuego icecap sitting on the Darwin plateau at 1800m elevation came to an abrupt end at the Beagle. The land plunged to the sea and the icy margins of the icecap peeled away, slamming into the water with a terrific rumble. We were told that this was the world's highest single drop icefall. The Navarino side was almost as spectacular. The land was covered in southern beech forest tipped with ice and veiled with spray from myriad waterfalls tumbling right across the channel like steam from a boiling kettle. A photographer's paradise.

Towards lunch time the wind increased to storm force and again we were making no headway. The long and straight channel provided no shelter save for one small bay on our starboard side. It had a broad, white-sand beach at its head backed by a thick forest. Battling huge wind waves magnified by the long reach of the strait, *Argonauta* turned towards the bay. Gusts of wind were blowing the ship backwards but with each brief lull we inched forward. Finally we came abeam of the small headland that sheltered the bay. Suddenly we turned sharply and sailed into calm, flat waters. It was like walking into the sunny, quiet valley of Shangri La out of the Himalayan blizzard.

Argonauta did not reduce speed as we reached the middle of the bay with the beach 500 metres away. We lined up for the middle of the beach as the engine vibrations continued. A small yacht, the only other boat we had seen apart from the warships, was anchored to our left. We were travelling at around eight knots as we passed the yacht, bearing down on the beach, now only 200 metres away.

Behind the beach lay a forest of southern beech trees, boggy groundcover and exposed sand dunes in the clear patches. A small creek emptied out into the bay. Behind the forest, the ground rose up abruptly, marking the escarpment of the ice cap plateau. Through a gap in the escarpment carved a small glacier with its terminus only 4km away.

Argonauta bore on. The engines cut out moments before we hit the beach. Sand was now beneath the hull, not water. Still *Argonauta* sailed on, as if floating on some magic carpet. Now she was plunging into the forest. The bow hit the first line of trees behind the beach. They snapped like matchsticks in the unequal confrontation with 3000 tonnes of moving steel. We rode on into the thicket like a gargantuan tank. Tree branches were crashing into portholes. We negotiated one more sand slope, then the combined effects of gravity and friction finally won through. We slowed, then stopped. A third of the ship was now inside the forest, the bow resting on a tangle of branches and leaves, a mossy thicket reaching to deck level with overhanging trees shading the bridge.

Most of the ship sat on the sand with a deep ditch recording the path of *Argonauta* out of the water. It was momentarily quiet, with the constant roar of the wind and the waves now distant. That respite was shattered by piercing Spanish shouting erupting all over the ship as crew ran in all directions like ants off a hotplate.

Alfonso burst out of the bridge door paralytic with rage, jumping up and down on the spot barely able to get his words out, shouting, breathing heavily and shouting some more. We gathered that this was not the spot he wished his ship to be parked. The Captain's gyrations on the bridge with the forest as backdrop added to the surrealism of the scene: gleaming white sand with glaciers beyond; southern beech forest reaching through portholes and the dancing, screaming, beetroot-faced captain looking more comical by the minute.

The ship was very nicely positioned quite upright, not listing but tilting upwards like it was mounting a wave that never moved. This attitude took some getting used to. The ditch that we had carved across the beach now filled with seawater enveloping the stern and the propeller.

The first officer, Julius Martin, who spoke by far the best English of the officers, had explained to us earlier what had been on the captain's mind. In these parts there were few sheltered bays and this one was ideal in a westerly gale, so Alfonso had decided to take refuge here until the storm passed. Going on was just wasting fuel, and at the rate of our progress under the current conditions, he had calculated we would run out of fuel long before reaching port. So he considered it preferable to stop in this little cove and give the strained engines a rest. But stopping in coves in this part of the world was not a matter of simply dropping anchor. The thick kelp beds that flourished at this southern latitude prevented anchors from taking hold so they were quite ineffective except for small craft. Instead it was standard practice for large vessels to use the beach as an anchor by running up the beach at low tide and re-floating at high tide.

Captain Adolfus had considered all this, considered the fuel situation, the food situation, the schedule, the weather forecast and the tide and he was a very experienced captain in these waters, with many successful beachings on his record. He knew the technique, the speed of entry, the tidal ranges of the bays the buoyancy of the boat and the strength of his engines to get us off when the high tide came in. He was good at this. That is where the explanation from Officer Julius ended. What had happened here?

I searched for an answer from the crew but none spoke. to me or the other passengers. I was sipping a drink at the bar when Julius took a seat next to me.

"This serious and bad blood," Julius said.

"Bad blood. What do you mean?" I asked.

"Best if you don't know this, but I want to tell you. Can you keep it?" Julius whispered furtively. I nodded. Julius then related the facts, in confidence.

"Gonzo, he flipped!" That was the explanation. Al's sister was an unhappy woman whose unhappiness grew the longer she was married to Gonzo. This was the Captain's sister no less and Gonzo was of course the ship's engineer. Alfonso and Gonzo were constantly arguing. What made Gonzo take that further leap we never found out. All we knew was that he saw his opportunity and took it. It is the job of ship's engineers in these parts to trim the ship, that is, to ensure the ballast is properly distributed. Weight shifts can destabilise a boat and make it stern heavy and bow light or vice versa. It is important to maximise a ship's stability in these storm-tossed waters. Gonzo was by all accounts a competent ship's engineer and was on top of this principle.

The ship's fresh water supply was a mobile form of ballast and could be directed to make trim adjustments. It was also an important part of the practice of ship beachings. You ran your ship up onto the beach at low tide so you would be sure of floating off again when the tide came in. But there was more to this. You also made sure that as you ran up onto the beach you had all your fresh water held in the bow tanks. This made the bow heavy and more likely to dig into the sand. When it was time to exit the beach the ship's engineer moved the water to stern holding tanks thereby making the stern heavier and lightening the bow. This greatly helped refloat the ship as it took the weight off that part of the hull sitting on the sand.

Gonzo did this in reverse and thereby stuck the knife into his captain who was responsible for his ship. Gonzo saw his moment and rerouted all the water to the stern. We arrived at the beach bow light and proceeded on through the countryside, stopping way too long and seemingly out of reach of the high tide. From Al's reaction I concluded that part of his rage was due to the fact that he knew Gonzo was behind this sabotage.

Latins are known to be fiery – emotional and demonstrative. But they don't stay dark for long. The smiles and the laughter return with the bitterness banished or at least under cover. This is of course a sweeping generalisation, but it did seem to apply to Alfonso. Mid-afternoon arrived. We had been parked for almost two hours. Now a jovial captain showed up at the bar.

"You go ashore," he said. "I get crew to man the boat and we collect mussels. Best in world here. Big barbeque around fire and have fun, fun, fun!"

"How's our ship? What's going to happen?"

"All OK, OK. You see. Big tide coming. We go in morning or night. You see."

Alfonso laughed, tipping his hat as he walked off. Was this the man who could scarcely breathe from rage two hours earlier?

The word was out: we were to go ashore and explore our little bay and the forest that lay around and beyond the bow. Our captain was turning this defeat into a victory of sorts by making it look part of a planned tourist 'event'. Boats were lowered, very efficiently I thought, as I presumed they were not used all that often. (How wrong that assumption proved to be.) The crew set up a shuttle for one boat of five passengers per trip, very quickly extended to three boats to cope with the demand as everyone wanted to set foot on the fabled island of Tierra del Fuego for the first time. By good fortune the beach was just inside Chilean territory. That was one less thing to worry about: no surprise gunboats showing up in the middle of the night. The passage to shore was brief – a mere 30 metres to the sandy beach. The beach and the rock pools on its margins were full of wonders, cold temperature corals, beautiful little shellfish, strange rock formations, sponges, vivid green mosses and lichens and a soft understorey to a magnificent beech forest behind the sand. The water was transparent and ice-cold. With a biting westerly wind blowing across the headlands, the weather wasn't exactly ideal for a beach barbie, but it was still sunny and we had four hours of exploring before our beach dinner at 8pm.

While the crew combed the shoreline for mussels, we passengers headed away from the beach, into the forest. Treading on the springy, spongy moss felt like floating on a brilliant green carpet. The vegetation gleamed in the sun, pristine, with a freshly washed look that comes from never having been touched by humans, never. Little birds hopped up to check us out, fearless birds observing just another animal of the forest.

We reached a rocky ridge which took us above the trees to an overwhelming view. Straight ahead was the terminus of an unnamed glacier spilling off the ice cap of the Darwin plateau towering 1000 metres above us and to the left was 20km of the narrow Beagle Channel hemmed in by massive sea cliffs. We could just see where the channel split into two, one to the north and the other bearing south around Isla Gordon. No one lived there. Further south, a pattern of forested islands quickly dissipated to open ocean south of Cape Horn, while to the north the Andes extended to the Magellan Straits. And at this latitude, 54 south, this was all the land there was on the planet. Past the western coast, 80km to the west, there was nothing but ocean. Moving towards the setting sun, all you would ever see was ocean until at last you would arrive back at this archipelago, the uttermost end of the earth, the well-known phrase that so aptly captures the feeling.

The light was fading as we returned. We picked our way between the trees until suddenly looming up ahead between two large Antarctic beech trees was the 12m-high prow of a ship. From the enchantment of our pristine wilderness walk, it was a shock to be suddenly confronted by *Argonauta* and the crew tossing the beech branches they had chopped down onto our campfire.

The wind was dying and stars appearing as we huddled next to the fire. The Captain had used the lifeboat shuttle service well in bringing ashore the ship's supply of good Chilean wine. The mussels were sizzling in the bowl as we nibbled on crackers and dips and downed the Semillon. This was the world's southernmost barbeque. Everyone was laughing. The ice cream arrived by shuttle boat fresh from the galley. It was sweet, cold and solid, its flavour enhanced by its location. Dessert wine followed and then hot coffee to end with more shuttle action. The captain seemed happy with the outcome of the misadventure and no one cared to ask him how he expected to leave. That would spoil a perfect night. Live for the moment, the South American way.

Walking along the beach that night, the stars blazed down out of a pure black sky with star patterns made strange by the latitude. The ghostly glacier gleamed in the starlight, which lit the jagged outline of the mountains. There was an aura of peace, remoteness. Strange to face the opposite direction and observe a ship on the beach.

My head was swimming from over-imbibing as I staggered back to my cabin to sleep. It was still dark when I was woken by grinding and thumping noises. They lasted a minute or two, followed by silence and then came again. I was becoming used to the life of this ship so the noises didn't seem out of place in a half-awake state, so I returned to dreamland.

The next morning *Argonauta* was still beached. There had been a high tide after midnight and Captain Adolfus had tried to back off, but the ship had not budged. I was with a group of Australian tourists booked to leave Punta Arenas by air for Santiago in two days. We requested that the Captain radio our situation and probable delay to our Punta Arenas travel agent so that alternative travel arrangements could be made if we looked like missing our flight.

"No, no. Be calm, Señor. There is no problem here. We have big, big tide today and we will be on our way. You see. It all OK. Everything sweet. We take you ashore for walk and early lunch, no?" The Captain sounded confident.

"Not good for Captain to say he delayed because we on land," Julius whispered. "Bad situation. Better for Captain to report delay because of engine malfunction in the channel. He doesn't want to radio ahead right now until he fixes this." Julius was in a serious mood. It seemed that the politics on board dictated that we should just go with the flow, or in this case, its absence.

All through the morning the water crept up the beach and flooded the ditch made by the ship on its arrival. Crew were on the beach with shovels, widening and deepening the channel, but after an hour of effort by several men, the channel looked the same. Water then wrapped itself around the boat and was lapping the vanguard row of trees at the back of the beach by lunchtime. The tide was truly a big one. It looked like it could go no further without inundating the forest. If this tide wasn't sufficient to float us off, we were indeed stranded.

That old familiar vibration started at 1pm as the ship's engines fired up. The propeller moved and foamed up the water. The vibrations became worse as Alfonso called for full power and the whole beach was now covered in a sheet of white foamy water. The ship did not budge.

“Chuta! Chuta!” (“Shit! Shit!”) Urgent cries from the bridge. Crew members race around the deck. The channel water froths into huge balls of billowing suds. The whole ship shudders like a drunk having a seizure. The engines rev and roar. The ship lurches slowly backwards. Suddenly it picks up speed and we shoot recklessly across the bay towards the rocks on the other side. Shouting. Screaming alarm bells. Crew running crazily around the deck, shouting, cursing. The rocks loom perilously close. As I steel myself for what seems an inevitable catastrophic crash, the bow magically turns and we are lined up with the entrance of the bay.

Relative peace returned aboard *Argonauta*. For the rest of the afternoon we made our way towards the western end of a narrowing channel with mountains encroaching on both sides. The crew resumed their normal duties; running the ship and looking after us. Those old familiar vibrations were back. Beer glasses hanging on hooks down on the bar shimmered as they swung back and forth. Stewards attempted to silence nervously rattling windows by stuffing window cracks with newspapers. Many of the ship’s doors couldn’t close, lights didn’t work, taps were stuck in the on position.

While our voyage was thrilling, the food became bland and monotonous, seemingly coming from the same giant stew pot but given different names for different nights. Irish stew became beef stockpot then braised beef and gravy, then beef soup. Now we understood the captain’s enthusiasm for fresh mussels.

Daily drinks and hors d’oeuvres were the saving grace. It was Frederick’s job to supply passengers from lunch time onwards with mini squares of hard cold toast served with Pisco sour cocktails. Pisco, an Andean alcoholic spirit, is mixed with egg white, lemon and sugar to make Pisco sour, a morish, gin-like cocktail popular throughout Chile, Peru and Ecuador.

After a while, we realised that this task wasn’t just Frederick’s duty; it was his *raison d’etre*. He saw to it that we were given our pisco sours regularly like medicine. The trouble was that it was very drinkable, too drinkable and one too many of these was easy to achieve by mid-afternoon with Frederick’s continuous supply. It was fun initially, but soon we resorted to hiding to avoid Frederick’s advances when we heard him coming. In a small ship this didn’t work out very well as he knew all the hiding places. It mattered not that he spoke little English, the tone of his Spanish was clear. When discovered, he wagged his finger seriously, his pleading voice exhorting us to stop trying to escape and take our mandatory medicine. His sad, hurt looks if we hesitated to down a dose forced us to comply. It was simply the courteous thing to do. There was no argument. We had to obey to change his doleful expression into a broad Latin smile of approval.

By day three I was getting desperate, and at the appointed hour my scouts gave word to me that Frederick was on patrol. I immediately dropped whatever I was doing. I had, after some investigation, found a great hidey-hole in the engine room, behind the boiler, away from the stairs. I didn’t have to wait long. A door swung open at the top of the steep and exposed ladder into the engine room from above. Into the entrance appeared Frederick, balancing his tray and scanning the scene. There was no escape, even here. He caught a movement. My shoe stuck out from behind the vent, and even from a distance, Frederick identified that it belonged to my foot.

"Roger, amigo!" he shouted above the roar of the engines and proceeded carefully down the ladder, one hand on the rail and the other balancing the tray like a circus performer. After such a show, I surrendered.

Apart from Frederick, the principle source of entertainment on board was the video cassette recorder, housed up in a small common room behind the bridge and Captain's quarters. More than 6 people in this room was a crowd so amongst the passengers we developed a roster. This didn't work because the crew would also pile in when a film was on and we had a crush of 12 or more at each film showing. VCRs seemed quite a novelty on board ships in the 1980s and they were a cheap form of entertainment since real television signals were hundreds of miles away at Punta Arenas and of course there was no shipboard entertainment program. It was a bit like a Prisoner of War camp where the inmates made their own amusements.

VCR choices included James Cagney in *White Heat*, John Wayne in *The Alamo*, the Marx brothers in *Duck Soup* and two local Chilean soap operas. I got excited when after rummaging through the dark reaches of the video cupboard on day three I unearthed *They Were Expendable* with Robert Montgomery, a title which was to have a prophetic ring to it. What made the filmgoing experience even more entertaining was that all but the Robert Montgomery epic were in Spanish and it became a source of debate to guess what the characters were saying.

"Aquí vienen!" said big John Wayne as the Mexican Army were at the ramparts.

"Ningún sir. Soy seguro que podemos sostener la barra de pudelar," replied Lawrence Harvey as the army colonel dismissed the threat.

"¿Usted no va a escuchar él es usted?" said Richard Widmark, playing Daniel Boone supporting his friend Davy Crocket. The crew laughed gleefully at anything that was said, no matter how dramatic it was onscreen.

John Wayne looked furious. He glared at the Army colonel and said, "No tomo órdenes de usted y usted es incorrecto. Olvídese de la muchacha."

We all agreed that this must mean something like, "Piss off, you boofhead. You know nothing about the strength of the Mexican Army, and I'll remind you also sir to keep your hands off Rita Hayworth."

The colonel looked out at the scene from the roof of the Fort and turned to Crocket slowly, "I can't piss off. We're surrounded." I asked the crew what they were saying, but got no help. They were doubled up with laughter.

We discussed what might be the actual words and I resolved to get hold of the English version of this film if we ever got out of the Beagle Channel. It was appropriate this was in Spanish with the whole Mexican Army starring in the film.

The next morning Captain Adolfus took a side excursion up an inlet to the north, part of the glacial valley from the ice cap and Mt Italia at over 7000 ft.

This was on the itinerary and even though we were running late we didn't want to miss out. As the sound narrowed towards its end, a giant glacier from somewhere above the low morning cloud base peeled off office-building-sized chunks of ice which tumbled with a roar into the sea. I could feel the vibrations in my feet as every so often a great white mass rumbled and tumbled down the sheer rock face at the head of the sound and crashed into the water with a gigantic splash, sending out 2-metre-high waves towards us. It was grey and cold. There were icebergs all over the sound and these increased in size and number the closer we edged to its head. The biggest of the nearby bergs reached to the bridge of the ship. Considering too that only about a tenth of icebergs are visible above water, it really was huge.

We spent about an hour drifting around. Then the Captain spotted the iceberg he wanted. Our group was lined up near the bow on the deck in front of the bridge.

"Look, look, big one!" shouted Alfonso, his body convulsing with excitement as he pointed to a mountainous berg as big as the ship looming up ahead. "You know Titanic! Ha, Ha! Watch out amigos!"

Bells clanged urgently, the ship pulsed feverishly as the engine vibrations returned, accompanied every few minutes by glacial vibrations. We picked up speed as we closed in on the big berg.

"This easy, no worries mate. You like a lot!" Alfonso guffawed. He then returned to his bridge duties, ensuring a well-executed collision, as any ship's captain would do.

We hit the berg on a sloping surface, doing about five knots. Immediately the whole ship rode up, repeating its attitude on the beach. As the grade on the iceberg's surface steepened, we abruptly stopped our forward progress and slid back into the water. Alfonso burst out of the bridge, jumping up an down with excitement.

"You like? Again please, yes, ha–ha!" The bell rang out again as he shouted more orders to the helmsman. Once more our vibrating ship lurched forward. This time it hit the ice at an angle to the slope. The ship rode up imperiously as the berg slipped under the ship.

Argonauta came to an abrupt stop and listed to port. The front half of the ship did a spectacular sideslip back into the sea with a great white wave erupting from under our port bow as we crashed back into the water.

During this manoeuvre shrill scraping sounds reverberated from the hull and below decks came the cacophony of flinging furniture and breaking glass. The ship's engine stopped as a battered *Argonauta* righted itself in the water.

Suddenly all was silent, save for the rumble from the glacier. Huge scrape marks appeared on the iceberg's surface as we now drifted away from it back on an even keel. Alfonso had delivered a very *Titanic*-like show, complete with the silence of the post-collision stopped engines. I feared that we were well away from the busy North Atlantic sea lanes where an equivalent to *Carpathia*, *Titanic's* rescue ship, could pick us up.

Now noise started coming from the davits holding the lifeboats. I turned around to see a lifeboat being lowered in a surprisingly efficient fashion. How much of the re-enactment was our glorious captain going to perform for us? Near the water the lowering stopped and the ship's cargo door opened. Out strode three crew members equipped with a chain saw, an axe and a bucket of tools. This wasn't in the *Titanic* script, no matter which film version I had seen.

With the crew safely aboard, the lifeboat settled into the water. They disconnected themselves from the lines and rowed away. So was it crew first and not the women and children? I liked the improvisation. The true purpose then became clear. They were rowing towards the iceberg.

Once alongside the berg, they roped up. The axe was passed out and crewman number one jumped onto a level platform and started to hack at a thin section of ice. The chainsaw was then applied but looked puny on the massive scale of the ice. Its irritating whining echoed back from the rock walls of the cove. What were they up to?

After several minutes, they stopped and carefully slid back into the boat, made fast to the ice. Before leaving, a crewman left a red mark where he had made his token incision. They rowed away from the iceberg. About 300 metres away they stopped. Silence. We waited.

Suddenly huge chunks of ice exploded into the air, rocketing off in all directions. The thunder reverberated off the cliffs, back and forth, back and forth as clouds enveloped the berg.

When they cleared, we could see a large ball of ice had separated from the main iceberg and was starting to float away. The crew then rowed back and began to secure the ball with lines. The ship's engines started and we inched towards the activity.

Alfonso's purpose was clear. He was 'capturing' the iceberg for us. Crew entered the control room for the forward crane. Its long arm moved across the foc'sle, extending over the water near the lifeboat. A hook was lowered and after some testing to see if the ice could be better secured, it was attached to the lines around the berg. The crane motor went under load as the crane took the strain.

The whole ship started listing to port as the crane started to lift. The crane cable was moving. The ice moved upwards and much more of it became visible. It was as big as a truck. The crew had done well.

The ropes held. The crane swung the ice across the railing and then inboard with the ship correcting its list. The ice was then slowly lowered onto the deck. As it thumped onto the steel, the Captain emerged from the bridge shrieking with glee.

Then came the big moment. Frederick appeared on the 'ice' deck with some bar tools, a martini ice pick, a chisel, a small hammer and a champagne bucket. Spontaneous cheers rang out from passengers and crew. Conscious of his audience, Frederick bowed graciously.

The pisco sour patrol started as usual right after lunch. This time Frederick didn't have to find any of us. He made an entrance in the lounge room around 2pm where we had gathered awaiting his offerings. They were the usual trays of cocktails, but this time shards of 10,000-year-old glacial ice had been added. Frederick stood proud. His smile was broader than ever.

"Señor Roger," he said. "You find me, I no find you." It was his great day.

In the long evening light we made our way out of the Beagle and were into the broader Ballenero channel which led directly to the Pacific and our turn to starboard up the coast to the Magellan Straits. The scenery was superb with the weather now becoming more settled and blue sky up ahead. After the day's events, we passengers were ebullient. Now for that warm shower before dinner. Not so. The showers no longer worked. The taps didn't work. There was no water anywhere, except in the galley. Even the broken taps that always dripped were dry. Our overworked crew was notified and a high level pre-dinner meeting was convened in the lounge.

"The Captain sends his personal apology for this situation," Julius grimaced. "The ship's owners have not given us the new tanks we have asked for so we have little supply as the old ones are small. So sorry. I can give you a little more water now."

"But Julius, what about later? What about tomorrow?"

"It has taken a long time to get to Punta, so more water needed than usual. A problem, eh?"

"But what happens after this last bit goes?"

"Ha, ha!" Julius beamed as if looking forward to getting that question. "No worries," he said, echoing his captain. "For our Captain this is no problem. He can fix it."

"But how?"

"You see, it will be fixed by morning, you see. See Captain tomorrow to explain, not now. I have to go. The Captain and I are sorry. Thank you ladies and gentlemen." Julius nodded to all the assembled passengers as he departed.

The shortness of water was overcome to some extent by the abundance of alcohol that evening. I fantasised about having a champagne shower but it would be too cold. We did get back some water. After dinner, the chief source of entertainment was musing over what 'fixing it' really meant.

I awoke at about 2am with a roaring sound coming from my porthole. I lay there for a while not wanting to get up, but the sound was getting louder. I climbed down the ladder from my top bunk and looked out through the glass. All I could see was rock. Curious, I opened the porthole a little. Heavy spray hit my face.

My door opened. In rushed my excited cabin mate.

"Come up on deck, quick! You gotta see this, you just gotta!"

I dashed up to the foredeck. I couldn't comprehend the sight that met my eyes.

In the dark I could make out that the ship was lashed to a steeply sloping rock face. There were crew racing around the deck with hoses and rope. A large plank bridged the gap between the ship and the rock face. People were scurrying about on the rocks next to the ship and high up, perhaps 100 metres up near the tree line.

"Look out!" I moved by instinct towards the door in time to miss a solid stream of rapidly moving water, hitting the deck with tremendous force. It came from the sky not the sea. And it was fresh. The deck was awash. Heavy deck gear was being flung around as if they were mere floating cardboard cartons. The rock face was lit dimly by a fading moon and by torchlight. As my eyes adjusted to the light, I could see that the rock face was part of an extensive waterfall system. Its main force shifted with the breeze and every so often it hit the deck of *Argonauta*, falling from hundreds of metres above us.

It was a dangerous place to be. Crew were in peril as they scrambled onto the wet rock. There were about 10 of them holding ropes and hoses. Several crew also had bottles of water under their arms to prime the siphon. With no free hands they were skilfully keeping their balance on a slippery, sloping surface. I couldn't see any safety ropes and a slip could cause a fall all the way down to the water where they might be crushed between rock and ship.

One crew member with thick horn-rimmed spectacles was negotiating the narrow wooded plank used to connect the ship with the rock face. The plank moved constantly as the ship shifted on its lines. Crew walking the plank, into a waterfall, at 2am, in the dark, was beyond my imaginings – just another 'event' not listed in our voyage description document.

The ship jumped forward. Thumping and scraping as the hull made contact with the rock face. The clinking and dinging of glass breaking below decks.

Alfonso had found his water.

"Captain's best water spot. Crew get water," explained the officer in charge of the operation. He sucked in his cheeks, mimicking the motion of someone siphoning water through a tube.

"You see." He pointed to the tangle of hoses on the deck, then towards some open hatches. "To tanks."

A gust of wind whipped the waterfall back. Like a giant hand it punched some unsecured deck chairs, flinging them across to the railing and then washing them through the open hatches.

"I think they may get more water from the sky than from the hose," I shouted above the roar, pointing towards the hatches.

"Very good," smiled the officer. He looked pleased. About the only loose object on the deck that wasn't being moved around was the ice, now melting fast.

Above me I could see the outlines of several crew as they moved around with their hoses to siphon the best pools. One crew member slipped into the whirlpool and was hauled back. It was a hard job, one hand holding a rope, the other a hose and no hands to hold on. I could make out that the rope was used to tie the hose into position.

We moved inside in case another few tonnes of fresh ice might come our way.

"Absolute craziness." My cabin mate was astounded.

"But the captain was right," I said. "He's fixing it."

As the sun rose on day 4, ship life returned to normal once again. The water was back, showers were on, breakfast was being served and the engine was vibrating as usual. The decks looked very clean and fresh that morning, and quite uncluttered. There seemed to be fewer deck chairs about than before, however.

It was a glorious day. Not a cloud in the sky. We were in a broad sound with open sea up ahead. Terra del Fuego's highest peak, Sarmiento, was visible to the north east, rising above a gleaming white ice cap. Mountainous islands towered around us. For once everything was proceeding normally. The Captain strutted the bridge, the officers smiled at us and Frederick's appearance after lunch was on cue with more supplies from the melting chunk of glacier.

We rounded Peninsula Brecknock and approached the Cockburn Channel as the sun was setting on a dead calm sea. The day was full of great vistas with seals, dolphins and albatross to see us pass through these wonderful waterways, stark and clean in their extreme isolation.

The plan was to arrive at Punta Arenas by lunch time the next day, leaving about two hours before our flight to Santiago departed the local airport. The Captain gave his assurances that this could be done. I could not doubt his sincerity. But by what method this might be achieved I could not guess as we were seriously behind time.

It was about 8am on day five when the bells started sounding. The vibrations had worsened and were moving the salt and pepper shakers across the breakfast table and causing ripples on the surface of my cup of tea. I was crunching into my toast, not worrying about the bells which I thought probably signalled some new crisis that our Captain would somehow manage like he always did. The bells continued and Julius entered the dining room looking serious.

"You must finish up here now. We are preparing to leave."

"Leave where?"

"Leave here."

"Go where? I'm having a piece of toast."

"Leave in the boats."

"What boats?"

"Our boats. They are being lowered down right now. See." He pointed to the window.

"Can you go to your cabin please? Collect your things." Julius frowned.

"Where are we going?"

"Over there." Julius pointed to the northern shoreline.

"Why there? I was a little annoyed as my toast was getting cold.

"Better there than here." Julius hurried out.

Just then my cabin mate came over after talking with another officer.

"He's right. We are abandoning ship. Let's pack up. Don't worry about breakfast. It's time we had a change anyhow."

Argonauta's overused lifeboats were seeing action again. They had been given a workout on this voyage, not like other ships where these boats just get to sit on their cradles forever. Searching for an explanation, I sought out Julius. He gestured hopelessness with his hands the way Latin people do so well.

"The engine, too much work. It is old. It is kaput."

I moved to shake his hand to thank him for his help. He gave me a weak and brief apologetic handshake.

"Best you go now. Buses await. You get to Punta before us now."

I then understood the strategy. From near Cape Froward, the southernmost point on the South American mainland a road parallels the Magellan Strait from Puerto Bulnes all the way into Punta Arenas. Alfonso must have figured that his sick ship could not make the schedule he promised us. Maybe he had known this all along since the beaching. His poor struggling engines already strained from getting off the beach were being strained again. His brother-in-law may have told him this was not sustainable, that is, if they were actually talking to one another. The buses could travel much faster than poor *Argonauta* ever could and we would then get into Punta at the agreed time. I imagine this was his best solution. Alfonso wouldn't contemplate losing face again.

I got my things together quickly and made my way down to a lower deck where the cargo door was opened and a lifeboat docked. Two lifeboats would shuttle all 59 passengers to shore. That was the theory.

I stepped into the lifeboat and left *Argonauta* for the last time with a sense of sadness. As we pulled away, I looked up at the Captain on the bridge deck. He sadly waved us goodbye. All of us in the boat waved back. One person stood up and saluted.

The helmsman turned the bow towards the northern shore near Capo Froward, the southern tip of mainland South America. We didn't get far. The outboard conked out halfway to shore with the buses visible and waiting for us. A crewmember started to poke the motor with a screwdriver. I thought about more photographs but my camera was out of reach. Then I realised abandoning ship might not look good on a promotional brochure.

Slowly we were drifting back to the ship. We dropped anchor to arrest our drift. We had no oars on board. A third boat was now being lowered from the ship as the second boat came alongside. We transferred to that, out of a sick lifeboat from a sick ship. Finally we were shore bound.

The mud flats extended out 100 metres or more from the shore at low tide. It was now low tide. The lifeboat slid into the mud, ending all forward progress. We disembarked into a muddy soup up to our knees. It sucked at our shoes as they sank at every laboured step as we attempted to walk with all our bags. Sometimes the mud won and the shoe stayed in the muddy hole while we navigated our next steps. Going back to retrieve shoes was difficult but had to be done quickly before the mud closed over the entrance, leaving no indication of where we should dig for them. I managed to keep my shoes to the end as the mud firmed up closer to shore.

Then came the last challenge. It was a swiftly flowing and deep stream between the mudflat and shore. It looked well beyond knee depth as the bottom was out of sight in the clear water.

Hooking my bags over my shoulder with one hand I launched forth with the other and waded into the icy water only, 10 metres wide. Halfway across, I could see a narrow but deep channel ahead, perhaps a metre wide. This was it, the last barrier to the finish line. Just knowing that was enough. I pushed on, and as the water deepened, I pushed with my free arm and kicked with my legs. My bags lifted off my back and floated along with me in my short swim in the Magellan Straits. The initial spurt was enough to take me over and my legs hit the shoreline of mainland South America.

Soon all us passengers had made it to dry ground. The rats of *Argonauta* had landed. Cold and wet and chilled further by the wind, we squelched over two fences and a long grassy field to make the road and our two waiting buses. I was a sodden, dripping, muddy mess. The bus drivers laughed at us but were ready with blankets, fresh white napkins, scones and thermoses of hot coffee.

I was one of the lucky ones. Other passengers had lost their shoes forever and had bags that couldn't float. When booking an *Argonauta* voyage, passengers should be advised to take on board only bags that float. Looking back, the deserted *Argonauta* was now making slow progress in the main channel with all lifeboats back to their davits. No doubt Gonzo was nursing his engines again as the ship vibrated its way north up the Straits.

The transfer to the buses took about 90 minutes. I don't suppose Alfonso figured on that but then there was little that was predictable on this voyage, our unforgettable voyage on *Argonauta*. The bus drivers drove up the highway, north to Punta at a speed we were unaccustomed to. I looked back at a very lonely-looking vessel out in the main channel. I felt we had been with her for a long time, not the four days of real time. Julius, Gonzo, Frederick and Adolfus Alfonso were back there and we were now not with them.

We missed our flight by 30 minutes. The aircraft was taking off as we approached the terminal. After furious negotiations, we got onto a flight the next day. The pilot remarked that was the only day in a year that the weather and the view over the entire Patagonian Ice Cap en route to Santiago was completely clear. Perhaps our remarkable *Argonauta* Captain could take the credit for that too.

Amazon Botanical Gardens –Filmmaker

After my *Argonauta* interlude, I headed off alone up to Lima, Peru, with no plans except to get into the mountains, the cradle of Incan culture. But it was a dangerous time with a coup d'etat in the air in Lima and the communist Shining Path terrorising the countryside, shutting off much ground access to the Andes.

Wandering the streets of Lima I had to be on my guard. At any moment troops and water cannons might show up in pursuit of protestors. One day my fears were realised. The street suddenly cleared of people. I was confronting an approaching water cannon on my own. Arms waved out of shop windows attracting my attention and beckoning me to run out of the street, out of danger. I dived through an open window, into a shop and then out the other side into an internal shopping mall sealed off from the street, thrust magically back into the seemingly harmonious environment of a modern western shopping mall where shoppers went happily about their business, worlds away from the street dramas beyond the shutters.

But Lima was not why I was here. The Andes were but an hour's flight away. So I travelled out to the airport and bought a ticket to Cusco, the ancient Inca capital.

The ageing DC8 of Fawcett Airways touched down at the 3200m altitude of Cusco Airport where I was greeted with a cup of coca tea to help combat altitude sickness. The city looked every bit an old capital with its Spanish influence married to the local Quechuan culture and architecture. Quechuan women in their bowler hats, long black plaits and colourful voluminous skirts walked through narrow stone alleyways selling alpaca socks, mittens and hats.

There were so many things to see in Cusco and the nearby Sacred Valley of the Incas. I also walked the Inca Trail to the iconic 15th century Inca citadel, Machu Picchu. Beyond this, my aim was to reach a place I had dreamt about for years, the world's highest navigable lake, Lake Titicaca. So after many days exploring the Cusco region, I boarded the train to Puno, the main Peruvian port for the lake.

Patrolled by Peru's navy on its western shores and the Bolivian navy in the east, immense Lake Titicaca has headlands, lighthouses, islands and even international shipping all perched four kilometres above true sea level. After visiting the famous floating Uros reed islands, I decided to submerge myself in Quechuan culture for a few days by staying with a family on the island of Taquile, one of the jewels of the lake, a 4-hour, 45km ferry trip from Puno.

This is a glorious part of the world. The colours of the lake are an ethereal iridescent blue, perfectly reflecting the snow-capped peaks of the Bolivian

Cordillera Real. The water sparkles in the strong sunlight. The air seems crystal-clear due to the clean, thin, high-altitude atmosphere where the ultraviolet in the sunlight has not been filtered out.

I stayed several days with a local Quechuan family, sharing their simple, agricultural lifestyle, with no electricity, no cars. I watched the women spinning wool and weaving yarn while the men knitted colourful, pom-pom-tipped hats. At night I bedded down in a candlelit thatched hut. Outside, the coastal lighthouses flashed their warning, and the lake breezes were frigid due to the extreme altitude.

On the return trip back to Puno, the overloaded ferry was taking on water and threatening to swamp the engine. All the passengers on deck, obviously used to this condition, ran a bucket brigade bailing out the bilge water that kept the water level below the boat's engines and vulnerable electrics. During the bailing, I struck up a conversation with an American woman, Helen Anderson, who was interested in my Australian accent. I talked about my ideas for making audio-visuals as an evocative medium for conveying impressions about a place, an inevitable subject considering the beauty that was all around us on this sea voyage. When I mentioned my experiences on *Argonauta* and how I was producing a promotional audio-visual presentation, she was very interested.

"I'll tell you what," Helen said. "I run an eco-tourist lodge just downstream from Iquitos on the Amazon. It's called Amazon Botanical Gardens. I'm just getting it up and running now and need to start marketing it to tourists in the US. I'm really interested in your concept which fits in perfectly with what I want to promote. So when you get home, can you send me a copy of your film? If I like it I may commission you to make a film for us."

Momentarily lost for words I beamed back at Helen unable to hide my excitement. "Wow! Yes! Of course I'll do it!"

"Good." Helen held out her hand. "This is a handshake agreement. Wish I had some champagne to go with it but bottles explode at this altitude."

On my return to Australia, I completed my promotional work for the tour operators of the South American and *Argonauta* trips, which was well-received. I sent a copy to Helen. Weeks went by, and even accounting for the slow postal service between Australia and Peru, it looked like nothing was going to come back from the Amazon. Maybe it wasn't what she was after, maybe she didn't run an eco lodge in the rainforest like she said. Perhaps the story was too good, too perfect for it to ring true. But months later, her approval for my Amazon Botanical Gardens promotion finally came through.

After a long flight via Auckland, Buenos Aires and Lima, made even longer by extensive flight delays due to rainstorms and poor visibility, I finally arrived in Iquitos, on the Peruvian Amazon, in the middle of a tropical thunderstorm. It was a relief to be greeted at the airport by Helen's partner and co-owner of the resort, Bernal.

"It's too late to go down river today," Bernal explained, "so we'll stay at our place in Iquitos overnight. Helen is at Amazon Botanical Gardens and looking forward to seeing you."

Morning arrived on the Amazon. From the city docks, I looked across to the river's far bank, kilometres away – only to be told it wasn't the far bank but a river island, barely a third of the way across. Already looking like a vast inland sea, it was amazing to think that this mighty river, some 6500km long and the biggest by volume in the world by far, had its massive mouth still 3600km downstream.

Surrounded by rainforest and mighty rivers, Iquitos is the world's biggest city inaccessible by road. The morning light gave the river a serene feel, as the calm, cool air turned it into a mirror. We launched after an early riverside breakfast of bananas and jackfruit. Once away from the banks, the strong current took over and swept us downstream. Soon, we rounded a bend and the city passed from sight with the riverbanks taken over with cultivated paddocks growing yams and tapioca.

The river widened downstream so that the opposite bank was almost over the horizon. It was really a moving inland sea, not just a river flowing eastward to the Atlantic Ocean on the opposite side of the South American continent from where we were. We passed many native villages, each with their forest of TV aerials atop bamboo thatched huts, still within range of the Iquitos transmitter.

After three hours on the water and 80 km from the city, a collection of wooden and bamboo buildings appeared on a hillside above the left bank. As we approached the ABG wharf, there was Helen waving to us.

"Hello, Helen, this is amazing! You've really built all this?"

"Yes we did. It's a very long story but there's time to go through that later. You need to settle in, and get a feel for how you would like to do the filming."

So her wonderful Amazonian rainforest sanctuary really did exist. I took it all in that afternoon. The large main building housing the dining and entertaining area was surrounded by a collection of thatched-roofed, bamboo accommodation huts with elevated, rickety bamboo bridges connecting each to the main building. The rainforest impinged on everything, with only the roofs of the buildings visible above the green canopy. Fronting each building were lush lawns and the mighty Amazon.

In their search for a site for their eco-lodge, Helen and Bernal decided that this hill, the only high ground on the river bank from Iquitos, and its surrounds was the place for their vision. They imagined an eco-resort where tourists could come to learn about the Amazon and the wonder of the largest rain forest on earth and the need to preserve it, so they could then spread that conservation message back home. They spent over a year getting the Peruvian Government's approval for the development, and even longer developing trust with the local Indians and recruiting builders from local villages to construct the resort, all from local materials. That trust was both hard won and hard to maintain. In the villages there was always an element of mistrust about foreigners, especially ones who lived there.

After many months organising the local labour force and going through all the government bureaucratic hoops, the resort started to take shape. It took a great deal of supervision – and all of Helen's and Bernal's savings – to ensure all the buildings were constructed well, beyond the standard that the local builders were used to. A year passed before it was ready to take guests.

I settled in on my first Amazonian night. It was an eventful one as a violent thunderstorm raged all night. Sleep was impossible. The storm slunk away at dawn as if reacting to the new light from the east. The sun rose on a sodden scene.

Feeling more jetlagged than ever, I sat down at the breakfast table with Helen and Bernal and a couple of guests from Philadelphia. Some hungry creature was nibbling on my toes! Looking under the table, I eyeballed a gorgeous, tawny-coloured animal, like a giant cat, with velvety fur patterned with black, leopard-like spots. A baby ocelot!

"That's Tiger," said Helen. "He's very playful, but if he gets too boisterous for you, we'll put him out."

Foot gnawing and massaging was an unusual breakfast accompaniment but I happily assured my hosts: "This is his domain. Let him be – unless he decides to make my toes the main course."

The parrots were screeching, enjoying the rain-sodden plants drying out with the heat of the rising sun. We shouted across the breakfast table, just to make ourselves heard. "Just like Australia," I laughed, "but at least your birds don't dive-bomb your brekkie like our kookaburras. Never get between a kookaburra and a sausage, they say."

"Turn around and you won't think it's Australia," Bernal said gleefully. Ambling up the path from the river behind me was a hairy sloth, slowly swaying back and forth. "This is a rare sight. He must have known you were coming," said Bernal. My camera always at the ready was by my side and I took several shots of the dawdling, round-faced animal. It must have suddenly realised there were humans up ahead, as it dived towards the nearest tree for cover and disappeared into the jungle.

Helen smiled broadly and pointed to my camera. "I want you to get familiar with the Gardens and the local area quickly, like the wildlife, so you can get an idea about your subjects for filming, which we'll discuss later. So William here will be your guide for the next few days."

William appeared out of the shadows of the nearby jungle and nodded towards me. He was a short, native Indian from one of the local villages who spoke the odd English word but whose sign language was very clear.

I spent an unforgettable week with William. He took me on native paths through the darkest rainforest to another giant river to the north, the Napo. We kayaked the river at sunset with pink dolphins cavorting around us, illuminated by a blood sun setting behind the gathering clouds. We took the runabout out on the river at night to fish for nocturnal species and look into the eyes of cayman with nature's light show beyond, a ring of distant thunderstorms with lightning flashes reflecting off the river and the glow from phosphorescent trees glinting in the pools.

We visited villages and met the locals and shared their food. We saw native cats, anacondas, monkeys and all sorts of giant insects including the notorious fire ants. I tried to capture the life of the villages and their activities at work and at play. Kids played in the mud, women were busy washing and cleaning and the men were out hunting or trading. We visited minute clearings in the forest no tourist had ever penetrated. The people were curious and gentle and some still used poison darts for hunting.

One hot morning William pointed me towards the local creek where a number of native boys were swimming. "You swim here, with boys." I was glad for the opportunity to cool off, but as I was about to plunge in, I noticed swarms of small fish swimming with the boys. I pointed to them.

"Piranha, but you OK. Be quiet," were William's reassuring words.

Against my better judgment, I very gently slid down the mud bank and into the water. I was now swimming with upwards of 100 piranha. I stayed quiet, very quiet, no sudden movements. The Piranha got the message and they were quiet too, swimming around me and between my legs, gently brushing against my skin. A myth blown like the other one, which said you never pee into the Amazon because vampire fish – candiru – swim up the stream of urine into a man's penis and nibble away at your genitals with their barbs. Ouch! I was very glad that was just a myth. But I felt sure that, had I frothed up the water and made lots of sudden movements, I would have found out very quickly that the piranha's fearsome reputation was not a myth at all.

Now that I was resident in my own hut some of the shy local animals became quite friendly with me. Apart from Tiger, the baby ocelot that chewed my toes at breakfast each morning, I now had a pet capybara – the world's largest rodent – named George. George was a very solid rat, about 1m tall and weighing in at around 60kg. He seemed more like a dog than a rat, and he loved to play Fetch. No ball throw was too difficult for George to retrieve. Even when I threw it into a pond inhabited with those man-eating piranha, George dived in without hesitation and managed to emerge unscathed, ball in his mouth.

At night the volume of rainforest life turned up several notches. The insects buzzed more loudly, especially the mosquitoes, the birds called more musically, the frogs croaked in a great chorus, and then there was the accompaniment of tree branches snapping and animals snorting as they made their way through the darkness.

As well as the cluster of huts surrounding the large dining and entertainment building, there was the gazebo on the hill. I walked up there regularly in the early morning. It was on the only hill which was tall enough to puncture the continuous canopy of vegetation and was the only true lookout on the river. From the hill, the river's gigantic size became clear with a 20km view up and down the river. At sunrise the faint mist hanging over the water signalled cooler air. From the gazebo I sat and simply watched the scene for long periods. Tramp streamers making their way up river hugged the shoreline where the current was less. Ships heading downstream stayed in the middle of the channel. Always in the background was the steady drone of millions of insects.

There was so much to film at ABG, I soon ran out of the precious Ektachrome. Luckily big city Iquitos held stocks in camera shops, so several packets were put on a barge that shuttled between the city and ABG.

After a couple of weeks, I had accumulated a mountain of still pictures and worked out a storyline for Helen. There were no facilities for post-production there, so we agreed I could travel to the US to do that work since that was where the film would be used for marketing. But we still needed footage of ABG guests arriving and enjoying themselves to market the resort aspect of the place. Four Americans were due to arrive during the week, so I waited for their imminent arrival to include them in the film.

We got word they were on the boat coming down river and I set up my camera near the wharf. The boat's skipper made a meal of the initial docking, bouncing off the wharf and then heading down-river with the current. He tried again and again, each time missing the wharf and suggesting to the worried passengers they could jump across the gap as he motored by the wharf. This would not look good on a promotional film.

Helen was getting increasingly angry. "Estas borracho, idiota!" she bellowed and shook her fist. This seemed to have a positive effect on the skipper, who then made a perfect approach to the wharf, secured the boat and assisted the passengers in disembarking. The passengers were smiling too, as instructed. A day's shooting with the guests finished off the material I needed. Titles, music, sound effects and voiceover script were then worked out. I had brought along a small reel-to-reel tape-recorder so I could record the wildlife and sounds of the resort for the soundtrack.

A month had passed. ABG seemed like home, and I hated to think of leaving it. I would miss my daily morning routine of rising before dawn, taking a cold shower to wash away the sweat from the previous hot and steamy night, trekking up to the gazebo on the hill and drinking in that fabulous Amazon view, returning for a ball game with the capybara and breakfasting on bananas, guavas and camu fruit while the ocelot chewed at my toes.

Inevitably the day came when I had to say good bye. It was quite a ceremony. All the cooks, cleaners, gardeners and handymen lined up to farewell me and of course William was there as well. Then there was Tiger to fondle having chewed my toes for the last time and the Capybara to hug and throw the ball for. The giant rat retrieved the ball skilfully and returned it with a pleased look on its rodent face. Everyone laughed. Helen positioned herself to be the last to say good bye before I jumped onto the boat.

The underpowered vessel struggled against the might of the current, and many hours passed before the buildings of the city appeared upstream in the distance. The clapped-out old DC8 wings flapped alarmingly as my plane took off from Iquitos in a thunderstorm and headed west towards the desert and the Pacific. And the next afternoon I was in the US, so far away from the simplicity and poetry of Amazonian life.

The finished film got quite a lot of US media exposure and did what it was designed to do, boost tourist numbers to Amazon Botanical Gardens. I was so pleased. Was this going to be my career?

The place was making a profit, and Helen's great vision had been realised. That feeling of fulfilment was added to when 46-year-old Helen, who had no children, discovered she was seven months pregnant – certainly a welcome surprise to find out that her swollen belly was not caused by stomach cancer! The next challenge was giving birth and having a new baby in such an isolated setting, with the nearest hospital being four hours-plus away by boat.

Early one Amazonian morning, with the equatorial sun just peeping above the trees and her baby daughter sleeping in her cot, Helen heard the distant shouting of a large group of Indians. The shouting came closer. The anger of the crowd as they approached alarmed Helen, Bernal and the guests. Helen grabbed her baby and ran up the hill to the gazebo with Bernal and guests close behind. A large mob of Indians wielding weapons entered the front lawn. ABG was overrun and torched, and in an hour was a smoking ruin, fuelled by the jealousies harboured by the elders in the villages and their envy of ABG's success.

Thunder on the Ohio – "One-Off" Mid-West TV Presenter

From the Amazon, I travelled to Evansville, Indiana, a small and pleasant mid-western US city on the Ohio River. It boasts a large cultural centre, art gallery and museum as proof the town has class, in fact several classes: a 'cultured' moneyed white aristocracy, a business class and the parallel poor white and black classes. I was there because my girlfriend at the time worked as the art curator of the Evansville Museum of Arts, History and Science. The place had several TV stations with studio facilities such as WEVV-TV where I purchased studio time to put together the ABG audio-visual at broadcast quality. The visuals and soundtrack needed a professional voiceover and the TV station asked one of their presenters to do the job. Her name was Helen too and she provided much more than just a good voice.

"Roger, I like your sounds of the jungle and your Latin music but I think you need a few more special effects with your storms. How does this sound?"

Helen signalled to a technician in the control room and suddenly the sound proved room was full of thunder, big booming rolling thunder befitting an Amazon storm.

"That's what you need to get some drama into the scene. And how about this?" Helen signalled again. The room filled with the crowing of Macaws and rainforest parrots followed by the sound of heavy rain hitting the broad-leafed canopy. I was very pleased.

"Say, Roger," Helen added, "we don't get too many Aussie voices in this neck of the woods. I think it would create some interest if you would be so kind to do us a favour."

"Sure, after all your help. What would you like?"

"Well, we have Thunder on the Ohio – a power boat race on the river – this weekend. Can you be our second presenter? You don't have to know much. You can just say things like, we'd go to the kangaroo races or crocodile wrestling before ever seeing a power boat race."

"Kangaroos don't race but I get the idea. I'll try to say all the right things about how great the event is."

"Good, you've got it. It's not so much about what you say, but your funny accent. People would love to hear it which shows up how international the event is."

Helen was pleased and I had a new job.

Saturday dawned and I fronted up to the Evansville shoreline near the Museum where the TV OB vans were parked. The folk from WEVV descended upon me.

"Good, you're here. Now inside the van to prep and be briefed."

I learnt that this event was big with millions of dollars of high-powered boats on display, hundreds of thousands of spectators plus TV ratings and sponsors. I was nervous.

"Just be natural, Roger. Just comment as you would naturally. You know, say things like 'Jeez, this is great mate', just like in *Crocodile Dundee*."

I could feel the vibrations coming through my shoes. The ground seemed to move as the big boats started up pushing ocean-sized waves towards the Indiana shore. There were crowds, there were helicopters but above all there was noise and the spectators thrilled to the thunder, the power, the spectacle. I was out on the shoreline standing just behind the presenter as I was told to do with cameras pointing to us both.

"It looks like it's between Ohio Power and Southern Power." The presenter was having trouble identifying the boats amid the huge columns of spray being propelled skywards by the seriously overpowered vessels. "Wow, we have a race on our hands now. Let's get an Aussie's take on all this."

Without warning the cameras swung onto me. I sparked into action. "Bloody beauty mate. Nothing like this down under mate! What a huge spectacle!"

"Not like your kangaroo races eh?"

"No mate. Our shielas would say give us the power boats, not the bloody roos." I could imagine Crocodile Dundee saying just that.

An incident in the race caused the presenter to continue the call. A few more similar comments saw the day out for me with the whole show repeated for the finals the next day. The producer told me the feedback was great.

"It was the right call to get you on the show. Everyone loves an Aussie accent, mate."

Too bloody right.

Assisting Enlightenment – Self Development Course Supporter

Girlfriends came with a set of beliefs and outlooks not apparent at first meeting, and often not for weeks or even months. In the early '80s I had such a girlfriend who, a year down the track, started a process of self-development, responding to the "Is that all there is?" paradigm about life. Courses that facilitated this proliferated in that decade. With a few of these courses under her belt, her higher self was telling me I needed to catch up or be left behind in my state of unawareness and spiritual ignorance, resulting in sans girlfriend. I wasn't too keen on signing up, as I felt I didn't need 'fixing' and might have to simulate catharsis to gain acceptance. I felt a fraud acting this out for the first time, shamefully dishonest, contrasting starkly to a course environment demanding ruthless honesty and "intentional vulnerability" to be effective.

So it became a race, always chasing, always seeking to attain a new 'level' in the hope that I had finally achieved that awareness plateau where my girlfriend had settled, content with her new self.

But no, this wasn't to be. She was never really satisfied and felt the need to go on, and on, always seeking, always moving towards that mythical end of the exploring self-journey where true enlightenment resided and the self was actualised. In the end, after two years of trying, my pursuit of enlightenment fell short, and she left. By this time I had completed all of the 'tough' courses and was looked upon by the self-development organisation as one of their 'successes' and invited to be support staff for the incoming raw, unenlightened initiates. With my apparent mastery over the limitations of my own character, the view of the company was that I was now qualified to help others with their discovery of their own road to happiness.

I signed up to be a staff course supporter with 'significant interpersonal skills' in the job description. This proved immensely fulfilling for the times when I actually made a difference and said all the right words. Most times I felt unqualified and out of my depth and simple empathy carried me through, something I had a lot of, well before I ever embarked on the self-development road.

The organisation saw things differently and regarded me as a shining example of what was possible with their particular approach. Their courses in fact drew on ideas from both east and west, such as transpersonal psychology and somatic psychotherapy; meditation and Jungian psychology through the work of Ken Wilber, Abraham Maslow, Werner Erhard, Carl Rogers and Alexander Lowen. Eastern influences were largely from Buddhist texts including the teachings of people like Sogyal Rimpoche and the Dalai Lama. I learnt a lot about the work of these people and was always impressed by the emotive delivery of the organisation's teachers. I just felt it seemed a bit wasted on me as I never observed any fundamental change in my personality or Shangri-La-type epiphany.

Graham Brown and Babette Hayes started up Self Transformation Seminars in Britain in the mid-1980s and the call went out for support staff for their *Turning Point* course, a very popular entry level course at the time. I had just come up from South America when I got the call and travelled to London to be a support for one of these courses. It was a revelation. I was assigned to a group of 6 people as their mentor and guiding light. These 6 were creative, high-powered, high-achieving people in the real world. A few were famous. They were here because something was missing.

The course ran for three days and three nights with few sleep breaks. The lack of sleep was intentional, designed to strip participants of their normal defence mechanisms. Stress levels were high and balanced by time out with meditation. Each member of my group started off firmly bound to their street persona, but as time went on, this peeled off like the layers of an onion as each confronting, course-designed process and challenge was met. By the third day I knew these people so well, I found myself dispensing a level of feedback that I never knew was in me. I was not a trained psychologist, so what was I doing here? Why were these people responding so positively? I had never felt closer to anyone more than in that moment, and in just three days. I was euphoric. We all laughed, rejoiced and cried together and when it was all over at the end of the third night and without sleep, we all raced up the staircase and danced on the roof top as the sun rose over a distant St Pauls Cathedral.

Mantras, meditation, never using the second person in speech (because you have to own your issue by using the first person 'I'), eye contact, the seven energy chakras, being 'grounded', balanced and centred, coffee enemas (particularly effective in eliminating toxins on the night of a full moon) and adhering to particular food and drink combinations were all well-trodden course concepts, which I tried to follow at the time. Although I questioned some of these beliefs, I felt fulfilled in being of service during my self-transformation period, and I made lifelong friends through sharing experiences, sometimes loopy and weird, sometimes hilarious, but also sometimes profound.

Paradise on Pittwater – Youth Hostel Warden

My Australian home was Lovett Bay, a water-access-only settlement on the western shores of Pittwater, part of the Hawkesbury estuary on the northern outskirts of Sydney's metropolitan area. It's a special place. People who live there are self-reliant as there is no water or sewerage service and the electricity supply is unreliable. You have to be tough, resourceful and very community minded. The locals always help each other out when tinnies (aluminium runabout boats) sink or other misfortunes occur.

Although regular ferries service the offshore communities, most offshore residents use their tinnies to commute to the mainland. Going to work and coming home can be time-consuming if you have to change from scruffy tinnie shorts to office outfits in the car park adjacent to the tinnie commuter wharf in the morning and vice versa at the end of the work day. One story that did the rounds was that on one dark weekday evening a policeman patrolling the car park flashed his torch on half a dozen semi-naked men in the throes of changing clothes. "Stop!" he yelled. One of the men putting on his trousers looked up and explained: "It's all right, officer, we're locals." The officer's reply: "That's OK then. No worries."

The western foreshores is a creative ghetto of artists, writers, producers, actors, poets, filmmakers and the odd philosopher and scientist. The Friday night drinkathon at Church Point, the mainland jumping off wharf, produces heated discussion on the meaning of life and the nature of reality, where the expectation from the collective intellectual bank of the participants is that an answer will be found prior to the closing of the bottle shop. The people living there were the most wonderful collection of people I'd ever struck, resourceful, resilient and funny.

Pittwater is breathtakingly beautiful. The shoreline and hills behind are cloaked in thick rainforest along the creek lines and dense eucalypt forest on the ridges. Native wild animals are everywhere, from wallabies by day, and bandicoots, possums and sugar gliders by night, to armies of reptiles, swarms of beetles, bugs and bees and fish that jump out of the water at you in the early morning mists. Every creek cascading down from the plateau above holds sweet, pure water that is then diverted into hoses connected to storage tanks at each house.

And then there are the birds. As dawn breaks the kookaburras start their raucous cackling. First one starts up joined soon after by 20 or 30 others. This wakes the sulphur-crested cockatoos, known for being on a permanent short fuse.

They squawk angrily at the disturbance. Magpie warbling is next in the wake-up sequence, their profoundly complex melody signalling all the other birds to join the chorus – rainbow lorikeets, crows, currawongs, whip birds and finally the magnificent lyre bird, the world's most accomplished mimic, copies all the previous bird calls plus the latest model tinnie outboard motor sounds. Nature's symphony. It's not surprising that all birdsong worldwide actually originated in Australia.

There is nothing subtle about Australian fauna. The mammals and reptiles claim the bush as theirs and send a strong message that humans are just visitors. The birds are imperious, never backing off. In summer, the shrill, thousands-strong cicada chorus can be deafening. (The noisiest insects on the planet, their piercing buzzing can reach a painful 120 decibels close up.) The sounds of Pittwater, filtering through the dense rain forest of cabbage tree palms, casuarinas and pink grevilleas of the valleys and the eucalypts of the ridges. So much life, so much natural beauty in a Sydney suburb.

This magical bush environment was the perfect place to be creative. I could develop my new audio-visual business, and develop my techniques, make some pilots and then go out and market them. I figured I had enough money left to make a go of this for a year before financial destitution set in.

I lived in a studio in the forest, up the hill a bit from my landlord's house, which was built on a pier close enough to the water for him to shift his furniture during a king tide. He was a concert pianist amongst many other things, and very Italian in every way. We had a wonderful relationship. When it was time to review the rent I told him I should be paying more for the absolute privilege of living here, while he argued against an increase because he claimed I was 'in synch' with the environment and 'knew' the bush.

I became well known in the community, especially to Phil Charles who ran the youth hostel further up the hill from me. Over a glass of red we discussed the issues of life regularly; something that was easy to do there as we both gazed over the magnificent panorama in front of us of the spotted gum forest with glints of Pittwater between the trees.

One day our conversation turned to something more personal.

"You know Terry, that Austrian girl who was staying here for so long," Phil said.

"Yes, she didn't want to leave Paradise, did she?" I replied.

"No, and neither do I, but I'm going to, for a few months at least. You see, we're getting married."

"Congratulations!" I interrupted.

"Thanks. Didn't think I'd ever meet someone so special. Only problem is she's back in Austria to see her parents and she wants me to meet them and stay for a while. So..." He paused. "How would you like to be the youth hostel warden?"

Opportunity knocked again. So two weeks later I waved Phil off on his love pilgrimage and became Pittwater Youth Hostel's second warden.

These were champagne days. My day started with a ten-minute walk through the rare spotted gum forest past the wallabies, kookaburras and magpies to my office. The office door was always open, which meant that from my desk I had an uninterrupted view of the waterways, coast and several pristine beaches. This is truly one of the most beautifully sited hostels in Australia, reachable only by ferry, surrounded by bushland and rainforest, no shops nearby – magnificent isolation.

I would allocate tasks for all the backpackers staying at the hostel. That was the tradition in the 1980s, though it has disappeared today – just as the strict-sounding term 'warden' is no longer used; now hostels are run by 'managers'. It was fun working out the jobs list. Swedish backpackers in particular seemed always keen to clean and keep the hostel looking beautiful.

During the day, the sulphur-crested cockatoos would arrive on the verandah railing and with them the rainbow lorikeets. A goanna often showed up too. In the evening the possums would arrive and hang around until bedtime, then keep everyone awake by conducting sliding competitions on the roof. The soft dawn light made visible the extensive network of spiders' webs, constructed industrially during the night by an army of small hard workers like the Golden Orb and St Andrews Cross. The nastier arachnids such as the deadly funnel web and slightly less deadly red back considerately stayed out of sight.

This was true paradise in my eyes. If the passing parade of animals wasn't enough, the hostel came with its own goat which had the job of keeping the grass down. After a few weeks of this, I expanded operations by becoming a sort of free tour operator, leading guests through the bush to lookouts and Aboriginal engravings and running kayak trips across to the deserted beaches using the hostel's very own fleet. These beaches were in the national park and fringed with palm trees; some had waterfalls spilling onto the sand. My tour program also included night-time spotting of all the nocturnal animals in the forest and sunrise bushwalks up to a lookout first touched by the rising sun followed by morning swimming at the beaches.

One of the duties of a warden was to ensure the safety of the residents. This meant periodic fire drills had to be staged and the dates for these were advised by Head Office. In my time as warden only one such date came up, a Monday when paradoxically no one was resident. And the reason for that was that I had booked the entire hostel out for an all-weekend party for myself and a few dozen of my closest and noisiest friends. They had all cleared out before the darkness of Sunday night descended on the last ferry back to civilisation.

Monday morning came and with it the shrill ringing noise when I pressed the big fire alarm knob above the door in my office. "Fire, Fire!" I bellowed so that all the sleeping residents, had they been there, would have woken up and fled to a predetermined congregating point near the wombat hole. As soon as I thought my shouting had been effective and all the rooms in my imagination would have been vacant, I opened the emergency water cock and the emergency fire hose filled with the life-giving water that would put out the fire.

With all the commotion, the goat was now in a high state of anxiety and was charging around the grassy ground in front of the building. The water then came gushing out of the hose with a solid stream reaching clear to the bush line. I now saw a clear purpose for my labours. I hosed down the goat, which, after getting a drenching, calmed down sufficiently to resume eating grass again. I turned off the water from the tank, as rainwater is precious and not to be wasted – except for drills like this. Then I walked over to the wombat hole and briefed the residents, had they been there, of the outcome and to tell them, it was now safe to return to their rooms, had any been occupied. I shut off the fire alarm and rang Head Office.

"Mission accomplished!" I announced.

"Well done, Roger. You're the first hostel to report in. Very efficient indeed."

Just another day in paradise, but with the bonus that I felt I had achieved something.

My education – the never ending story

Part-time university was like walking through quicksand. Every inch of progress I made only came with a mighty effort. And if the pressure wasn't maintained, I slipped backwards. I was still ignorant about career choices as an undergraduate majoring in geophysics. I liked the subject until someone asked me what mining company I was wanting to work for. I was shocked. I didn't want to work for a mining company. I wanted to save the planet, not dig it up. So I immediately changed my major to climatology, much more logical for me if I had ever given it proper thought.

My slow progress eventually saw me get my first degree, then go on for a Masters and years more work. My thesis subject was "The Behaviour of Sound Waves in the Early Morning Atmosphere, which neatly combined two disciplines as required: meteorology, which I loved, and noise which I didn't understand. Macquarie University lacked the expertise to field an appropriate supervisor, so I was farmed out to Sydney University where the doyen of environmental acoustics, Professor Fergus Fricke, was available and ready to drill me in the art of extreme perseverance. The Professor's reputation was formidable so I was lucky to have him in the hope a little might rub off onto my work.

I was looking to build on the knowledge around how the characteristics of the atmosphere in the morning resulted in sound travelling further and appearing noisier. This meant a lot of field work, producing hopefully a lot of data, which would also hopefully provide the detail on the nature of sound wave refraction leading to the increased noise. I measured the atmosphere and sound levels over an entire winter. I wrote it all up and produced my analysis to the Professor. He said it looked interesting but I needed more data to back up my preliminary findings. So I spent a summer doing the same. I saw the Professor again. He said it looked interesting but I needed more data to back up my preliminary findings. With a sense of déjà vu I headed outdoors again for another season. Back to the Professor who said it looked interesting but I needed more data to back up my preliminary findings. Groundhog day. This time I held up my protest flag. Not enough statistical consistency, not enough good correlation was the response. I must have looked dangerously downcast because suddenly the Professor changed tack. One more period in the wilderness was enough. If I came back with the same sort of data next time, I could call it quits and write the whole thing up.

Seeing it was only a Masters and not a Doctorate I could get away with statements like 'there was insufficient data to provide a rigorous analysis and more research would be needed in the future', or words to that effect. A doctorate was for original thinkers, but a Masters was for plodders who hoped that sufficient plodding might lead to an original thought.

A year later, I produced my 300-page thesis. An eminent panel of scientists passed it with some reservations about lack of data. I had my precious piece of paper, my higher degree and I now considered myself, finally, as completing my education that had started all those years before at the Balmoral Beach kindergarten. It meant I could now go out and get 'a proper job'. At last!

Selling the Vision in the Bush – Audio-Visual Producer

Narrabri is a medium-sized town on the northwestern slopes of New South Wales. Nearby is a magnificent range of volcanic mountains, the Nandewars that rise 1500 metres into the clouds, directly out of the plains. There are few places in Australia where mountains do that on that scale so abruptly. From the highest peak, Mt Kaputar you can see 10 per cent of the entire State and at nights the lights of several towns shine forth far out onto the plains, towns such as Wee Waa and Moree. Also nearby is the Australia Telescope Compact Array, a major radio telescope facility delving into the far reaches of the universe. Narrabri is also a key centre for one of the main cotton-growing regions and is just to the north of the Piliga Forest, the largest remnant temperate forest in eastern Australia. If all this makes the town sound like an exciting place to visit, you would never have known it had you stepped into the Narrabri Council Tourist Information Centre back in the 1980s.

In 1987 the Centre was in a partially renovated, party dilapidated early 20th century cottage. The carpet was worn and old. There was a brochure stand half-filled with out-of-date brochures for nearby restaurants and motels. A permanent slide show was set up in one corner showing historic pictures of cattle down the main street and the first steam train to reach the town. An elderly gentleman tended the shop where a few curios were on sale. He may have been a local but had little knowledge or enthusiasm for Narrabri's main attractions and appeared to be mainly there to book accommodation. My first impressions were completed by the small library where books could be borrowed, not practical for travellers and in any case, these books were the ones you would find in garage sales being thrown out for a dollar a dozen. Narrabri wasn't unique in this presentation. The same disconnect applied to most council-run tourist information centres for most towns throughout the country at the time.

I had a vision. It was the technique of the audio-visual as a powerful promotional tool with the capacity to convey the essence and excitement of a place to draw tourists in. I could see the application working once Helen Anderson had ticked off this first film. Her business judgment told her it would work in the US, a very tough marketing environment, confirmation for me that it could work even better back home for the regional tourism market. Back in the 1980s, this market was run by local town shopkeepers and business people quite inexperienced in the requirements of this sphere of business.

Several months after the launch of my Amazon Botanical Gardens promo on American television, I drove up to the Narrabri Council Chambers for my meeting with the town's tourism sub-committee. That comprised George the butcher, Fred the real estate agent and part-time farmer, Geoff the lawyer and John the farm equipment dealer. We all shook hands, I ran my film of Amazon Botanical Gardens, told the group where this film had gone, extolled the virtues of Narrabri and surrounds and how that excitement could be communicated to visitors through an audio-visual presentation made specifically for them.

My presentation was greeted by deafening silence. George looked at Fred and Geoff. John looked bored. Geoff was fidgeting.

George cleared his throat. "Very nice, Roger," he said. "How much did the film cost?"

"Audio visuals are cheaper than video so a five-minute show can be done, all up, for about $3000." Silence descended again. Eventually John chipped in.

"We have to fix the toilet in the Centre, remember. I think the inlet plug's had it. And then there's the plumbing with the sewer connection, remember. There's well over a thousand in that."

"Plus the carpets," added George.

"But how about the show itself?" I interjected. "There's so much here in Narrabri that is exciting to tell others about. This sort of presentation does that perfectly. Just like how in my Amazon presentation you really get the feel of a thunderstorm on the river, here in Narrabri it could be about the mystery of the stars with your astronomical facilities and the grandeur of the high peaks of the Nandewars piercing the cloud layers. You know, stuff like that makes people excited and want to visit these places and that is good for you and your businesses."

"There are just those telescope dishes out there. Nothing really to see," said John.

"Better get onto them about the foxes," said Fred. "I've seen some passing the property, and they're getting into my sheep across the road. Bloody poor management, just like the National Park where all the pests have a home."

"Have you been to the top of Mount Kaputar?" I asked. The sub-committee members looked at each other. They all shook their heads.

"No, wait a minute," said John. "I was in the Scouts, I remember, and the scoutmaster organised a camp up there. I remember it rained. I was miserable."

"Well, anyway, it's one of those great spots in the entire country to go to and only 45 minutes' drive from town. The audio-visual can capture that," I said, keeping up my enthusiasm.

"I hear what you're saying, Roger. What do you think, boys?" said George, looking at his colleagues.

"Well, we're not the Amazon here. We're just Narrabri. I just don't think we're ready for this," said John, looking at the others.

I changed tack. "If you got more tourists in Narrabri, say double the current number what would that do for your businesses?" That remark seemed to animate the sub-committee.

"I'd love it. I'd deliver much more meat to the motels," said George.

"I can see it would be good for the hospitality industry here, may even raise property prices in the town. I know what you are getting at and it sounds good, but we may not be well set up for greater numbers of sightseers," Fred added.

The sub-committee hummed and harred until George spoke for them all.

"We really appreciated you coming all this way to make this effort for us and we really see what you are getting at. Look, best we can do right now is to put the idea to our next Council meeting and get back to you about the result. That's the best we can do. OK?"

I left the town that afternoon realizing the lack of vision was the cause of regional tourism languishing in the country at the time. It happened in much the same way in Albury, Tamworth, Grafton and Nowra. In fact it happened everywhere. The decision-makers were not tourism professionals; they were local shopkeepers and business people used to the slow lane of country town life. But the slow lane spelt death for my vision. I expanded my sales pitch to interstate markets with the same result. In the end it died. The money ran out too. The time had come to get some employment, but where to now?

Alpaca in Australia – Alpaca Garment Importer

I needed income. The spectre of being the recipient of unemployment benefits was looming. There was one hope and I had already sown the seeds for it four months earlier in the old Inca stronghold of Cusco, Peru.

Sitting in a café sipping my superb coffee, I had observed the typical scene of native women in their bowler hats guiding a flock of alpaca across the Plaza del Armas. These were truly noble beasts, gentle yet dignified and assured. Their wool was vastly superior to sheep's wool for garments as the fibres were hollow and thereby gave better insulation. This meant that an alpaca sweater offered far better protection against cold than a sheep's wool garment in addition to being more comfortable. Every Indian in Cusco wore alpaca. A thought struck me then. I walked over to one of the many clothes shops and tried on a few sweaters. They were so warm and soft. I had never seen garments like this in Australia. In broken Spanish, I asked the shopkeeper, Sisa, where she had bought them. Sisa explained that it was a family business. Her cousins were shepherds in the high Andes where they tended huge flocks of alpaca. Her cousins also spun their wool and knitted the sweaters at their farm to sell wholesale to the shop.

I spent days in that shop and arranged with the cousins for the supply of 200 sweaters of various styles, colours and sizes over a season. Then I took the documentation for this business arrangement to the government office to secure an export license. Communication with the Andean shepherds was difficult as the shop owner in Cusco had to travel by donkey up to the high plateau to see them. Securing a business arrangement, including ongoing orders stretching for more than one season, was painfully slow. Eventually the shepherds came out of the mountains to meet me. This was important as face-to-face meetings meant a lot in this culture. Sisa them sold me several sweaters to show retailers back in Australia.

It was an exciting venture as the tightly knit Cusco community told me I was their first Australian importer, and I later discovered I was one of the first alpaca importers into Australia. (This was the 1980s. Today, not only are alpaca garments on sale everywhere, but there also numerous Australian alpaca farms.)

Four months later, I was on a Sydney bus, lugging a suitcase full of alpaca jumpers for an appointment with the buying department of David Jones, the venerable upmarket department store. I was dressed appropriately for the occasion, sporting clean and clipped fingernails and polished black shoes.

“Good morning. I am Felicity from the Buyers here at DJs. I was intrigued by your phone call. I must say we haven’t ever stocked alpaca before so I have brought in an expert, John, to help me.”

I pulled the sweaters out of my suitcase for John to examine. I felt intimidated. John ran his fingers over the fabric and spent a lot of time checking the measurements and sizes. He then started to strip.

“Good heavens, John. What are you doing?” asked Felicity.

“What does it look like? I’m trying them on.”

His gestures and smile indicated his approval of the garments.

“Felicity, tell your management that this is an opportunity to steal a march on your competitors and I’ll tell you why,” he enthused. “Simply put, these jumpers are superb. I’ve never felt a fabric like it. They are unique. My recommendation is to buy heavily for winter. Just go for it, Felicity. These will sell. Focus your marketing on the quality and where they come from.”

“What for, in your opinion?”

“Between $200 to $300, I’d say.”

Felicity turned to me. “It looks good Roger. I’ll make my own inquiries with the management here so I’ll contact you. Please be ready to get onto your suppliers about giving us the volume we need. I’ll advise on volume as soon as I get the green light.”

On the way home that afternoon, I calculated my profit for several scenarios, considering I could get each for $30 including shipment and import duties. I then had to figure out how fast I could contact Sisa and then for her to reach her cousins in the mountains. I was excited. This was a real business venture, exploring a new market. But it worried me that the lines of communication were so tenuous.

I rang Sisa with the good news. I imagined her on her donkey the next day riding up towards the snow to tell her family of their great fortune. I waited and waited. Days went by. Weeks went by. David Jones was pressuring me.

Then one day I received a letter festooned with foreign stamps and postmarks. It was from Peru. I opened the letter. It was from Sisa but was in Spanish. Not trusting my own grip on the language, I took the letter to a local Spanish-speaking friend. He read it out to me.

“Dearest Roger, I am very sorry about this news but we have had trouble. The Shining Path has killed many of our flock and burnt down our farm. My cousins are here in Cusco with me. I thank God they are safe. Please excuse writing this in Spanish. We cannot help you now as I don’t think my cousins will want to go up there again for a while. – Sisa.”

For a long time I wondered whether the good news I had sent to the cousins had got out and was the reason for the attack. For a long time I felt not only very sad for their predicament but swamped with guilt for any part I might have unwittingly played in their misfortune.

Reunion and Rescue – Taxi Driver

When the money supply dries up and there is no identifiable source of funds, but the cost of living remains, where do you turn to grab much needed cash? It's what a lot of people do in this position. They go where employment is almost guaranteed. They become taxi drivers. For the small outlay of the training course, the exam and the driving test, getting the license was as good as printing money.

At least that's what I thought when I applied. But it wasn't so simple. My first few shifts behind the wheel of a taxi taught me something I didn't know. The taxi world is tough, unrelenting, competitive and somewhat dangerous. What I earned was dependent on getting jobs. This was entirely random. There were bad evenings and nights and worse evenings and nights when no one seemed to want a taxi or several cabs ahead of me got all the jobs or I was at the airport along with hundreds of others, soaking up precious time and finally getting a customer who only wanted to go down the street.

Slowly, I became street-smart and learned to be in the right place at the right time, but then so did all the others. I was at a low ebb. But I stuck it out for a few months before a new opportunity arrived, as deep down I knew it would. Yet though those few months were hard, there was a reward, and a big one. It was in the people I drove to their destination. Some of my passengers drove me crazy – the ones who were drunk, abusive and those who did a runner and refused to pay – but at times the passengers made it a worthwhile, even emotionally enriching, experience. Sometimes I was the anonymous and safe person to talk to or share something with, a sounding board. I was someone who wasn't going to impinge upon their lives for more than a few minutes or impose on them in any way. This seemed to give some people the license to tell their stories.

There was, for example, Mr Estaban, a well-dressed old man who appeared to be jumping out of his skin with anxiety as we drove towards the address he had handed to me on a slip of paper.

"Are you OK?" I asked, noting how he was repeatedly pulling on his tie and checking his nails.

He looked puzzled at my question. "OK, very OK, is very exciting," he replied in a heavy foreign accent.

I smiled. "Why are you excited, Mr Estaban?"

Mr Estab took this as an invitation to talk. "I meet my sister today. First time 55 years. I now go see her. Very exciting."

"Why so long?" I asked.

"Great War come 1941. Our village invaded. They take my sister away. I look and look but never find." Another WW2 veteran I assumed.

"Second World War?" I asked. Mr Estaban looked puzzled.

"Second World War?" he repeated. "No no, the Great War 1941 – invasion of our country by Peru in war. I am proud Ecuadorian and fight Peru."

I looked this up later. In 1941 Ecuador and Peru were at war. It had nothing to do with WW2. Neither country took part in the Second World War. This was a world apart. They were having their own war. Peru's superior army soon overran the weak Ecuadorian ground forces to force a capitulation. In the invasion many Ecuadorians went missing. It seemed that Mr Estoban's sister was one of those.

"Looking for Benita long, long time. Look all over Ecuador, all the time, many years. Long time later they say she in Australia, in Sydney, so I come here."

As we neared his destination, I slowed down to give Mr Estaban time to compose himself, to get ready but savour the moment of excited anticipation. The odd house numbers were on the left and increased. The road was straight. Up ahead I could see someone standing on the side of the road, looking my way. As I approached, I could see it was an elderly woman. Mr Estaban then saw her too.

"Si, si, si!" he shouted, bouncing up and down in his seat, his head almost hitting the ceiling.

The cab was still moving when Mr Estaban flung the door open and shot out like a slingshot. Mr Estaban bounded over to his sister, arms outstretched. She was crying and shaking with emotion. He smothered her with hugs and kisses. They stayed locked together without speaking. Finally he wiped away her tears. They were completely oblivious of my presence. Quietly I drove off, not wishing to intrude on their joy of reuniting by asking for the fare for the journey. In the excitement of the moment, Mr Estaban had forgotten to pay. I wanted to give him something for enriching my day, and this was it.

There was another unforgettable moment. One evening when I had just driven off after dropping off a passenger, a woman suddenly raced out in front of my cab, waving violently. I slammed on the brakes.

"Thank you for stopping, I thought you mightn't," she said, frowning and sighing. "I need to go to 17 Albany Crescent, East Killara as quickly as possible, please."

Feeling her urgency, I sped off as soon as she hopped into my taxi.

"I'll go as fast as I can by the quickest route."

"Whatever way you think, driver."

"You sound worried. Something's wrong?"

"Oh dear, yes. My daughter rang me up to tell me her little boy has gone missing. It's been a few hours now and it's getting dark." She cupped her face in her hands.

"I know East Killara. There's a lot of bush. He could have just wondered into it just off the road there and perhaps then couldn't find his way out again."

"If only I had a mobile phone," she said. "Then I could talk to my daughter and see what's happening."

"Have the police or emergency services been called?" I enquired. "If not, I can do it on my radio now."

"It's OK, driver. They've been called. The little terror is a wanderer but only up or down the street, never the bush."

"How old is he?"

"Three."

I pushed down hard on the accelerator, through several amber traffic lights turning red. Almost there, just a bit further.

"My daughter can't cope. She's had a miscarriage too. She's looked everywhere, door-knocked all the houses too. She's sick with worry, sick with worry."

A bank of police cars blocked the entrance to Albany Crescent. Lines of police tape barring the way suggested a crime scene. My frantic passenger screamed, a loud, continuous wail. A burly policeman put up his hand right in front of me.

"Turn around. You can't get through here. It's blocked off." He eyed my hysterical passenger. "What's the matter with her?"

"She's the little boy's grandmother, if that's what you are here for."

"Just a moment." He walked back to the huddle of other police. My passenger was still wailing uncontrollably, unwilling to get out of the cab to see what was going on.

"I can't get any closer, maám. I think you should get out to see what is happening. Perhaps your daughter may be looking for you."

Sniffing, coughing and crying, she eventually opened the door and eased herself out onto the road.

Ahead of me there was movement. Three policemen started to walk towards the cab. The woman grimaced.

Then without any warning a little figure sprung out from behind the three giant policemen and ran towards my cab. My passenger then let out an almighty piercing shriek. It was the precious little boy! He sprang into his grandmother's waiting arms.

The three policemen grinned broadly. I did a thumbs-up and they returned the gesture. I took in the scene in for a few moments, wiped away a tear, then reversed my taxi and drove off. Another free taxi ride, a gift worth giving in exchange for the euphoria I felt. Being a taxi driver was not always monotonous and could be intrinsically rewarding.

Ending a Race – Motor Sport Regulator

It was 1989 and I was 43. I now had my degrees. Two of them. In a short speech at my graduation party my proud mother finally exorcised her fears for my future.

"I must say I lived through desperate times," Norma said to my assembled friends. "I never really thought he would make the grade, not after missing out here and again in England, failing end-of-school exams. He had lots of jobs of course but no real job, not one that you could say needed real qualifications. And then years after leaving school something happened, I don't know what, but he suddenly knuckled down and passed the HSC with flying colours. God knows how this happened. No one was more surprised than me. And that led to this moment." Norma looked at me, smiling through moist eyes. "And now he can get a real job."

I was ready for sure. Ready for something professional befitting the letters after my name, and something outdoors, something to do with the environment. What job could tick those boxes? I looked in the job ads in the morning newspaper. There it was: an ad for an environmental assessment officer with the State Pollution Control Commission. The area of expertise was in environmental noise, which was what I studied.

Noise is a weird specialty. Few people understand the science. Fewer people work in the field. It is over-specialisation, but employment is guaranteed, because it tops the list as the most commonly complained about type of pollution. The science of acoustics is totally unglamorous and conceptually opaque and so there is little competition for jobs. I only had to show up for the interview to get one. This 'real job' was about going to commercial activities and checking that they were complying with the noise conditions on their noise license. It sounded simple enough.

So after a week of settling in I was off with a team of people to a motor racing facility called Amaroo Park. The motor racing circuit used to be in the bush but bad planning allowed residential development to encroach onto the park's boundary with the inevitable stream of noise complaints from residents starting soon after. I was there for their big race meeting of the season, watching the park managers running their measurements of noise from the racing cars. With us regulators present, they were particularly assiduous. Perhaps a little too much. A few cars had been pulled over for being too noisy but nothing dramatic happened. Not until the final race.

Off they went. The lead car was manoeuvring furiously to maintain its lead. It was an exciting tussle. The winner would be hailed the season champion and be invited to start in more prestigious races in Victoria. A worried official came over to our group. "Jake's pushing the envelope. He's two decibels over. I'll warn him, then we'll see." The official went back to the track.

"They wouldn't bother about this if we weren't here," observed my colleague. We had a great view of the race from our vantage point next to the control tower. I watched as Jake, the leader, started the bell lap. He passed the finish line for the last time. The bell was struck. The official moved forward onto the verge of the track and waved a black flag of disqualification at Jake.

The noise was about to crescendo.

"My God, what is he doing?"

Jake revved the motor and suddenly swerved, seemingly aiming to hit the terrified official, who thankfully leaped out of the path of the speeding bullet. The car raced furiously up the hill beside the track, Jake did a screeching burnout and stopped near our group in a cloud of dust.

The official ran towards us, shouting. "Hurry up, get inside the tower! Quick!" Panting, he caught up to us and pushed us inside the control tower, then locked the door.

Within seconds the door was being pounded furiously from the outside. Then came the booming voice. "Open up, scum! Don't hide like rats! Open up, cowards!" Hammer, hammer. The door was just holding up to the thumping battering. We ran up the spiral staircase to the top. The official was on his walkie-talkie. From the top we then saw Jake run back to his car and redline the engine.

"Oh Christ! He's going to ram us!" yelled my colleague. Now a fire truck with siren blaring plus three race officials' cars were speeding up the hill. Jake let the clutch out and powered toward the tower. But the fire truck blocked his assault just short of the door. There was pandemonium. People rushed around crazily, three storeys below our tower hideout. Jake was surrounded. His race was over.

That was my not-so-quiet introduction to my new job. Perhaps noise wasn't a dull field after all.

Moving Mountains – Mining Noise Regulator

I was now known by all the industry people as 'The Regulator'. I was the government man whose job was to order them to turn down their noise and comply with the conditions of their licenses. There were two ways of doing this: reactive, as in motor racing, and preventative, as in building a coal mine. I had done the car race; now came the mine.

The Hunter Valley of NSW has high quality black coal easy to access with open-cut mines. In the early 1990s mines were being developed in the Hunter at a frenetic pace. One of the biggest proposed new mines was Gallathorpe[1] near Murrurundi. Court hearings were under way in that town leading to an approval to construct the new mine. I travelled there as a regulator to ensure that the noise from the operating mine would not go above a specific level. To achieve that, the mine had to build a huge wall, designed to block the noise, between themselves and the nearby residents.

The court hearings were going badly. The mine operators couldn't convince our lawyers that they would comply with their current mine design. Things got heated and the Commissioner chairing proceedings called for an adjournment at lunch time so that everyone could take a breather. The Commissioner suggested everyone work out a technical solution with the regulator. Into the lunch room came the smoked salmon sandwiches and the start of the most surreal board game I have ever played. The 'board' was a model of the mine showing in detail all of the holes, barriers, access roads and infrastructure, all made up of hundreds of small, loose, wooden blocks that could be moved around inside the model to change the mine's architecture. Sitting around the board were the mine operators, their lawyers, their noise consultants, the government lawyers and me.

"Now Roger," said Peter, the mine's noise consultant, "you and I know how to do this so we will have to explain it to the others." I just nodded, not knowing exactly what to say, especially seeing I didn't have the knowledge Peter thought I had. In fact I was winging it.

"So this is our mine model. These red blocks are the new noise barriers and the other red blocks you can see are barriers in other directions. Can you see all that?"

"Yes, I can Peter," I said with hidden relief that I was able to understand at least that process. Peter and I moved blocks around just like I had learnt back at

[1] Not its real name

Balmoral Beach Kindergarten. The lawyers said nothing but studied the board intently.

"It looks like we have to raise this barrier quite a bit," I said, hoping I made sense.

"Yes, Roger," said Peter, looking irritated. "We all know that. The problem is that we only have these blocks to play with. That's why we stick to this model. In other words, we can't get fill from outside the site to build up. Any corrections have to be sourced from our own site. See now? That's the problem."

I stared at the model trying to take in all the detail. I didn't want to ask the obvious question as to why they couldn't import fill for fear I would look even more a fool for asking a silly question. I continued to study the model. There was silence in the room. Then I had a light-globe moment. "Look Peter, this is our problem area."

Excitedly I pointed to the residential development. "So we move blocks to here and build up the barrier to this height." I piled blocks onto blocks. "There is a cost for doing that which can be offset by taking blocks away up here because there is a natural hill there you can take advantage of. And if you can purchase that property at position X you cancel out any barriers to the northwest, giving you more blocks, you see. That gives you your cheaper access road as well."

I moved blocks from the inactive barrier and piled them on the critical one in our lunchtime board game. I then played with their positions until I was satisfied I had redesigned the model just right.

Peter stared at the board and fiddled with the blocks, as if contemplating his next Monopoly move and how many hotel blocks he could accumulate. "Hmm, hmm." He nodded. He was seeing the light.

"Now calculate the reduction in noise by the barrier at the new height and see what we get," I said.

Peter made a quick calculation and looked up smiling. "We make it! By Christ, we make it!" he exclaimed. A Eureka moment. "In theory, this works. But do you realise what you've done and why your option has been dismissed before, never going to this detail?"

I looked vacantly at Peter, not knowing the answer.

He continued: "You have just recommended what could be Australia's highest and biggest noise barrier. It's a bloody mountain. And you may have just added $20 million to the construction cost."

"You're welcome to look for a low-cost solution that complies. I'm just showing one solution. It may not be the only one," I reassured Peter. The consultant wasn't listening. He was already briefing his lawyers about the outcome of a very expensive board game.

Gallathorpe built the massive noise barrier. It dominates the landscape to the north from the road that heads west from Muston. It just goes to show what the construction industry can do with the right-sized shovel and a few board game blocks.

Hyperactive Neighbours – Local Government Advisor

My job as a scientist with the NSW Environment Protection Authority, previously called the State Pollution Control Commission, had several aspects. Firstly there was enforcement. This was where we went into the field and measured whether a licensed activity was complying with the operating conditions. This was what I had done up to this time. The other major part of the job was framing the conditions themselves. This policy aspect was more satisfying as it had permanence. Once a policy had been written and approved it might stay on the books for a long time. After my adventures with motor racing and mining, 'the powers that be' thought I might be less dangerous by writing policy rather than running it. I agreed. I really didn't want to cause a fuss with anyone, least of all racing car drivers and coal miners.

On top of this, there were domestic issues. These were controlled by local councils but often their staff needed guidance from us. I recall a typical call for help to me from a council noise ranger: "This guy uses his leaf blower at 6am to move the leaves off his driveway and the neighbour's getting real upset and ringing us up all the time. He says next time he hears the machine starting up that early he's coming over to job the guy. So how do I control leaf blowers?"

"Tell the leaf blower guy he is too early and can't start up till 8am," I replied. "Even after that, if the machine's noise is offensive, same result, a fat fine. Got that? Before eight it shouldn't be heard at all and after eight the offensive noise test applies. You know how to do that, don't you?"

Council noise ranger: "Shit yes, that's easy. And I'll tell the neighbour that too so he'll know, and tell him the fine for jobbing someone is much higher."

This council ranger had an extra query: "Someone is complaining that his neighbours have noisy sex early in the morning. What do I do about that?"

My suggestion: "Get the neighbour to tape the noise so you have evidence and get a statement from them. See if the neighbour can move rooms. If no joy, then tell the couple to either tone it down, move it to office hours or insulate their walls."

Council noise ranger: "Gee mate. That would cost thousands. They'd tell me to piss off I'm sure. What do I do then?"

"Tell them it's the law, and if they don't comply you could fine them for every time they do it and disturb the neighbour."

Council noise ranger: “Come on, that’s not in the Noise Act – that’s the Bluff Act, isn’t it?”

“Right on, but it could put the fear of God into them. It works most times. Try it. If that doesn’t work, tell them the neighbour is taping their pillow talk.”

My job at the EPA had aspects I could never have foreseen.

Noisy Bikies and Noisy Bikes – Motorcycle Noise Control Policy Maker

I arrived into the noise policy arm of the EPA at an auspicious time because policy-wise we were at ground zero where every noise guideline, rule or standard needed radical updating.

All of the noise guidelines of the time were in one large tome called the Environmental Noise Control Manual which had a rule for anything, from quarrying to suburban inclinators, from barking dogs to paperboy whistles. The host of policies were of the 'written-on-the-back-of-an-envelope' genre. A total revamp was obvious.

I was given a choice on what policy area to target first: industrial noise, road traffic noise, construction noise or motorcycles. Motor bikes were the obvious choice. They were far noisier than a typical car and often ridden or designed to accentuate their noise. They didn't have to be. So I went to town on developing a regulation which set motorcycle noise levels lower.

The work was meticulous. A lot of worldwide research was needed to support the noise reduction. Then we had to assess the economic impact on manufacturers. After that, we had to look at the effect on road safety for the rider. Every possible objection had to have a well thought-out response already prepared. Finally we needed to predict if there was any political fallout and counter arguments from that perspective. Only then would we be ready to release a draft for public comment.

Within four months we had a proposal worked out, reducing all motorcycle noise by about four decibels, a significant drop along with complementary field test procedures and an economic analysis. We showed it could be done technically and economically and was practical. The arguments put forward were compelling, considering the huge number of people affected by loud bikes. The EPA executive approved the public release of the draft regulation and associated explanations. So we published the draft and invited public submissions. We were quite satisfied with ourselves, perhaps even slightly smug. The trouble was that all this commendable work was done in a policy ivory tower. Our last step was to venture outside into the real world.

All hell broke loose. The *Daily Telegraph's* headline warned: *Bikie war on noise crackdown* with the EPA's PR people inundated with phone calls the morning of the article. The PR boss then came to see us.

“Tell us next time you are going to do something like this, just give us a warning please,” he pleaded. “The Motorcycle Riders Association is coming here to see you this afternoon. Did you know about that?”

“No.”

“Look, ring their President and sort it out quick. The media will be here for sure. We don’t want any ugly incidents. Do you want police backup?”

“We’ll talk to the President and see if we can have a discussion. Let’s try to keep it normal,” my boss said.

At 3pm out on the street outside our building bikies started arriving on their Harley Davidsons and other shiny chrome-plated noise monsters. We descended in the lift, nervously preparing to meet the contingent. I took a deep breath and swung open the lobby door and emerged into the noisy city street.

Five machines were revving up, each with its highly adorned leather-jacketed rider on top. Amongst all the normal motorcyclist’s garb I spotted a clerical collar.

“Hello, you must be Roger. I’m Tom, the Anglican pastor of Mt Matthews Church in Annandale.” He swung his bike around and motioned to his bikie mates. “Hey, shut your bikes down, boys!”

Then he faced me again. “Now the boys here are all upset, Roger. I’ll tell you why. You see, it just isn’t safe to ride around without noise.”

“A noisy bike is a safe bike,” blurted out one of the other bikies.

“He’s right. Drivers don’t see us unless they can hear us.”

I decided to speak up. “This is only a draft. The idea is for you to comment on it so we can improve it. Everyone gets a say.”

“Well, my son,” said the clergyman, “the best improvement is to rip it up. We’re here to tell you that. We’re not going to get into an argument about it. We’re just telling you. We’re off to Parliament House now to see our bikie-riding pollies. That will kill it. So don’t bother to do any more work on it, right? Think about that.”

All five engines started up simultaneously and revved furiously. The bikies swung their handlebars around and accelerated up the street in the general direction of Parliament House.

He was right. It was killed, killed by the undue influence bike-riding politicians had on the government because of their numbers and their key positions in the balance of power. As it turned out, motorcycle noise control was our only defeat, and much bigger and vastly more complicated government policies made it into law. A new Industrial Noise Policy was the flagship and was to be a launching pad for me later on into an entirely different work environment.

The Steinway Evacuation – Firefighter

Summers in Eastern Australia are mostly delightful, but there are years when the threat of bushfires becomes very real. The summer of1994 had just started when I saw the local rural fire officer walk down to the fire shed housing the fire engine and all the fire-fighting equipment and move the danger sign from high to extreme. The bush was dry and thick. On the western foreshores of Pittwater we were particularly vulnerable because of 30 km of uninterrupted bushland to the west, the direction most fires came from. The heat built up over the weeks until on one Saturday morning I awoke to the very Australian smell of burning eucalyptus. I ran outside my Lovett Bay studio. Smoke was shrouding the hillsides.

The phone rang. It was the captain of the local rural fire service station, warning that a fire was burning along the ridges and heading towards my house.

"We need your help seeing you did some training when you were the hostel warden. If you are safe to help your neighbours please assist but evacuate if it looks out of control. Keep an escape path free so you can make for your boat and if you can see that the neighbours do the same. We may not be able to get to you to help. Got that?"

I raced down the track to my landlord Enrico's house. He was anxious and agitated, more than I had ever seen him before. A demonstrative Italian, Enrico was pacing up and down his private jetty, fearfully eyeing the nearby smoky, bushy ridge. "I don't know, I don't know. What can I do? What can I do?" Shaking, he covered his face with his hands.

As I went to place a reassuring hand on his shoulder, a thunderous crackling split the air. We looked up at the ridge. It exploded. The entire ridge line above us, over 100 metres long, suddenly erupted in lashing tongues of red and yellow flames.

Enrico fell to his knees on the jetty. "My life! It is ruined!" he cried repeatedly both in English and Italian. "La mia vita è rovinata! I am ruined! Ruined!"

It was useless to try to talk to him. He was a heaving, choking wreck. Even his partner Judy couldn't rouse him to action. She turned to me.

"There's really only one thing that is so important to save," she said. "Just one thing. His Steinway. He's had it all of his professional life. It's been to his most important concerts. It's his life. That's what's upsetting him."

I could appreciate that urgency. Indeed I had often listened to the harmony of his Steinway grand piano wafting through the bush, making me feel that indeed I was living in paradise and all was well with the world.

But now the fire was starting to leap down the slope, heading straight for us. The smoke was getting thicker. We left a prostrate Enrico and walked inside to inspect the grand piano.

"It must weigh a tonne," I said. "At least it has castors."

Enrico had house guests so I could enlist them to help move the grand dame, but to where? I picked up the phone and rang a number that many offshore residents rang when moving, the Hawk.

In the middle of an emergency I didn't expect the phone to answer.

"Hi Jake. It's Roger from Lovett Bay. We need to evacuate a heavy piece of furniture ASAP. Is the Hawk available for a jetty near Woody Point?"

"We're shitting ourselves, there's so much on at the moment – but you're bloody lucky. We're near there now and have a bit of space on board. What is it?"

"A grand piano. A Steinway."

"You're joking, mate. What's it weigh?"

"A tonne. I don't know, but it's bloody heavy."

"All right, put up your flag. We'll be along in 30 minutes or less."

"Make it less if you can. The fire's half way down the slope towards us."

"Christ. Sure, ASAP, mate."

I turned to Judy and the house guests. Enrico was still heaving.

"The Hawk is coming to pick up the Steinway. It will be here very soon. We need to move the piano out onto the jetty within reach of the crane."

"What's the Hawk?" asked a house guest.

"It's the barge everyone uses here to move house and heavy stuff to and from the mainland," I explained.

Four of us could barely budge the huge instrument, but it started to roll when we all got up one end. Enrico was brought back to reality when he saw the Steinway move.

"The Hawk's coming to rescue the Steinway, Enrico!"

"Excellent. I'll help direct it out onto the wharf," he said, suddenly roused to action.

The Hawk was in sight as we edged the piano out onto the jetty. A few minutes later the barge was alongside. Three beefy-looking men jumped off, house-moving cradles, straps and ropes in hand.

"So this is it mate, eh? The boss said it was going to be big. He wasn't joking," one of the moving guys said. Within minutes these professionals had strapped the piano tight and hooked the straps to the crane. Dense smoke clouds billowed across the jetty, cutting visibility to near zero.

"Lift!" called the crane operator. The ropes around the piano became taught as the crane took the load. The whole barge listed to the right with the imbalance.

"Keep going!" The engine revved loudly under the strain as the Steinway lifted off the jetty and was swung across the gap between jetty and barge. The fire had edged closer and was burning about 200m away. Every few seconds the hanging grand piano disappeared in a cloud of smoke. The sight bordered on the surreal. Enrico was on his knees again. But when a smoke blanket momentarily lifted, we witnessed the Steinway making a safe landing on the deck of the rescue barge.

"Gotta go, mate. We're needed in Elvina."

"Thanks are not enough. You blokes are just bloody great," I said.

"Thank you, thank you." Enrico shook everyone's hand until they were out of reach.

And the Hawk was gone, piano safely aboard next to a trench digger and several outboards.

Thankfully a slight wind change halted the fire front's race down the slope before it could reach Enrico's house. Fire trucks managed to eventually contain it. But 11 homes were lost as well as numerous boatsheds, jetties and boats, some exploding on their moorings.

Weeks later, when all the fires were a memory and a rainy period had set in, Enrico quietly had his precious piano returned, floating back on a millpond Pittwater morning, all glistening and clean and free of smoke particles, ready to be played again, perhaps some Chopin or even the Rach 3. An evacuation to remember.

The Great River Walk Expedition – Walk Leader and Routefinder

With my passion for bushwalking and geography, I love poring over maps and investigating possible routes through pristine bush. For a long time I had thought of tracing the course of the Hawkesbury River on foot, from its source on the Great Dividing Range some 170 km southwest of Sydney as a trickling tributary called the Wollondilly, through gorges and wilderness to the ocean entrance of this now grand river at Broken Bay in the most imposing estuary on the Australian east coast, around 500 kilometres downstream and 40km from Sydney's centre.

So when I read a brief note in *The Sydney Morning Herald* that a quasi-government committee had been formed to investigate the potential for establishing an entirely new long-distance walking track for Australia following the Wollondilly-Hawkesbury-Nepean river system, I immediately contacted them. As a walks leader with Sydney Bush Walkers, I wanted to find out how they were going to address this idea, so I went along to one of their meetings.

To my surprise I found that no one on the Committee was a true-blue bushwalker. No one had actually got out from behind their desk to walk any of the route. This meant that they didn't know whether their concept was physically practical.

"Can it actually be walked?" I asked the Committee.

"We assumed it could," the Chair answered.

"Have you had a look where the river goes? It flows through quite remote country, including a 40km gorge. I don't know whether there is a way through. Then in the lower reaches it goes through very rough bush – no tracks, no roads."

"Well, yes, that is a problem." The Chair scratched his head.

"The trouble is we lack the capacity to walk the walk, as it were. In truth it needs recognised bushwalkers. So, I have an idea. If the Committee agrees, why don't we request Roger and Sydney Bushwalkers to walk the route, if they are agreeable. It would be best if we could get Committee endorsement."

All the Committee members looked to me for a response.

"To be clear, you want me to officially find a feasible route that can be walked all the way from source to mouth, right?" I asked.

"That's the idea, and if you could document the route and report on the conditions and recommend alternatives, we would be eternally grateful."

"Wow, that's a tall order, Chair, sort of like asking Captain Cook to discover Australia and report back," piped up another Committee member.

"Look Roger, we'll provide whatever resources we can throw at this project," added the Chair, "and you can take as long as you need. What do you think?"

It was certainly a tempting offer, but I cautioned: "You realise that no one to my knowledge has ever walked this route as a single project before, so it may take me some time and I may not get through."

"Well, better we know earlier rather than later that the whole thing is impossible than to go on in blissful ignorance. So what do you think?" the Chair repeated. "We can officially commission you, to give it official recognition. That might help with any negotiations you end up having along the way."

"OK, I'll do it. In fact I think I can even make it an official walk in the Club's program so as to get a team together to walk the distance."

The Chair beamed. "Just great. We'll organise a big send-off party at the start of the walk."

"I'll look forward to the welcoming party at the end," I said, thinking of the epic commitment I had just made.

Thus began my next job of sorts, to be undertaken while I working at my real job. My first task was reconnaissance to locate the actual source of the river.

Standing on a windswept ridge on the crest of the Great Dividing Range, the longest mountain range in Australia dividing east and west flowing rivers, I looked west to the beginning of the Lachlan River system whose waters flowed to the vast inland and eventually the Southern Ocean. Then I shifted my gaze to the east, to the trickle of water marking the source of the Wollondilly River, the major tributary of the Hawkesbury-Nepean, which eventually reaches the Pacific Ocean near the nation's biggest city.

I thought about the early Australian explorers. They were tough, really tough and courageous, heading off into a total unknown. How different would be our little expedition in a thoroughly mapped, online GPS world? And yet there still remained an element of mystery about our journey. No one had walked the whole way. No one could tell us whether we could get through or not. No map could tell me what conditions would be like on the ground, either through the Wollondilly Gorge, through the Blue Mountains or the trackless country near the coast. No one I could find had done all that. There was a sense that our project touched on the past with the element of the unknown lurking somewhere ahead.

This beautiful river's beginning is quiet and bucolic, flowing through rolling hills dotted by grand 19th century homesteads owned by the descendants of the early explorers. Its mood changes as it cascades through an inaccessible 40km long gorge hidden away from the world in uninhabited country before spilling out into a forbidden lake where even an approach is against the law because it is the principle source of Sydney's drinking water. The river runs on, growing into an estuary steeped in the history of the early colony where the British rowed up in their longboats desperately looking for fresh water and arable land to feed the soldiers, convicts and settlers back in the new Sydney town. It then approaches the ocean through a second wider gorge in rugged country where seven national parks meet. The river's course is as strange as its mood changes. Unlike most rivers that head for the sea, the Hawkesbury, having left the mountains for the coastal plains turns back to re-enter the mountains, not once but twice and then describes a semi-circle that surrounds Sydney to the west before finally forcing its way seawards through a plateau.

The start of the walk was an event for the local townspeople from Goulburn and Crookwell. But the Committee Chair wanted something that was newsworthy, so he asked the local indigenous tribes to formally give permission to access their spiritual lands. The Gandangara and Dharuk peoples came together for the permission ceremony, a rare event in itself as the two groups were in a long dispute about the location of their common border.

A Gandangara elder turned to me. "I know you will respect our land because you are walking over it, slowly, so you will know it. More people like you should walk, then they might understand."

How different life was for Aboriginals from all tribes around the vast 22,000 sq. km Hawkesbury catchment before British colonisation more than 200 years ago. Then, with the arrival of the British, they had lost their land, so many of their people and their traditional way of life. This was something our group pondered at times later en route as we observed aboriginal rock carvings and shellfish middens near the river.

After showing respect to the traditional custodians of the land, the local mayor gave a speech, the local politician gave us a handshake and the local butcher put on the inevitable sausage sizzle. And then we jumped the fence next to a small muddy pool which began the trickle of water bound for the Pacific Ocean.

The Committee had handed me two jobs: to find a way through to the river mouth and to harness local support for a permanent route down the river. While the first job proved tough going, the second was a delight. As almost all of the first 150 km was through private property, I negotiated one-off access with over 90 property owners. They all loved the idea. They all seemed to see that the people who took the time and trouble to walk through their country were connected to it so much more than the casual car driver burning a high speed path though the dusty back roads. This was what bushwalking was about, not just walking but being immersed in the bush, moving quietly across the land and noticing its minute details, like a platypus rippling the river, an old goanna sauntering amongst some trees, mobs of kangaroos in the paddocks and the noisy squawks of cockatoos flying above.

Only occasionally were there any roads, houses or power lines to modify this view as we made our slow way down to the coast. On that first day, a pattern was established that lasted the whole period of the walk. Farmers whose land we crossed came to meet us as we walked through their fields and across their fences. They came to be social, to have a chat and to walk with us part of the way. Many farmers' families went back to the early days, as pioneers opening up the wilderness in the early 19th century, only a few years after the first explorers had gone through, owning their land from the very beginning. Jeff

Prell's historic homestead *Gundowringa* dates from the 1830s. As we moved across his bottom paddock near the ever growing stream, Jeff appeared ahead of us pointing to picnic tables laden with hot, freshly baked scones with strawberry jam and cream accompanied by silver-service tea.

At John Deal's Gibraltar Rocks property we were offered cold beer at the end of a hot day. At James Pascoe's small sheep station we slept in the shearing sheds after indulging in a huge meat lovers' country barbeque and being entertained by the farmer's guitar-playing son. And then there was Hans (surrounded by his harem of three women) presenting a full on whole pig spit roast in an outdoor pit full of glowing red coals, perfect for a cold winter's night.

Securing permission to cross private land following the river bank downstream meant visiting each landowner weeks before the actual walk. On each visit, I received much more than mere permission. They told me their stories.

Fay owned the Far Reach Homestead, often used in films because it looked like the grand mansion Tara from *Gone with the Wind.* She talked about her three sons. Only one son, Tom, was interested in carrying on the family tradition of running the farm. He loved it and managed it well. The other sons went into the city to work behind a desk, attracted by the big money from big corporations. One day Tom was running his tractor across the paddocks. As he crossed the rail track, the wind whining through the stand of casuarinas that he was riding through masked another noise: the oncoming Melbourne train, *The Spirit of Progress.* He was killed instantly. Fay despaired for the future of the property with no family member wanting to take on the 160-year-old tradition of running the farm and mourned the impending loss.

Further down the river at the beginning of Canyonleigh Gorge I met Stan. He lived in a tin shack surrounded by acres of metal scrap, car bodies, truck parts, old refrigerators and old tyres, all rusting refugees from the industrial past. Stan was the archetypal bushman, wrinkled, tough and wiry with skin baked brown from a lifetime under the sun. Stan knew the river better than anyone else in these parts. On my reconnaissance of a possible route downstream, I knocked on his door to get advice as well as permission.

I introduced myself and he motioned me inside, limping to a very worn couch with its stuffing escaping onto the earth floor.

"Don't mind me," said Stan. "I'm a mite slow. Stepped on a nail a few days back and it ran right through me foot. Bloody painful. I got it out with pliers but I bled like billio."

"Have you seen a doctor about that? An old nail might cause tetanus unless you've been immunised."

"Immunised? Nah, don't go in for all that stuff. Haven't seen a quack in 30 years. Don't need them, mate. Look all I need is this tea towel. I just fastened it around my foot real tight covering the wound. Bleeding's stopped now, so I'm better. So don't worry yourself because of me. She'll be jake, no worries mate."

Stan talked endlessly to me about his river and how we could get through, how we could tackle the block-up, where all the snakes were, the platypus, the emus and the wombat holes. Stan knew every rock from one end of the gorge to the other. The message was clear. We could get through, slowly. “But don’t think to yourself you’re the first to get through. Not by a long chalk,” Stan warned. “Others have walked it too, back in 1956 I think and canoed it in the ‘60s would you believe, although those crazy people didn’t make it. Go slowly, watch where you’re putting your feet and you’ll do it. Gee, brings back memories talking about this.”

Stan paused and looked through the window to the river. “I had a girlfriend once who lived down the gorge, name’s Sheila. She used to rock-hop up river to meet me. I danced on those river rocks with her. Really did, sometimes in moonlight too. Never wrong footed, never. Gee, that was a bloody long time ago now. Sheila’s passed on now, but I’ll never forget her, never.”

I left Stan to his chores, armed with all the knowledge I needed to plan the gorge stages of the walk. Eight weeks later we officially walked the river past Stan’s place. I was eager to introduce the bushman to my group. As we approached I could smell a fire and I became concerned. Then, rounding a bend in the track, we came to Stan’s property. The burnt grass was still smoking, but far worse was Stan’s shack, burnt to the ground, just an ash pile covered by blackened corrugated iron. There was no sign of Stan.

That afternoon I rang Stan’s neighbour Jack, the owner of Nandi Station.

“Stan’s OK,” Jack said. “The tough old bugger’s in hospital nursing some burns. His stove caught fire I think, probably from all the accumulated fat dripping from it. We saved some of his stuff, I think. I don’t know what he’ll do now.”

We sent some money to Stan and flowers for his hospital bed. He may have never received flowers before in his whole life, and yes, I asked the hospital to have a look at his foot as well.

The going was easy for the first few stages, walking across grassy paddocks, but when we hit the boulder-strewn gorge we had to rock-hop and progress slowed and route-finding became important. We eventually conquered the gorge and entered easier country near Goodmans Ford.

Alan and Judith lived in a modest house right on the river with views right down a long reach past the ford. I explained the walk concept and asked for permission to walk across their lands in eight weeks’ time. They both smiled broadly at me.

“So you understand just how special this river is if you want to walk all the way next to it. Isn’t that wonderful, Alan? Just like the way we think it is special. You know, we don’t get to meet that many people who think like that these days, so of course you can walk through,” Judith said. “Come and have a cuppa and we’ll talk.” Judith kept on while she busied herself with tea-making. “You know, we didn’t know this existed, even though we lived in Mittagong for years, just up the road really. But once we saw it, we said right away, we’ll buy it. We put our money down the same day, so no one else could get ahead of us. And it’s ours now.”

"We've never known such peace," Alan chipped in. "I've never been this relaxed, at peace with everything." He gazed out of the window at the river scene before him, with the sheoaks on the bank gracefully bending with the breeze. Then he sat down, looking pensive.

Judith broke the silence. "I'd like to explain. This was the last throw of the dice, our last chance. You see Alan had cancer, leukaemia actually. The doctors said it was terminal so we went to different doctors, second and third and fourth opinions. All were bad. Alan went through the mill and had chemotherapy. And for all the suffering he endured, nothing changed. They kept telling us the horrible prognosis. Then a friend thought what we needed was a complete change of scene, of lifestyle. It might just help. We got support from a lot of friends about that. They all thought it was better than the horrible treadmill Alan was on."

"It wasn't just me," Alan said. "I could see Judith was at the end of her tether. We had to do something different and quickly. Then we found this place. Been here now for getting on to a year. I often go down to that white rock in the middle of the stream and just sit there and look at the majesty around me. And guess what?" Alan looked at me animated. "It's gone. The cancer's gone." Judith left the room whimpering quietly. Alan got out of his chair "Please excuse Judith. It's certainly been hard on her but it's over now. I've beaten the bitch. It's this place that did it, and that river."

The valley widened at the southern entrance to the Blue Mountains World Heritage area as the river approached Lake Burragorang. It was in this part of the walk that we came across a totally unexpected sight. As we ascended a small ridge the view ahead spread out into an awe-inspiring panorama of grasslands sprinkled with eucalypts in one vast parkland setting, all contained within the vertical sandstone cliffs of the Wallanderry tableland to the east and the jumble of ridges known as the Blue Breaks to the west. It had the feeling of Conan Doyle's Lost World. Inside this amphitheatre stretching 30km to the north were countless native animals: goannas darting up trees, mobs of kangaroos munching on the grass, emus dancing across the plain, flocks of galahs and rainbow lorikeets painting colourful ribbons in the sky and the melodious warbling of magpies overpowered by the cacophony of squawking cockatoos. Eagles circled high above, ready to swoop down onto some small hapless mammal. All this life was hidden away in a vast, secret valley less than 60 km from the centre of the nation's biggest metropolis. This was the Serengeti of Sydney. It existed because of the total prohibition of any public access for over 40 years, as it was part of Sydney's drinking water catchment. The native flora and fauna had free reign, and nature, given half a chance, had been bountiful.

After passing Alan and Judith's property above Goodman's Ford we walked into Yerranderie, surrounded by National Park in a true designated wilderness and owned by perhaps the most unorthodox landowner of all. Val Lhuede was an architect specialising in restoration. Her father had purchased the entire town of Yerranderie in the 1940s which Val inherited. It was a mining boom town back before the First World War extracting silver, lead and gold. Its 2000 residents had a school, three churches, two butchers, one hotel, a police station, a court house and a silent movie theatre. Yerranderie fell on hard times in the 1930s when the price of silver plummeted. It became a ghost town and stayed that way until Val's Dad bought it. After his death, Val began restoring the entire town to its former glory, a project that was to take her more than 50 years. We visited Val in the old hotel on our way through. It was with much pride that she gave us a Cooks Tour of her town.

All sorts of people lived by this river, we discovered, from oyster farmers, fishers and boat operators, to an ageing Bavarian couple running a low-key nudist colony, an astrophysicist running a heritage homestead and a bipolar hippie managing a paintball skirmish operation. Then there was the minimum security prison on an island in the river where at night the prisoner officers locked themselves in, allowing the prisoners to roam free all over the island, a sort of reverse jail. (There were escape attempts, like the men who swam across the river, climbed up the cliff face on the opposite bank, then bashed their way through thick bush until they eventually came to a road, where they flagged down a passing car – only to discover it was a police car, which speedily transported them to a much more secure jail.) All of these people who lived and worked by this river were typical of the bush mosaic of life, all colourful and typical characters permeating the Australian bush all over the country.

Getting to know some of the people rooted to the river helped make the walk particularly enjoyable. But the watercourse itself is magnificent. We meandered along it through rugged sandstone cliff lines; we rock hopped across cascades and pools; we passed the Blue Mountains' famous landmark, The Three Sisters ; we drank in the sights as well as the wine from a historic riverside winery; and we reflected on the past by the oldest church in Australia at Ebenezer before forging on into the trackless country nearer the coast, where we needed gaiters and gloves to bash our way through prickly bush so thick we could see neither the ground nor the way ahead.

We had entered the lands of the Dharug indigenous peoples and then the Guringai people near the coast. By 1850 few of these people remained, devastated by the white man's small pox disease and then his guns. One of their greatest legacies was to leave behind one of the richest assemblages of rock art and engravings. Almost every time we came to a rock ledge with a view there were the Aboriginal engravings cut into the sandstone, representing one of the biggest collections of Aboriginal art in Australia.

We pushed on, until one day we sighted the shimmering sea. On that final day, we ascended the track leading to the very end of the walk, Barrenjoey Lighthouse, guarding the southern point to Broken Bay. For the final 100 metres my 4-year-old son Lachlan led the way. From the lighthouse we had a sweeping bird's eye view over that vast waterway. We looked back over the wild country beyond the estuary, towards our highlands starting point. To the south was a fabulous view stretching over Pittwater from Sydney's famous Palm Beach (and *Home and Away's* Summer Bay) over numerous beaches and headlands to the city skyscrapers, jutting above the horizon. It was a moment to savour: we had come through.

Changing the Industrial Landscape – Environmental Noise Policy Maker

After the motorcycle noise fiasco, the Noise Policy Unit needed a win. The most important policy we could improve on initially was control over industrial noise because it had the potential, if left unchecked, to make whole regions unliveable. It needed years of work, to understand the problem, to see where improvements could be made at least cost, to see what the public wanted, what industry wanted and to work out how to explain the science to politicians.

It took two years to come up with a draft policy and another year consulting with industry, government and community representatives before we could present the draft policy to the Minister for approval.

"Would you like me to run through the details of the policy and how it will work?" I asked the Minister.

"Hell no!" he exclaimed. "It's all Double Dutch to me. I'd have no hope with you boffins. I just want you tell me how you think it'll ride with the industry guys and the public."

The Minister's reaction confirmed our strategy: explain the science to industry, the politics to the Government and the processes to the Bureaucracy and never the other way around. This third pillar of the strategy was the real killer. A full description was needed so the full horror of the process could be grasped.

Here is a summary of the process. It is not satire; it really happened.

How a government policy is made - the real story of the NSW Industrial Noise Policy

Phase one – The birth of a "policy concept"

It's Spring – the season of hope and promise. A policy concept is born. It will be called the NSW Industrial Noise Policy, the most complicated piece of science-based public policy the government has ever seen.

Phase two – Seeking approval for work to begin

Spring turns to summer. The challenge is to reduce the explanation of what it is about to half a page for Executives with short attention spans.

Phase three – In House Research

The real work starts with field work in the coldest autumn and winter in 10 years. There are concerns by management that policy people have emerged into the real world and are distancing themselves from theory.

Phase four– Writing the policy document and working papers

After 6 months of data acquisition and analysis, management tell us without warning they would like the policy paper written over the weekend to adhere to some efficiency expert's schedule established three years earlier.

The policy paper is written for the purpose of gaining internal endorsement. The working papers contain the real policy in technical detail that acoustic practitioners appreciate but internal management do not understand and do not read.

The Executive Summary is the document most read by internal decision-makers and is made easy by being split up into bite-sized chunks easily assimilated, short words and a blank area at the end which can be used for scribbling or colouring-in.

The scientific paper is for presentation at the next scientific conference and is essentially a job application in the hope of securing an escape route if the process goes pear-shaped.

Phase five – The Cabinet Submission

The document then languishes for three months, which are needed to get the words just right, plus another three months to answer the Minister's questions about what logarithms mean before it can be passed. It is deferred twice in Cabinet due to the need for Cabinet to sit in Eden (to announce a new forest deal to strip forests to create jobs for the timber industry in time for a local by-election), and on Lord Howe Island to announce a new Lord Howe Island wood hen breeding program (to highlight the government's green credentials).

Phase six – Printing the draft policy

The draft policy goes to the publications section. The editors don't like the use of the passive voice and convert the document to second person active without using the tracking facility in Word so that the changes cannot be easily picked up. Converting back is slow work.

Phase seven – Consultation

A briefing note is written seeking approval for the consultation process. Several drafts are needed. The final draft describes a different program altogether. Four more weeks pass to get this right.

Over 1000 stakeholders are identified and sent complete information packages in a most thorough effort to involve all interested parties, but the Natural Therapists Association was not identified and they complain they were intentionally disenfranchised. This group never understands the policy, despite several one-on-one meetings, and write to the Minister to complain. A week is spent in writing the Minister's response, giving it the appropriate sincere spin.

All issues raised are genuinely taken into account. However, we are viewed by some stakeholders with suspicion because we are constrained in saying how well we have taken views into account until the final draft comes out. Additional work is needed to manage nervous stakeholders. This includes further workshops. Other stakeholders get wind that a further consultative stage has started and want to be included. Add two more months onto the process.

Phase eight – Final Approval

The revised policy package is now ready and approval is sought from the Minister. The package is lost in the Minister's office. An extensive search fails to find it until the cleaner moves the goldfish bowl and finds the package next to the fish meal holder.

Management tells us to be careful and avoid certain words when talking to the Minister. We asked what these were and were told 'controversial' and 'courageous', citing a passage from the BBC comedy *Yes Minister*. Management stressed this needed to be taken seriously. It was not a joke. And to the quote:

Sir Humphrey: *If you want to be really sure that the Minister doesn't accept it, you must say the decision is 'courageous'.*

Bernard: *And that's worse than 'controversial'?*

Sir Humphrey: *Oh, yes! 'Controversial' only means 'this will lose you votes'. 'Courageous' means 'this will lose you the election!'*

Two more weeks pass.

Phase nine – Communication approval

Another briefing note, several drafts of the press release and the letters to stakeholders. Summer turns into autumn.

Phase ten – Publication

The website design is not going well. The hyperlinks are playing up because the editor has introduced some weird controls that come from an ancient version of Wordperfect that were preserved in the conversion to Word.

A debate then rages as to whether land use should be hyphenated. Amongst the editors, the 'progressives' want it hyphenated, the 'moderates' don't and the Department don't want it used at all as it introduces a new idea about planning policy.

Phase eleven – The release process

All is ready except for the foreword. This is recognised as a good news policy so other politicians want to be included in introducing it. Ministers' offices are chaotic and weeks pass before it is sorted out as to who gets included. The foreword is redrafted more times than any other part of the policy. Then two more weeks pass because the photo of one of the Ministers is assessed by a minder as not suitably serious enough.

Five minutes before the final go-ahead, the Environment Minister reads the one-page brief for the first time and is horrified that the included picture of him was taken before his stomach stapling operation. A new trim picture is substituted, involving a three-day delay.

Finally, all is ready. The document is printed for release and a release date is set.

The Minister's office then realises that it is now too close to the general election to release as new policy announcements are not appropriate during election campaigns because the government switches to caretaker mode. The government campaigns on the platform of government efficiency and is defeated.

The new Minister from the incoming government orders a review of all policies approved by the previous government. A reworked submission with the printed policy is presented but languishes in the Minister's office for months because of the high workload and steep learning curve that all new governments have.

Sir Humphrey: *"After all Bernard, ministers come and go, but you and I are here for the long haul." – (Yes Minister – BBC 1986).*

There is now a danger that because of the time lag, the package may need to go out to consultation again. The idea is floated but impatient stakeholders tell the Minister to get on with it and that Rome was built in less time (but more than a day).

Finally the new Minister releases the policy highlighting it is part of the new look high-efficiency government. The Minister doesn't like his picture, so the initial run of 3000 copies gets pulped to make way for 3000 fresh copies with a new smiling and sincere photo, and of course a new foreword, which happens to be almost identical to the original foreword written four months previously.

The new policy is welcomed by some parts of industry as an example of the way a 'can do' new government can produce its initiatives so quickly, justifying the need for a change of government with fresh ideas.

***

We started all over again with other policy areas such as road traffic, construction and vibration. But with all these years of work, the novelty of a real job dreaming up government policy was wearing thin, and there seemed to be years of more of the same dance ahead. Creating new government policy seemed too hard won. The process would have been funny had it not been serious, soaking up the years without a hint of change.

I knew it was time to get out and do something new, something different and something fresh.

Moving On

My mother died in May 2004. I had no other family, no sisters and no brothers, making it a good time to seek new horizons for my family – my wife and four-year-old son. Canada looked an enticing prospect, with a similar lifestyle and outlook to Australia, though so different in some ways.

So I decided to advertise myself on the Canadian Acoustical Society's website. Within a week I was contacted by Hilder Associates[2]*, a multinational environmental consultancy firm about a possible job with their team in Calgary, Alberta. Emails flashed forwards and back with mounting likelihood that I was the person they were looking for, someone with government policy clout to help*

[2] Not their real name

them understand the soon-to-be-released Alberta noise policy, partially fashioned on ours.

In the end it came down to an interview by international telephone hookup. That was the start of a great adventure quite different to what had gone before.

Into the Commercial World and a New Country – Scientist

I was entangled in peak-hour traffic on the Sydney Harbour Bridge, the nation's busiest road, when the conference call from Canada came through. My four interrogators in Calgary were impressed that they had caught me on such an identifiable piece of Australiana. I was relieved that at least I had a hands-free phone so I wouldn't be fined for talking while driving. I tried to drop a hint that this was not a good time to carry on a job interview, with me multi-tasking the interview while navigating through the horrendous peak-hour traffic. It didn't work.

"How do you see yourself contributing to the Hilder objectives?" It wasn't easy to focus on the question while I was being squeezed by a big prime mover merging into my lane on the bridge.

"So what do you think of the government's draft noise policy here in Alberta?" A bus turned suddenly into my lane in the middle of the bridge, cutting me off and making me swerve suddenly into the neighbouring lane. Horns beeped angrily.

"How do you think it compares to what you have Down Under?" I fought to get back to the right lane for my destination.

The interview continued for 15 minutes and finished just as I pulled up in my car space in the office car park.

"I'll email you with our formal job offer," concluded Teresa, the head interviewer. "I don't think I'll have too much difficulty in proving to the government here that you are not taking the job of a Canadian. That's the rule here. As I see it, no Canadian has your policy qualifications and experience."

I slumped in the car, wet with sweat and feeling stunned at the end of the most unusual job interview I had ever had.

A few months later my family and I were winging our way to Canada.

Calgary is Canada's powerhouse, the focus of the flow of money coming from the huge mineral reserves of northern Alberta, the oil sands deposits and the North West Territories' gold and diamond mines.

It was a logical base for Hilder, a large employee-owned international consultancy dealing with environmental impacts and engaged by miners to handle their regulatory requirements regarding their environmental management.

Hilder had provided us with temporary accommodation in a lovely top-floor suite looking over the city, the Bow River and, on the horizon, the Rocky

Mountains. We arrived on a weekend. Still jet-lagged, I dressed in my business suit on Monday morning to travel the 6 city blocks to my new employer. I was nervous. Was I going to be good enough? This was the profit-driven commercial world, not a laid-back government office.

Windfarms and the World Bank – Scientist

Within a few days of starting my new job, I was propelled into the international scene with my first customer: the World Bank.

"The World Bank finances wind farms and Brazil is their first big wind farm project," my boss explained. "So to get off on the right foot they want to make sure Brazil does the right thing and complies with noise standards. Being a bank, they don't have any noise expertise and wouldn't know what a noise policy looks like if they fell over it, so they want us to give them a wind farm noise policy they can use and understand. That's where you come in. Give them one."

I had come a long way from sussing out sex noise in Mosman for the local council. This is a test, I thought. It's my first big job so I'd better not stuff up. South Australia, always progressive in policy making, had already developed a world-standard policy, so I decided to phone the SA Environment Protection Authority to ask if they minded the World Bank plagiarising their intellectual property.

"Do we mind? You say The World Bank wants to use our little policy?" Peter shouted into the phone from the EPA in Adelaide. "Did you hear that boys!" He was now shouting to his office staff. "This is crazy. It's all yours, of course!"

Meeting with World Bank Executives, it didn't take much explanation for them to get the idea about how the policy worked. The South Australian policy document was written so clearly and understandably that even an economist would understand it.

So the World Bank adopted the policy and the hundreds of wind farms planned for Brazil would be designed to be quiet where the local people lived.

At the end of the meeting with the World Bank one executive got up out of his seat and shook his head. "I dragged our science guy here along to act as interpreter for us because I thought you were going to use some esoteric science language to explain your policy. Well it's clear to me, surprisingly clear. So I didn't need him, after all."

The Great Caribou Migration – Resident Caribou "Expert"

My second job was to investigate whether constructing a diamond mine, planned to become the largest in the world, would affect Canada's massive caribou migration. The mine would be developed in extremely remote subarctic country about 300 km north of Yellowknife, in Canada's Northwest Territories.

The warming weather of spring in the remote Canadian North-West triggers the greatest mass migration of large animals on earth. Millions of caribou are on the move northwards into the tundra to graze on the rich grasslands and snow-free herb fields to fatten up for the following winter. They are split into vast herds, each with up to a million animals on the move. This is bigger than the wildebeest migration on the African Serengeti.

The extensive documentation for the mine's environmental impact statement was being prepared and it seemed at first that there would be no issues to hold back development. It was situated on First Nation land and leased to the miners subject to a long list of conditions.

However, there was one major stumbling block. A group of First Nation activists opposed to the mine raised concerns that the proposed site was in the path of the annual caribou migration and could disturb their movement north, not just because of the location of the mine, but also because its predicted noise, foreign to a caribou's ear, could possibly make them panic, stampede and be injured. These First Nation people maintain the caribou are sacred and they must not have their migration disturbed. The noise of the mine could also affect the First Nation people's hunting practices.

"What do you know about caribou?" my boss asked.

"Not much," I replied, "but I sense from your question I'm going to need to know a lot more."

Peter handed me a file plus a collection of posters. "Hang these great pictures of caribou around your wall here," he said. "As of now you are our caribou migration expert. Bone up on it and work out what the hell we do with this one. The clients want answers, but the answer they really want is that their mine has absolutely no effect on the migration backed up by the science. OK? The Dene First Nation people up there are saying interference with this migration would cause a significant loss to their culture and their food source because they have lived with and relied upon the caribou for centuries, so they have to be happy with the outcome too. It's all yours. Happy hunting."

I soon discovered that, despite this being a world renowned phenomenon, little was known about the actual pattern of migration, apart from the fact that herd numbers were declining. Would that mean that the mine might disturb less of them? But even one animal disturbed was unacceptable to the First Nation people. I needed to know more about the actual migration path. I felt way out of my depth. So when desperation sets in, there was just one thing to do: call a meeting.

The large table at the centre of the meeting room was festooned with maps and photos. There was Henry, the caribou expert from the biology unit, Jonathan and Jason, both noise people and myself. We pored over the maps which included aerial photos of herds on the move and the tundra country around the proposed mine.

Henry explained: "We have three herds tracking through the mine area and nearby Lake Kennedy – the Bathurst, Akiak and Beverly herds – totalling over a million animals. Just to tell you the scale of their run, the mine area represents just one thousandth of one per cent of their run, so it's not much of a disturbance."

By comparing photos of the herds' tracks over several migration seasons, we could see that each year they were shifting further away from the mine, moving slightly further to the east.

But any disruption to their migration pattern caused by the mine would be a huge concern not only to First Nation people but it could also disturb the area's ecosystem. Caribou are important to predators whose presence is essential for maintaining a healthy ecosystem. The survival of these animals, who are already suffering declines, is at least in part dependent on them having access to their natural habitat. So even a small disturbance could be critical.

"Do we know why they are avoiding the mine?" I asked the caribou expert.

"Don't know," Henry replied.

"Do you know if noise affects them at all?"

"Don't know," said Henry again. We all stood in silence, gazing at the photos taking from low-flying aircraft showing the whole scene below dotted with animals.

"Also, on the edges of their path their density is quite low. You might expect to have only one animal per square kilometre. That means you could walk through the forest and never see or hear one. Even a million animals can spread that thinly because of the vastness of the land mass. So you might wait for days to see one bumping into the mine fence or perhaps hearing the machinery. But don't ask me those questions. It's just guesswork, which won't impress the lawyers if this development is challenged."

"So what do we do?" asked Jason. "The client wants answers. We have to work out a reasonable critical path for this – you know, a risk assessment. We need to talk to someone who knows a lot about caribou – and someone with status and credibility."

Henry raised his hand in acknowledgement. "That's it. We go and see Alvert Tanaasa, a Dene Nation eminent elder. He's old, which means he knows everything about the land. He'll give us stories about the caribou that we can use."

"But aren't we doing this to counter their objections?" I asked.

"Not Alvert. He's for the mine because of the money," replied Henry. "I know he'd be happy to talk."

"So where is he, how do we arrange this?" I asked, running through the logistics in my head.

"Simple, ring him on his cell phone and arrange a time. We fly up there and take gifts for the children and him. He's quite convenient really. There's an airstrip near his village north of Lake Kennedy. It's just below the Arctic circle."

Henry pointed to the location on the map. "The strip would be ice-free by now. Can you arrange all that, Roger?"

"I suppose the budget will take it?"

"Oh yes. You're the new kid. There's no budget. It's 'whatever it takes' on these projects."

Avert gave us all we ever wanted to know including why the caribou numbers were decreasing, why they were shifting east and whether the few caribou that came close to the mine would freak out.

"You guys worry too much. The herd likes the harder ground to move through. The Permafrost is thawing near the mine and in the valleys around there, so it's boggy. That shouldn't be happening. That's why they're shifting east. I suppose you could say the mine's responsible because it pushes climate change. I wouldn't say that. Keep the mine out of it. OK?"

Alvert looked at each of us with his sharp Inuit eyes. "And another thing. Caribou are not stupid you know. They know right away a mine is not a wolf. It doesn't look like a wolf, doesn't smell like a wolf, doesn't move and doesn't make wolf sounds. One is a threat. The other isn't. So they ignore it. The mine could be pumping out Elvis Presley, wouldn't matter unless it drowned out wolf sounds. I said before, you guys worry too much. Mine's OK."

Avert's advice was gold for us, especially as it was coming from an eminent First Nation source. So we had our assessment, and the client had their analysis and opinion ready for their lawyers to feast on. Hilder was pleased again.

Copper in the Congo – Environmental Assessment Author and Global Co-ordinator

The challenge of the Monday staff meetings was to keep a sharp mind in dealing with all the issues discussed around the table while the body attempted to digest the calorie-laden sludge of fresh iced donuts with coffee and slices of heavy chocolate cake for afters.

There was the usual whip around on progress reports on projects, big and small. Then it came to me and my recent brush with First Nation. Teresa handed me a file with the words Milawayo DRC Copper[3], and a photo of a large open-cut hole.

I glanced through the pages to find out where Milawayo and DRC were. The list of abbreviations at the end told me. DRC was Democratic Republic of the Congo.

My job was to co-ordinate the Environmental and Social Impact Report for one of the world's biggest copper mine. I was to direct and co-ordinate a global team of experts including: legal eagles in Houston and London; a team in Johannesburg examining the social impact of the mine and a community development plan; air quality management from Perth; a mine operation strategy team in Dallas; waste strategy from Toronto, transport and access from a contracted study group in Paris; project alternatives and worst-case scenarios from New York; water and tailings management from BHP in Melbourne; energy and power from Dublin, noise from Singapore; work force and labour management from a group in the DRC; and communications from Hilder's expert in Calgary. All these groups had to be pulled together and their work checked and reviewed.

I had to firstly build relationships with all these people and get an understanding of their field of work and their contribution to the project. Numerous video meetings with these global experts helped build the big picture. I had to work a time schedule for myself that fitted in with whatever group's time zone I was in. The only local was the communications expert.

One factor was emerging that concerned me. The mine was to take up a lot of land, erasing three villages, home for centuries to many families of Congolese Tutsi. The Social Impacts and Community Development Plan being written by

[3] Not its real name

the Johannesburg group didn't have a plan for resettling all these displaced families and developing a new community centre for them.

I chased up this omission with the leader of the South African group. "We were told that's being handled by the labour people in the DRC," he said. "It's their people, so we were advised by London to leave it to the locals to work out."

"We can't leave it to them," I said. "Nothing's happened so far. No responses, no plan. We have to do this properly. Can you imagine how this will look to the world if a rich miner digging up the biggest lode of copper and cobalt anywhere in the world doesn't do the right thing to Tutsis, of all groups, after the genocide of their cousins in Rwanda? They need to have their villages re-established with better facilities, including access to fresh water, school and health facilities, an employment program plus a community centre and access to their traditional lands. Their people also need to be on the mine's relocation committee."

Eventually all the strands of the project came together with the assistance program to the Tutsis written into the planning documents. I felt satisfied that we had steered the development towards doing the right thing for the locals who had for generations endured hardships and tribal conflict in one of the poorest countries in Africa. In terms of my job, it seemed a far cry from my days digging holes in a suburban Sydney road.

Team bonding and Calgary life

Hilder assumed all its staff could bond with their clients. This ensured happy clients and ongoing contracts. Ensuring this happened led to interesting 'refresher' courses. One was a short course of fly fishing where clients and Hilder staff frolicked together on the river bank being guided by instructors in the gentle arts of whipping the rod and dangling the lure, in order to catch the elusive salmon. As an ignorant Australian novice, I struggled in acquiring the skills but was helped along by our clients who knew a lot more than I did. Hilder people came over to my group and whispered to me, "Keep it going. The clients love helping you. It's building a bridge." Eventually my technique started to form and my instructor gave me just a little praise. "You won't catch any fish but your casts are getting more graceful. Remember working the fly is like good ballet, all movements are smooth but purposeful. Keep it going." The bonding fared better than the fishing, especially after we abandoned fishing for fishy tales and drinks in the hotel.

Then there was the need for internal bonding so we could then act as a team, one for all and all for one. This meant hide-and-seek games in Calgary's Olympic Stadium, running up and down the bobsled track and similar 'return to childhood' games devised by sports psychologists to deliver a win-win outcome only possible through teamwork. The more obese members of the group were seriously challenged.

Calgary is a dynamic international city, an exciting place to live and to work. There was so much happening in the city, especially in summer, such as the spectacular Calgary Stampede, the numerous free outdoor performances in the square below our apartment, rafting the Bow River rapids and exploring the nearby Rockies. Those long summer days allowed plenty of outdoor family fun, like canoeing in the twilight until 11pm.

But as an Australian I had no concept of what the Canadian cold was really like. The first incursion of Arctic air was in the first week of October when on one night the temperature did a free-fall below freezing. We woke to a morning of minus 15 Celsius and a thick carpet of snow outside our apartment. Our son Lachlan was by now enrolled in the kindergarten class of an inner-city school, a rather austere-looking school with one large old grey stone building surrounded by a sea of asphalt dotted with playground equipment, now transformed into a gleaming white snow blanket studded with ice sculptures. This was where the kids played until the big front door to the old building opened, indicating school starting in the warmth of the interior. Only on really cold mornings – there defined as below minus 18 – did the doors open early. This was the school's minus 18 policy. Any morning warmer than minus 18 was fine for keeping the kids outside until the bell sounded.

On the local ski field at Olympic Park, the rules seemed more extreme. Lachlan and other small kids, wrapped up like bean bags, were out in the snow learning to ski until the ski instructors considered it too cold to keep them outdoors. That was set at minus 23. And where were the parents? They were indoors scoffing hot chocolate.

By December, the Bow River was frozen over. Then there was the opportunity for ice-skating in the city square next to our apartment, where Lachlan was taught to skate by a kindly member of the renowned local ice hockey team, the Calgary Flames.

Strangely enough, I often felt warmer working and living in Calgary in winter than at home in Australia, because the heating is always on high it seems, so in offices, at home and in the city's linked underground shopping malls, people are often clad only in T-shirts, having shed their layers of outdoor clothing.

Visiting neighbouring Edmonton's huge indoor mall in November, we were surreally transported to a tropical summer inside their World Waterpark. There we were, catching warm waves and lazing on the palm-dotted beach, gazing up at the snow falling on the transparent roof.

Being in Calgary in winter had many upsides, like being so close to so many ski resorts, and cross-country skiing on the local golf course. But there were downsides too, like having to plug the car into a powerpoint overnight to keep the engine warm enough to be able to start the next morning, when it had to be dug out from the snow for the morning commute.

The temperature plunged to an icy minus 42 with wind chill as we viewed Calgary's Christmas lights and ice sculptures. Even the hardy locals were not able to endure the frigid conditions for long, and like us, soon retreated to their cars with frozen nostril hair and numb hands clutching their cups of once-hot chocolate.

My agreement with Hilder was to transfer to Vancouver from Calgary after 6 months and work from their Vancouver office. So in December 2006 we migrated to British Columbia and a new life by the sea in 'Van'.

Power and First Nation: The BCP Project[4] – Project Coordinator

Hilder's Vancouver office had none of the camaraderie and cupcakes of Calgary. In Vancouver I was the sole noise expert in the office and no one else understood this mysterious subject. It wasn't just the office culture that was different. Where Alberta had clear environmental regulations, BC had none. There were no government rules about limiting the environmental impact of developments.

My first project was assessing the impact of a proposal to deliver hydro power generated in the remote interior of BC to the major south-east cities of Victoria and Greater Vancouver, the British Columbia Power (BCP) Project. The high tension power lines to be erected would make a low-frequency hum, especially in humid and wet weather. The greater the voltage, the greater the hum and these were to be very high voltage lines at 500kV. Looking at the map of this remote area, it seemed that very few people would be affected. It seemed a straightforward project. I soon found out how wrong that assumption was.

The first issue concerned the First Nation people. The line was near several of their settlements and they were objecting to the noise the line might make. My job was to identify all the settlements, work out their impacts and points for negotiation. As the line was on their lands for most of the way, they had the ability to shut the route down. The second problem was the possible effect of the line on marine life where the line was in a submarine cable from the mainland across to Vancouver Island.

The line passed over land owned by four First Nation tribes. A 3-hour 'chopper-cam' film of the entire route enabled me to identify the different tribes' forest settlements and even individual dwellings.

Agreement had been reached with three of the tribes, but the Katzie Nation of the Fraser Valley had voiced their strong opposition to the line because of buzzing, and they were after compensation. Rerouting the line off their land would be a major task if negotiations broke down.

"So what do we do?" I asked.

"Let's go and talk to Terry, a key Katzie elder, and sound him out, excuse the pun," said John.

"But we're not meant to see any First Nation people until we have a position to negotiate," I said. I was alarmed I was stepping out of my role.

---

[4] Not its real name

"Hell no, we're just having a discussion, not a negotiation. He knows me but bringing along the noise specialist from the Study to meet him would impress him a lot."

John left and I was worried. I sorted though some scientific papers on transmission noise and a thought struck me. As the Katzie had one main settlement affected, it was possible they might sign up if they could be told they would have zero noise at that village.

"How could you tell them that when you know we can't reduce the noise any more on a 500kV AC line?" asked my boss when I told him of my idea.

"Just a moment. I'll run that past a few guys and get back to you," was my boss's response. All it took was another 10 minutes and he was back on the line. "Go for it boy! Bloody expensive but we still have a route, and it would be much cheaper than rerouting the line. Go and make the offer to the Katzie."

A few days later First Nation specialist John and I were thumping up a dirt track in the hills north of the Frazer Valley.

"Let me do the talking," John shouted above the din of tyres on gravel. Stick to your specialty. Don't make any comments unless invited to, OK?"

"Yes, of course. I'm on my best behaviour," I said with tongue in cheek.

The road flattened out after a long climb, and we came into a clearing in the forest with a scattering of old huts. A tall brown man with white hair emerged from a hut and walked across to our vehicle.

John jumped out of the car. "Terry, it's been a long time." John held out his hand but Terry ignored it. He was focused on me.

"I know him, but why are you here?"

"I'm Roger, the noise guy. Pleased to meet you." I held out my hand.

"I'll only shake your hand if you are here to help and not just to sweet-talk me."

Terry ignored John entirely. "I am here to help. Can you explain your problem to me? That will help me work out a solution for you."

Terry smiled the supercilious smile of a disbeliever.

"Come over to my hut and we'll talk for what it's worth."

John cut in with an air of desperation "I can tell you Roger's background, Terry, and what he is…"

"Hey, John, don't hassle me." Terry turned to me. "You want to know our problem? This is it."

He produced an old tape recorder and pressed the button. A low continuous tonal hum sounded.

"Now that goes on all day when it's wet and it's wet most of the time. You go and put a line right though my village and that will happen here. Don't bullshit me. I've read up on this. I know there's no way you can shut it up. So how are you going to help me, eh?" Terry demanded.

"There's no way, so I'm sending you guys across the river. You can run your line there, not here. You guys knew that, so why are you up here except to sweet-talk us into signing our lives away." Terry glared at us. He looked like he was on the warpath. "You're all just pathetic."

I stood up and walked to the edge of the clearing. I motioned Terry to follow me. Looking curious, he did so.

"I can hear what I think are four different bird species and a distant waterfall. Am I right?"

"It's five. There's two alike, and that's not a waterfall, it's the pump overflow."

"Well, that's what you'll hear if the line goes through. Nothing will change, even on rainy days."

"OK, I'll swallow the bait. Tell me how."

"Simple. It just doesn't exist on the surface, because it's underground. Way underground, where it's safe and remote from you."

"Underground, eh." Terry looked surprised and stood there silently for a few moments, scratching his chin. "You guys serious?"

"Yes we are. I came up here to tell you just that."

He looked at me and held out his hand. "I'm ready to shake your hand now. Shake."

Terry and I shook hands. "But listen to me," he cautioned. "Be true to your word. Otherwise it's war. Tell your boss that."

John and I left with a friendly wave and bumped our way back down the potholed track.

"Bloody hell, Roger, I was having kittens back there," said John. "You don't know Terry's moods. The thing could have gone pear-shaped despite your underground ploy."

"But it didn't, and it's not a ploy. The Katzie will sign. I know. I've done this sort of thing before."

"I thought you were just a noise guy."

"I hope I'm more than that."

Counting Orcas – Killer Whale Research Coordinator

What does electricity do to marine life? This was my next issue in dealing with the environmental impact of constructing high tension power lines from the interior of British Columbia to the coast and Vancouver Island. Accessing the island meant running the lines underwater across the Strait of Georgia from Howe Sound just north of Vancouver. I had to find out what impacts that line would have on the whole marine ecosystem.

I had not a clue how to start. I had zero expertise. I was saved by Jim Fellows, Hilder's naturalist. He told me exactly what to do: "Count orcas – and for as long as you can."

It had to be orcas because they were the easiest marine mammals to spot from the shoreline and could act as an indicator for population numbers of other species. Orcas – or killer whales – are actually large dolphins, not whales, and they are fierce predators, known to hunt and kill sea lions, dolphins, sharks and whales as well as smaller aquatic life. The idea was to count orcas where the old existing submarine power line crossed, also count them where our proposed line was to cross, and to then compare the numbers recorded for each location. If the numbers were less at the existing power line that was evidence that orcas avoided that area. If that were the case, there might be a lot of opposition to establishing a new underground cable.

My first task was to help Jim set up cameras at each location to spot surface incidents plus sonar for below-surface monitoring. Then I had to physically observe orca sightings in both locations to back up the camera and sonar data. That involved going backwards and forwards between the two sites for a couple of weeks, at all times of the daylight hours and in all weathers.

And so it was that I found myself camping out in bitter cold on the northern shoreline of Howe Sound in the company of seals, bald eagles – and orcas. Day after day I sat on windswept rocks surveying the sea with my binoculars and pressing a counter button whenever I saw a large black fin on a black back and white chest.

On some days, dark clouds enveloped the sound and the gloom of typical wet Canadian West Coast weather took over. Heavy showers often obliterated the opposite shoreline from view as well as any orcas surfacing in the storm. I was chilled to the bone. Then on other days the sun shone through and optimism returned.

My clicker finger was quick on the trigger. I sighted hundreds of orcas, usually travelling together in pods. I did notice that there were more to be seen in the 'no line' location and they appeared to be travelling in larger pods, often of around 20. There were fewer orcas near the existing line, but any confirmation would only be found on analysis of all the data.

I was on this project for about two months, enough time to have amassed sufficient data to make an assessment. Back in the office, Jim shuffled the papers and computer printouts, eyeing the spreadsheets.

"Hey, numbers are down, definitely down near the line. Higher at the new site without the line."

So what did that mean for the proposed new cable? Orcas obviously didn't like the existing one, and probably many species of fish didn't like it either.

We couldn't just note this in the assessment and leave it. There would be hell to pay if the media found out we were interfering with orcas and not doing anything about it.

"You will have to recommend a solution," said Jim. "That's your job."

I felt lost. All this work seemed to lead nowhere. But thankfully that wasn't the end of the line. A bunch of research papers I had delved into pointed to a solution.

There was evidence that marine life was affected by the alternating electrical current of submarine power lines. Specifically, it was the associated magnetic field which reversed 50 times every second, the frequency of the alternating electrical current of the line. Research suggested the alternating current of the line meant the magnetic field was reversed at the same frequency of the alternation. And the orcas didn't like that.

Suddenly a light bulb moment flashed before my eyes. It was simple really. Design the underwater line to run direct current, not alternating current, so there would be no magnetic reversal. I wrote up my Orca adventure, added my recommendation and emailed it to my boss. The reaction came 10 minutes later.

"What's with you and underground power?" shouted an angry Graham down the line. "First you force us to sink the line at huge cost near some pathetic First Nation dot on the map village, now you tell us we have to convert to DC for the crossing to VI. Do you have any idea how much that will cost? No power company in Canada has ever done that."

I drew a deep breath. "We don't have to do anything if you are happy with running the risk of the media finding out about our non-action with the orcas. What do you think Vancouver TV will do with this story? How much harder will they make our lives? What will the client think of us if we put him in the poo?" There was silence from the other end of the line, then a loud click as Graham hung up.

But very quickly my recommendation reached the draft report stage, then the final report. I found out later, much later, that the submarine DC line was constructed, the only one in all Canada. In my dreams the orcas of Georgia Strait said thank you.

The Straits of Georgia Revisited

Sitting on a rock along the shoreline was one job, but I experienced the strait a bit differently on another job when I helped fly a plane over it. I had to get to Victoria, BC's capital on Vancouver Island as I was to lobby government ministers for possible contracts, surprisingly at their invitation. The office told me there was no need to catch public transport as Barry Weston, the office economist and eccentric, would fly me there. Barry lived in Nanaimo on VI and commuted to the office each day by flying his Cessna 182 from his back yard into Vancouver's light aircraft field at Boundary Bay and driving his car from there to the office. He did it in all weathers and often the weather was filthy.

"Welcome aboard!" called Graham as I climbed into the cockpit of his Cessna at Boundary Bay aerodrome. "One thing though. You'll need to help me fly the plane."

"What? I don't have a license."

"You won't need one. Here's the map, and it's a headache. It's only a 20-minute flight but we have 6 changes of call frequency. I'll have too much to do so I want you to work the frequency settings for me. Here's the list. When I signal you to change, you go ahead and change them. We have B-Bay departures, Vancouver area control, US western airspace control, US military, Victoria area control and Vic airport arrivals. Got it? You see, we fly into US airspace because we cross the international border twice, once into, then out of the US in about five minutes. We need military clearance as well, otherwise we might find ourselves getting buzzed by phantom jets. You understand?"

"Wouldn't it be easier to just catch the car ferry?"

"Silly boy. This is fine. Don't worry about it."

And off we flew. True to his word, I was kept constantly busy changing frequency dials, establishing radio contact, signing off and holding the mike near Barry as he was struggling with the crosswinds 2000 feet above Georgia Strait. The American military must have been asleep when we flew into their airspace, as there was no response. Five minutes later we had left the US and the focus was on approach control at Victoria and getting the plane cleared for landing. I was exhausted by the time Barry switched off engines.

The flight back to the mainland was far more relaxing as Barry thought it a good idea to fly up the Vancouver Island coast and cut across the Straits of Georgia to Boundary Bay Airport, avoiding the United States.

"Avoiding the US is always best, and in more ways than one."

Barry summed up my thoughts exactly.

Cruise Ships and Turbines – Technical Specialist

After working for Hilder without much of a break from June, my holidays were due and Vancouver was the perfect base, with magnificent mountains and stunning coastal scenery at its doorstep. Taking a cruise north to Alaska via the fiords, glaciers and remote towns of the Inside Passage certainly appealed. It was Hilder's version of a holiday, meaning I took work along with me. For Hilder, our likely stop in Prince Rupert was the key. A wind farm was being proposed for Mount Hays right next to downtown Prince Rupert, with the noise from the farm most likely heard on residential Digby Island, just offshore from the main harbour. As I was heading in that direction on holidays, this was a job for me.

The developer wanted a number of wind turbines to be built on Mount Hays. All I had to do was to work out which was the best geographical arrangements of turbines to minimise noise to the people living in the city or in direct line of sight at Digby Island. For this exercise I had a program called Cadna, a noise prediction model. It was like a board game. I could virtually shift turbine site locations on the mountains so that their cumulative total of noise changed with each turbine configuration. It was a roll of the dice. If I played around long enough, I was sure to get lucky and discover the best arrangement. In addition, because I was meant to be either in or passing Prince Rupert I was to take copious numbers of photos of the mountain from every angle possible to work out turbine sightlines. My last week in the office before our cruise departure was about solving the 'board game'. I hadn't finished before departure.

"Take your laptop with you so you can while away those lazy hours on board finishing off the modelling, and don't forget your camera," called Brian.

Vancouver departures by sea are spectacular affairs, similar to sailing through the Sydney Harbour heads. Our monster ship glided silently under the peak-hour-choked Lions Gate Bridge and out into the long channel separating Vancouver Island from the mainland. Life was easy. People were lazing in the pools and spas, lounging on deck chairs, playing games, feasting at the multiple food outlets or shopping – and there was one solitary person in the library, absorbed in the wind-farm turbine-site board game.

It took a day to clear Vancouver Island and cross patches of open ocean, long enough to finish all my modelling and send off the draft report. Technology is a wonderful thing making our lives much easier in so many ways. Sadly its reach didn't extend to ship internet, slow, intermittent and dreadfully expensive.

Poacher Island was coming up on our starboard bow and the lead into Prince Rupert. The sun was low in the western sky when Mt Hays came into view in the far distance. Just as the coastal hills stuck their heads farther above the horizon, the ship did a slow turn to port and headed for Dundas Island further up the coast, on a bearing for the Inside Passage. Oh no, that meant no turbine pictures. But then I had a light-bulb moment. From my work on Mt Hays I had a contact, Jack Martin. He lived on Digby Island right next to Mt Hays. I pulled out my cell phone, found his number in my phone directory and rang him from the deck of *Diamond Princess* 25 km from the Prince Rupert cell phone repeater. I had a signal. It was weak but it was a signal.

"Hello Jack, it's Roger from Hilder here. I'd better be quick before the line drops out."

"Roger who? Speak up!"

"Roger from Hilder in Vancouver, except I'm on the deck of a ship off Poacher Island near you. Hilder thought I'd be able to take decent pictures of the Mount Hays turbines, but the ship isn't going near there after all, so I'm a bit desperate. Could you do me a big favour and dash out right now while the sun is shining and take lots of pictures of Mt Hays from as many angles from Digby as you can. So it looks like I did take them after all. I'll organise something nice for you, just name your price. How about it?"

"Ha-Ha. You Aussies are funny. Sure I'll do it. Looks like I have half an hour with the light so I'll go now. Gee what a crazy call. I'll tell you what I would like. Get me a crate of 4X, you know, that Queensland beer. Then I'd be happy. No one in this town would have ever seen it."

And on my return to the office two weeks later I got the pictures and Jack got the 4X.

Farewell Canada

After being away from Australia for almost two years my leave from the Environment Protection Authority had expired and I needed to return to save my superannuation. I had felt very much at home in Canada, and there are certainly many similarities between Australia and Canada. Both are vast countries, rich in natural resources; both have First Nation issues; and both are former British colonies run almost exactly the same way, with a Westminster system of government and comprehensive welfare system. And as a vast generalisation, Canadians and Australians share a love of sport and the freedom of the outdoors.

But for me, as far as my work was concerned, there was one big difference, and that was the organisation I worked for. This international commercial consultancy, which was concerned with environmentally responsible development, provided me with big jobs and international projects I would never have had back home. My horizons had expanded exponentially.

My biggest adjustment Down Under was driving on the left again and getting a sense of direction with the sun in the wrong part of the sky.

Then came the day I fronted up to the old office, on the same floor, in the same building, with most of the same people, doing the same sort of things that I did before. It was like a time machine stuck in 2006. I spent the first morning back writing my resignation letter. It was the only thing I could do there that was original.

Counting Heads on the Peninsula – National Census Area Supervisor

Nature abhors a vacuum and will attempt to fill it at the earliest opportunity. My career path had been a bit like this. After Canada and after the EPA came another empty space but within a few weeks something new popped up and my career vacuum was filled again. I received a call from a friend telling me I ought to think about ringing someone in the Australian Bureau of Statistics because they needed people to help run the national census.

"It's a simple job. You count how many people live in Australia. Can you count up to 24 million," he joked.

A phone call and a quick interview was all it took for me to become a census manager. "You'll be responsible for running a team of collectors counting everybody who, on the night of 9th August 2011, will have slept somewhere between Avalon Beach Surf Club and Barrenjoey Lighthouse at Palm Beach, about 15000 people in 6000 houses," said the interviewer. "How do you feel about that?"

"Always happy with a job that includes a lighthouse," I replied.

Over the next two months, after completing my own job training, I recruited and trained my local team of collectors.

We all pored over the aerial maps of our area. "Is that a house, a shed, a chook house or a garage?" asked Tom, one of my Collectors, pointing at a smudge on the map.

"You'll have to check every doubtful building on these photos. Any one of those could have people living in them. That's why you can't beat an on-the-ground inspection."

"What about in here?" Tom pointed to areas of thick vegetation. "Someone could be camped in there or a house hidden by trees."

"All houses should have a letter box to give them away. As far as camping is concerned you'll just have to get lucky to spot someone. Ask the neighbours. They may know of someone hanging out in the bush."

The terrain of my area was very hilly with houses perched on ridgetops or buried in deep valleys. Physical contact with people had to be made, necessitating arduous walks up and down steep driveways all day. Some houses had an inclinator, a platform lift making access up a steep slope to their hilltop eyrie a breeze, saving a weary, panting collector hundreds of steps – if it wasn't locked.

The 9th of August 2011 was the key date. We census officers had already delivered detailed questionnaire forms to every house in our area to determine how many people were staying at that address on census night and also to answer residents' questions. The real challenge was in getting responses back, either via the new internet method or the old-fashioned way of manually collecting completed forms, so we could eventually find out who the recalcitrants were.

People's responses fell into five groups. The first class, and it was first class, were the 'nothing is too much trouble' people with their immediate electronic response or properly completed form left out for us to collect as early as the next day. Then there were the 'I'm not sure what I am doing' people who had trouble filling out the forms and needed help or the technology for uploading the electronic form was a little beyond them. Overall, though, they were a well-meaning group. These first two groups thankfully formed over 80 per cent of the total. Then beyond that and in the great minority there were 'the nasties'.

The main troublesome group was the 'I won't be put out by the bloody government so I'll only co-operate when I'm good and ready, if at all' people. That group caused the most pain as it created the most work for us in constantly going back to their houses where the blank form had been blown by the wind into the garden and was now collecting dead leaves from the nearby trees or alternatively the form had disappeared and no one was ever at home, no matter what time of the day or night we visited. Five visits back to the ghost house was the limit. After that they were reported for non-compliance, possibly punished with a fine.

There were two variations to this group, the first being 'I'll make your life impossible' sub-group. For my team this group was represented by occupants of the house hiding when we knocked at the door. There might be washing drying on the clothes line, but strangely whenever we visited, there was never a soul to be seen. Sometimes we could hear voices inside, but no-one responded to our repeated knocking on the door. Sometimes, they were not good at the hiding game. I recall glancing inside a front window of one house where I had returned for a response on five occasions and seeing a foot suddenly protrude from behind a sofa. It helped the evaders' cause if a snarling dog chased the collector off the property.

Many houses in Palm Beach and Whale Beach are among the most expensive in Australia. Many mansions cling to cliffs offering superb coastal views, justifying the outlandish rents charged by the owners during the summer holidays, some over $10,000 a week. In winter, however, more than 50 per cent of all the houses are officially vacant, as the owners consider them holiday homes. At more than one house it was obvious that, unbeknown to the non-resident owners, squatters had moved in. No-one responded to my calls of "Anyone home?", although from the eerily flickering light and whispering inside, someone certainly was, enjoying their rent-free luxury accommodation.

Then there were the people who, according to our detective work (asking neighbours), were actually at home on census night, so had to be counted, but whose questionnaires were not returned, despite repeated visits to the residence

– like the man who had flown off with his completed census form in his travel bag the morning after the census on a research mission to Greenland to study glacier retreat rates. Greenland is a country not noted for its mobile phone or Wi-Fi coverage, providing us with a problem not covered by the manual, which immodestly purported to cover all situations.

The final two classes were really difficult. The first was the 'You'll never take me alive' group barricading the fortress to repel intruders. One resident did not answer the door, but peered out from behind a curtain and shouted that he would blow me into oblivion with his shotgun if I dared come near his house again.

The second class in this extreme category was the Martian group. I called them that because they seemed to inhabit a different planet. Census night had come and gone. My team had managed to get responses back from all but two houses, the ABS documentation from the previous census and documented development since then confirmed that we had missed no one. The air photos also confirmed this. All was fine, my regional director told me. I had done my job as had my team. Congratulations all round. Yet I had an uneasy feeling something was wrong.

Barrenjoey Road makes one final magnificent sweep around a cliff as it enters Palm Beach. Behind the cliff is dense bushland. I had a feeling there might be a building up there that hadn't been counted. I had a long look at the cliff and figured out a way up. Ever the keen rock climber, I clambered up the cliff with the help of a strategically placed rope anchored to a rock. Who had put that there? I felt a bit like Jack climbing the beanstalk about to be confronted by the giant. I then found narrow ledges and inched my way along them and up shallow steep gullies until after a little exposure I reached the top and the beginning of the forest. The ground cover was very thick as I moved away from the cliff, eventually reaching a flat area. There I discovered a power line, hidden by ferns. Following it, I came to a small, two-storey, dilapidated wooden cabin, shrouded by creepers and surrounded by trees which arched together over the roof, covering any evidence of the existence of a house from above. I climbed the weathered wood slats leading to the verandah and knocked on the door.

"Hey-hey, what do we have here? Someone at the door, my my!" A wrinkled old man with a long, white beard appeared. He looked quite jovial. "Hello, son. Are you lost? Fancy seeing someone up here! Well, well! Come inside and I'll check you for injuries."

"My name is Roger. I'm OK, but I'm here because we've having a census and I have the job of counting everyone. So now I know you are here I can count you."

"A census you say? Well I never. No one has ever counted me before. I tell the neighbours to send away intruders and they do, you know. A census, eh? Didn't hear about it. Don't have TV or the wireless. Don't have time for those things."

"Do you live alone?"

"No I don't. Come and I'll show you." The old man took me through two dark rooms before we reached a small greenhouse. "Say hello to the census boy, Harold." Harold looked up at me and then looked back to the old man for guidance. Then Harold meowed. "Percy's here somewhere, probably hiding. Percy's shy you see."

I made a wild guess. "Is Percy a bird?

"No, no, sonny. Not just a bird – a sulphur-crested cocky, son. There you go now. You can count us all on your forms. I hope I have helped you. So me and Harold and Percy get counted. That's a nice thing to do, a nice thing."

And that was the 2011 census, possibly imperfect but streets ahead of the 2016 census, when I was also employed as a collector. This time there was no interaction with people before the big night; no invitations from a few confused residents to come inside for a cuppa to explain how to answer particular questions. This was the first online census. All forms were accessible through a website and it was expected that the vast majority of people would submit their forms online. However, the website crashed on census night and went offline for two days. A fiasco. And this time we were only to start our rounds two weeks after census night, theoretically giving residents ample time to complete their online forms. This late start posed problems for us. Many people recorded as non-responders who answered our door knocks at their homes weeks later had no recollection of where they were on census night, and some were on an Airbnb holiday and not in Australia on that date. Chatting to people, like the man with his sulphur-crested cockatoo, in the low-tech 2011 head count, was a much more positive experience.

Specialisation – the double edged sword

Specialisation is knowing more about less. This process can evolve to the point where what you know is only shared by two scientists in Geneva and a PhD graduate in Cape Town, so the rest of us who don't appreciate your worth consider you unemployable. It comes down to the perceived usefulness of your specialisation. If you are an expert in the mating habits of the corroboree frog, then the NSW National Parks and Wildlife Service may see you as an essential member of a team formed to preserve Australian alpine ecosystems. However, a government running a very large deficit and urgently needing funding for run-down hospitals in marginal electorates may see funding corroboree frog research as being off the radar, so the mating expert gets specialised out of existence.

Then there is the other side of the sword. I accidentally amassed experience with environmental noise monitoring and analysis, a specialisation mysterious to most people. "What do you do? What sort of work is there in noise?" people would ask. Others would say: "I tried to understand noise once but never got the hang of it at all. It's very abstract and technical." So again suspicion mounts by the non-specialist as to the usefulness of acousticians in the labour force.

But this specialisation is in high demand because people are very voluble about noise and its impact on their lives. Politicians know this, so respond by funding study groups, policy units and enforcement officers to show they are keeping noise under control for the good of the citizenry. When I started out in this field, I had no idea that I would be able to be employed for as long as I wanted and never be made redundant because I was one of the few who chose a field where knowing a lot about a little counted.

Woodstock Down Under – Pop Festival Noise Monitor

The Woodstock Festival held in upstate New York in August 1969 was a turning point in popular music culture. Its effects changed popular music in America and beyond. Its reach extended to Australia where an Australian version of Woodstock was staged in 1973 near the town on Nimbin on the far North Coast of NSW. It was called the Aquarius Festival. The influx of counterculture changed Nimbin forever. People came from all over for the festival and stayed after it was over. Their alternative lifestyle and philosophy then spread across the region to affect other towns and villages like Mullumbimby and Byron Bay.

So it was inevitable that some pop concert promoter would see a business opportunity in reviving the glory days, stage a new outdoor festival and rake in the money. It was called *Music in the Forest* – though after 50,000 feet had walked over it on the first day of the three-day concert it was more like *Music in the Mud.* Like Woodstock, *The Festival* was staged on a rural property with pop bands following pop bands almost continuously from Friday to Sunday. The location of this mega-concert meant that a whole town might be pulverised by the amplified music as well as all the surrounding countryside. Consequently noise criteria were set by the government. Their strictness was modified a bit by the beneficial effect the show was anticipated to have on the local economy.

So for the whole show to go ahead, the government decreed the music level must be monitored and if some enthusiastic DJ pushed it over the limit, then the person monitoring the noise level would order them to tone it down and warn of the huge fine they could be hit with if they repeatedly failed to comply.

I was asked to join the team monitoring *The Festival.* In a military-type operation noise officers were assigned day and night to monitor noise levels both inside the concert area to deal with the out-of-control disc jockeys and in the surrounding areas, where we could also investigate residents' complaints.

We had to familiarise ourselves with the local roads in our particular areas. There was a big road network, not surprising for the most densely populated rural area in Australia. Some roads climbed the hills and ran through thick rainforest, others followed the banana plantations. Locations where someone had complained about the noise of some previous pop festival were marked in red on my roadmap. I was meant to rush to the address of the complainant as soon as I could to take a noise reading or two. It was a great way to discover the countryside.

The government had given special noise limits for the nearby Billibar Nature Reserve. My boss Susan pointed out particularly sensitive areas in the middle of the forest, far away from the road. "Don't worry, there are tracks in to these spots marked by a cairn on the road and a cairn at the end of the bush track in the rainforest," she said. "You'll need a really good torch – it's black as pitch in there without a moon. And check yourself for leeches afterwards too."

"So what's in there?" I asked.

"OK, here's a list." Susan reached into her bag. "We have here the Wallum Tree Frog, Laughing Tree Frog, Wompoo Pidgeon, Yellow-Eyed Cuckoo-Shrike, Black Bittern and Comb-Crested Jacana. There are more on this list."

"So what do we do with these animals? Are they meant to be protected from rock music as well?" I asked.

"Yes, and more so than people. Their criteria are stricter. So you have to monitor the forest as well to see how much festival music spills over Jones Road into the Nature Reserve.

"Can't we give them free tickets? You know, the same deal as for some of the houses. The laughing tree frog probably has one."

I spent the next four nights running the circuit. Rarely did I hear any festival music. The freeway noise masked whatever was running on stage. The nights were cool with a moon that set early. Festival control texted me occasionally with a complaint. I would respond by measuring noise outside the complainant's house and invariably it was wind in the trees, road traffic or the territorial screech of brushtail possums defending their turf.

Then there was a complaint coming from the very end of Middle Pocket Road, beyond where it turns to slush and the rainforest closes in on all sides. It took a long time to get to the end of the road as I was sliding on the greasy surface just after a shower. I turned off the engine and all lights. It was coal-mine dark and profoundly quiet. So quiet that the ultimate background noise of oxygen and nitrogen molecules bumping into each other was the only noise to register on the sound level meter.

"You the guy checking the noise up here?" The disembodied voice puncturing the inky blackness startled me. "You should have been here an hour ago," the voice continued. "It was going good then. You could hear everything. There, hear that? By crikey, it's on again."

I strained my ears, but all I could detect were the air molecules, breathing and a fart from the invisible body. "Can't say I can hear it."

"Write down in your little book there what's happening here. It's bad for us. We normally enjoy the quiet. You say you can't hear it. Get yer ears tested, mate." The invisible body started moving away now, dimly illuminated by the red glow of a cigarette. "And get a guy up here without fucked-up hearing. D'ya hear!"

Suddenly he was gone and the quiet returned.

By contrast, Billibar Nature Reserve was full of noise, the haunting hooting from owls, the twitter of small birds, the hiss of possums and snapping of twigs as they scurried up the eucalypts and many other sounds of the forest from animals unknown. Added to this was the pounding surf and the confused cacophony of several sound stages simultaneously belting out conflicting music genres.

By midnight, in accordance with noise regulations, the main acts had packed up and softer recorded music was playing. One final complaint to attend to and I was done for the night. I had no trouble finding the address. I could guess it to be the lit-up house with the shrill barking dog. Knocking on the door just made the dog bark more ferociously. No one responded. No chance of hearing relaxing, after-midnight recorded music with this din going on. Time to call it a night.

Three more nights, and the festival was over. I hoped the wompoo pigeons and laughing tree frogs had a better time than some of the drug-affected festival crowd or small cell of embittered locals.

Bats Out of Hell – Bat Scarer

Bram Stoker's Count Dracula was meant to scare the pants off anyone who had the temerity to visit certain parts of the Carpathian Mountains in Rumania. On those fog-shrouded peaks the vampire bat ruled, so the story went. The Count himself was meant to be a vampire. But I was to turn the tables on bats as I became the scarer and the bat, the scaree.

When the great naturalist and botanist, Joseph Banks arrived in Australia on Cook's Endeavour in 1770, he immediately recognised the uniqueness of the local flora and began the long process of documenting it. A product of this process was the creation of Sydney's Royal Botanical Gardens with its very extensive collection of native trees and shrubs, including many species of magnificent eucalypts and the recently discovered new genus straight from the dinosaur age, the Wollemi pine. Many of the Royal Botanical Gardens' trees were heritage-listed. But in 2015 they were under attack. Many precious trees were sick and some were dying.

The reason for this was that grey-headed flying foxes – actually giant bats with wingspans up to a metre and fox-like heads – were colonising these heritage trees, feeding on them and stripping them bare. This flying fox colony was several hundred strong. Considered pests by the Royal Botanical Gardens staff, they were in fact a protected species as they were listed as endangered. But the trees they were stripping were protected too.

The NSW Government decided that the trees were more important and the bats should be evicted but in a humane way that would not interfere with their life cycle. That meant driving them out of the Gardens before the females became pregnant, meaning before April. The question then was how to evict them so that they would fly to another colony or create a new one well away from the Gardens. Research suggested noise was the answer, making their normal roosting site untenable without physically damaging the mammals. But what noise, and when? This is where I came in.

Past experience didn't indicate any particularly successful sound, so we applied a little common sense. Music seemed part of the solution but not classical like Debussy, nor Chopin – that was all too gentle. How about Wagner? – loud, yes, but too symphonic. Tchaikovsky's 1812 with canons – that was more like it – but not enough. Rolling Stones, Midnight Oil and lots of heavy metal rock – getting closer. Add some real heavy metal hammers on garbage bin tin covers to the musical mix. Surely bats would find that cacophony truly objectionable.

The only trouble was that the billionaires living down the hill might find it offensive as well, leading to our ejection instead of the bats. So once we had the noise right, the next step was to set a level that annoyed one type of mammal without disturbing another more influential one. So we predicted how high we could go, without it being heard down at the palatial finger wharf, praying it was still loud enough in the Gardens to put off all the Draculas.

Timing was crucial. Our bat expert suggested the time when the pathfinders were coming back to roost after a night fruit picking. This would be about 30 minutes before dawn. In other words, 5:15am. Strategy meetings and instrument checks added to the preparation, so our work began at 3:30am.

The big day arrived. All of Sydney knew it was about to happen as television news gave blanket coverage, including on-the-spot reporters giving up-to-the-minute accounts of proceedings. The clock ticked past 5am. All personnel with sound reproduction gear were dispersed through the bat landing areas. All the garbage bin holders, hammers poised in hand were 'on station', as they say, and I was in the centre of it all, ready to measure the noise levels produced at my designated positions.

Someone gave a signal. Like an orchestra conductor, I raised my hand then decisively slammed down on the big red button. A volcanic roar erupted, spewing our thunderous symphony into the black sky. The vanguard of the returning colony was due at this moment, but in the blackness we had no idea what was happening overhead. The noise went on and on. I waited for complaints. None came. Amazingly, the Finger Wharf crowd were still asleep. The eastern sky started to light up. Soon it was light enough to see the silhouettes of bat wings overhead. They were hovering, not landing. More bats joined the holding pattern as *The 1812* played, with the impulse of Russian cannon fire holding off Napoleon's armies echoing off the east face of Parliament House. This plus the garbage bin accompaniment proved too much for the bats. They left. The grey-headed flying foxes turned around and appeared to set a course to the south-east, towards that other great stretch of inner Sydney green space, Centennial Park.

After a couple of boisterous hours, we called a cease-fire. Only a few stragglers were still circling. Bat numbers still in the trees accommodating the colony were down by 80 per cent.

But this could not be counted as success. We might have won the battle, but not the war, as the cliché goes. So the next night we did it all over again. Dawn broke a second time, and some bats obviously in temporary digs that day tried to return, only to be greeted by the same racket of discordant musical genres and garbage tin renditions. This time the holding pattern had fewer bats, and they dispersed earlier. They now had knowledge of their new home. For four consecutive nights our dawn chorus split the sky. Before the fifth, the Royal Botanical Gardens Director called a final cease-fire.

On that fifth dawn, all our recordings were switched off. All our garbage bins were left in the waste compound. All the hammers were back in the tool shed. We waited. The sky brightened in the east. Then one, then two, then three bats appeared. We waited and waited for more, but all we saw was an empty sky. There were only ever three. Three out of hundreds. Where were all the others? Reports came in that the colony had split; some were in Centennial Park and others in smaller colonies in other parts of Sydney, in Gordon and Avalon.

The Garden's colony was now down to just a few individuals, not enough to cause more damage to its precious trees. Over the next days and weeks, colony numbers were carefully monitored. Only a few bats returned. Never again did they threaten the Garden's treasures. The operation was a success, although some argued that all we did was to transfer the problem, not resolve it. But for us the problem was never the bats, but the trees.

News of our success spread, and noise was used to disperse bat colonies elsewhere, but they never achieved The Royal Botanic Gardens' level of success. I heard the noise character was different in these other cases and the music choice was different, so perhaps special thanks for our success could have gone to Pyotr Ilyich Tchaikovsky.

The Bob Miller Story – Editor and Compiler

My father was not cut out to be my male role model. He was also very temporary, departing the scene with the divorce when I was 10. My search for a replacement father figure didn't last long. In my mind I settled on Bob Miller a year after my father left. Robert C Miller, a Yank, was a well-known journalist for United Press International and arrived in Australia to cover the 1956 Melbourne Olympic Games. Norma met Bob soon after he arrived as a work colleague and their friendship blossomed almost overnight into a relationship. The clash of egos made the liaison very rocky. It was on again, off again continuously for almost half a century. It did mean Bob was always in my life, in the background somewhere but always accessible and there to give advice. At one point Norma rang me from Honolulu late one night asking whether it was alright with me if they got married, Hawaii being one of Bob's bases. They never did.

Norma died in 2004 and Bob went downhill from the moment I rang him in the USA to tell him the news. He died several weeks later. But before that, long before that on his last visit to Australia he left me his entire collection of diaries. Being a journo, the diaries were a complete account of the stories he covered and the observations he made about life, the universe and everything.

Robert C Miller was initially a war correspondent for United Press International. He was one of the great journalists of his time, covering both the European and Pacific theatres of the Second World War and then both the Korean and Vietnam wars. His reports started with the death of Carole Lombard and went through to the rise of Bill Clinton. He was friends with several WW2 generals, including Patton and Macarthur, along with US presidents like Nixon, Johnson and Reagan. The great war correspondents covering the conflicts of the 20th century typically went on to write books, most becoming classics of their genre. Bob did not. Most of his peers covered the war from command posts, from general headquarters, with General's aids or in hospitals back away from the front. Not Bob.

He was in the front line and sometimes ahead of it, writing eyewitness accounts about the hand-to-hand fighting and how the battle developed through the tactical decisions of field officers and the effects of individual valour. It was a miracle that he survived the war but Bob was always lucky.

He was the only American reporter captured by the Vietcong who lived – because he convinced the VC he was an Australian journalist aiming to get the Viet-Cong perspective on the war. In his effort to appear to be a 'true-blue'

Aussie, he even whistled the Australian 'anthem' *Waltzing Matilda* during his capture which had a positive effect on his captors.

His diaries are gripping, bringing history to life. Take, for example, his account of the storming of Guadalcanal Island in the Pacific by US troops in World War 2. Bob was embedded with the first wave of invading Marines storming a beach just before dawn on the Japanese held part of the island. His platoon dug in near the tree line above the high-tide mark. There was no resistance. Feeling around in the darkness, Bob found a wet life jacket. His platoon found more. Someone shone a light illuminating a whole pile. The instructions for use were in Japanese.

Ahead, in the trees, was the newly arrived Japanese Army waiting for first light to slaughter the even-more-newly-arrived marines. The marines knew this. The landing craft had left. They were trapped. But then came a miracle. Just as it was getting light enough to see the beach, the headlands and the ocean beyond, three fully fledged American destroyers appeared around the headland. It would have looked to the Japanese like very significant reinforcements had arrived. So the Japanese General made a decision to withdraw into the forest and stick to his orders to attack the American enclave further up the island from behind. He didn't want to lose men engaged in a battle he was not authorised to initiate.

Bob found out later that the three warships had nothing to do with their operation and were simply relocating. The captain of the fleet could have chosen a number of courses to go from A to B, but decided on a whim to choose the only course that would be visible from Bob's beach. Part of this miracle was the timing. Had the warships appeared 15 minutes earlier, it would have been too dark for the Japanese to appreciate the size of the fleet before it moved past the beach and out of the picture, telling the enemy the warships had nothing to do with the landing. The Japanese would then have attacked. Had the warships arrived 15 minutes later than they did, the attack would have already occurred. The warships' arrival was at the pivotal moment.

So this was Bob's great story. In his words: "Completely by accident these two mortal enemies had conducted the flawless execution of two independent amphibious operations at exactly the same spot, on the same night, without a hitch or a casualty, and without a shot being fired, on a precise timetable that enabled each landing to be made exactly as planned, without ever knowing they were within yodelling distance of each other."

Bob's diaries are peppered with real stories like this and his life story screams out to be told. Writing his biography is one of my current projects.

Jobs of the Future – An Outback Mystery

I was having a drink in the hotel in the outback town of Marree near the vast Lake Eyre salt pan and was intrigued by a local's story of the mysterious sounds of the lake. A big muster had been on at Anna Creek, a remote South Australian outback cattle station a little larger than Belgium. Teams on horseback had been scouring the country looking for cattle that hadn't seen a human being for over a year. The riders were heading north along Lake Eyre's western shoreline. It was late afternoon, a quiet, still afternoon. That was when the riders heard the lake speak. It was a deep low rumble, like distant thunder, coming from the lake. The stockmen were not surprised. They had all heard it often, whenever they were near the lake on still days.

The eminent geologist Dr John Dulhunty and his wife Roma had also heard this rumble. They spent months camped on or near the lake in the 1970s and 1980s exploring its features. Roma wrote three books about their experiences. They loved this harsh and often dangerous environment. The days when nothing moved, when the wind stopped blowing and all was silent, when the shimmer of the lake's surface blended into the sky and the mirages hid the horizon, were 'spell days' as Roma called them. It was the spell of the Lake. That was when they heard the rumble. Even Dr Dulhunty, a world expert on Lake Eyre, could never figure out a likely cause, and where the rumble came from. And it only occurred here, and no other salt lake. Roma had asked stockmen from Anna Creek about the rumble and they had confirmed her experience.

The world has many salt lakes. Most have a little water in them. The dry ones are generally smaller and have a small catchment to match, meaning no large river channels. This is the pattern around the globe with one big exception, Lake Eyre, a dry salt lake but with several big river channels and a catchment the size of Europe. These are dry channels draining an arid desert but every few years the northern monsoon penetrates south far enough to fill these rivers and then the lake itself.

Eventually after the rivers dry up the lake water evaporates returning the giant playa to its natural state with a new salt crust and with millions of tonnes of fresh sediment. The scale of these processes set this lake apart. Once dry the rumble starts again. Many researchers have come and gone and no one has an answer.

Reading Roma's books fired my imagination. What would it really be like out there on a featureless totally quiet flat salt plain with no living thing, no point of reference? It would be getting close to true sensory deprivation. Then in the quietest place on the planet, Lake Eyre on a 'spell day', the deep, forbidding rumble might then start up.

I wanted to find out for myself whether the rumble really existed, so I applied to the South Australian Government to conduct research on the lake to detect the source of the strange noise. It was the only such permit to be granted. I planned to cross the dry salt crust on snow shoes and had already started to seek out funding. However my attempts were thwarted in the following years because the normally dry lake had unexpectedly filled with water. In fact, tourists were taking flights from Marree for a 'once in a lifetime' view of the thousands of birds, including sea birds, flocking to this outback sea. I am still waiting to capture that elusive dry lake rumble.

"You could interest the Australian Acoustical Society in that sort of work because it sounds original and different," suggested a colleague at a Society conference. "You could then get some financial support. So write up a proposal, see where it goes. Talk to people about it – you never know who might take on your idea. But I tell you this. It won't happen if you don't try; if you don't believe in it."

And that's the truth behind all odd jobs.

This job may or may not happen. If it doesn't, something else will come along. The show goes on.

Each job in my long list of jobs has presented me with a new set of challenges. I have always been up for a challenge, new problems to solve and new people to work with. I still am. Eventually when a particular job became too familiar and no new challenges presented themselves, the job felt stale and I knew it was time to move on. I felt the anxiety of not knowing if a new and interesting job would come along. But it always did. The process was helped by me remaining optimistic, open to any opportunity, however fleeting, and harbouring a warmth for people.

I always found that people were the lifeblood of the jobs I had. They all invariably enriched my experience of working. When recalling the past, it is the people that come to mind first before the actual tasks that I undertook.

My father had the same job all of his life. He was recruited as a junior office boy by General Motors Acceptance Corporation in his teens and retired from the same company and from the same line of work after 40 years when his health failed. He spent his whole life there apart from his time fighting the Axis powers in WW2. The firm gave him more than a gold watch at his retirement, in fact it was a gold clock. I didn't want that to be me.

I was not limited to what my resume said I could do. I was told once that if I argued for my limitations, then they were mine; if I didn't have the courage to move out of my comfort zone, there in that predictable environment I would stay. The corollary was that if I truly believed life could be exciting and jobs could be an enriching experience, then there was a good chance they would be.

My mother got me started. She was the most important single factor. An old acquaintance, Antony Penrose wrote about his famous mother, the noted war correspondent and photographer Lee Miller. His book was published and brought his mother's accomplishments into the light. His achievement in writing the book gave birth to the same idea in my mind about setting out what Norma did as a high-powered career woman journalist and diplomat: A true female pathfinder, almost unprecedented for her day. She led the way of grabbing onto opportunities as they flashed by, leading to the sort of cockeyed career path that I learned from and ultimately emulated. I am still learning. Thanks Norma. But no thanks to my vocational career advisor who, when I was 16, suggested I could become an accountant.